RICHARD RORTY'S NEW PRAGMATISM

Continuum Studies in American Philosophy
Series Editor: James Fieser, University of Tennessee at Martin

RICHARD RORTY'S NEW PRAGMATISM

Neither Liberal nor Free

EDWARD GRIPPE

continuum

Continuum International Publishing Group
The Tower Building, 11 York Road, London SE1 7NX
80 Maiden Lane, Suite 704, New York, NY 10038
www.continuumbooks.com

British Library Cataloguing-in-Publication Data
A catalogue record for this book is available from the British Library.

ISBN–10: HB: 0–8264–8901–X
ISBN–13: HB: 978–0–8264–8901–2

Library of Congress Cataloging-in-Publication Data
Grippe, Edward.
    Richard Rorty's new pragmatism : neither liberal nor free / by Edward Grippe.
       p. cm.
    Includes bibliographical references.
    ISBN–13: 978–0–8264–8901–2
    ISBN–10: 0–8264–8901–X
    1. Rorty, Richard. I. Title.

B945.R524G75 2007
191–dc22

2006038317

Typeset by Aarontype Limited, Easton, Bristol
Printed and bound in Great Britain by Biddles Ltd, King's Lynn, Norfolk

To my wife, Susan, whose patience and support are a constant blessing

Contents

Part I

Chapter 1

Introductory Overview: The Premises Underpinning Rorty's New Pragmatism

The Impossibility of Essentialist or Foundationalist Realism

The search for a way to access that which is real has been the grand hope of Western philosophy and science since before the Platonic era. Knowledge was thought to be a matter of finding the right way to structure language so that it would rationally capture the world and its objects as it and they are, and truth would reveal itself to our minds through this linguistic scheme. The world and its contents are found to be what they are, in that reality is already *there* either through participation of particular objects in a transcendental realm, or due to an immanent essence or nature residing 'within' these entities, or again owing to a sub-standing continuity.

However, Immanuel Kant conceived of a constructed world, one in which the subject, by an active engagement with sensible *materia*, structures perception. Reality, the noumenal thing in itself, forever is beyond human understanding. Interpretation of pre-scheme noumena is out of the question, but with the employment of schema perceptive cognition was possible. Held in common by all rational entities the *a priori* categories of consciousness insinuate a structure on to the primal 'stuff' to form jointly the content of experience. However, a price is paid to preserve for the realm of the senses a law-like character: the objects of our perception are reduced to an orderly and consistent *appearance*. This construction imposed upon *materia* allows for interpretative acts to take place and for consensus to form as to what will pass as knowledge of the perceptual realm, but the interpretative act becomes alienated from any grounding source other than human reason.

In recognizing the three antinomies of Self, Cosmos and God as limits of thought, however, Kant underscored the finitude of human reason while not establishing that any of these three limiting concepts exist in ways other than as abstractions (hence, the need for a faith separate from reason). And by including the Self as one of the antinomies, Kant inadvertently brought into question the *a priori* nature of the categories. How could one assert that there are immutable, definable categories that are 12 in number if the rational self, their constitutive ground, is beyond comprehension? Given Kant's bifurcation of noumena and phenomena, all claims about the nature of the self would have to be constructs themselves. Therefore, the limits of human reason must extend to all interpretations concerning human reason, including Kant's own. That is, the *a priori* structure of perceptive cognition ought to be seen as a useful construct serving the purpose of undergirding the possibility of scientific knowledge and not necessary aspects of a transcendental reality poking through, so to speak, the shroud of phenomena. Richard Rorty concurs:

> Kant was a turning point in the history of Western philosophy because he was a *reductio ad absurdum* of the attempt to distinguish between the role of the subject and the role of the object in constituting knowledge (Rorty 1999a: 49).

Rorty maintains in the spirit of *psychological nominalism* that all awareness is a linguistic event; that is, every sentence about an object can only be a description, explicitly or implicitly, of its relation to a web of other (linguistically delimited) objects, and that nothing can be known of these objects without appeal to some symbol system. There is no possibility to step outside of language and take hold of reality unmediated by some linguistic description (Rorty 1999a: 48–54). The Kantian transcendental ego must fall victim to this historicist[1] restricted nominalism. Its description, like all other descriptions, was a social construct whose function was to serve a locally perceived social need. That need was to reconcile religion and science by demarcating exclusive zones of relevance for each. Nevertheless, Kant 'fell between two stools', as Rorty puts it, allowing the infiltration of the monotheological into the philo-scientific phenomenal realm when Kant argued, in an effort to stave off a slide into subjectivism, that Reason was the one and only determinate source for scheme reservoirs. For even if one conditionally grants that there is something prior to the use of any symbol system, nothing can be said about its composition given that it would be undifferentiated, and hence beyond numerical or logical characterization. So even from a Kantian perspective it ought to be undecidable as to whether the human consciousness is one 'object' distributed transpersonally, or that it is, rather, plural, and more properly understood as diverse and idiosyncratic sources from which flows a variety of (possibly incommensurate) schemes (Krausz 2003: 19–20).

Rorty's Anti-representationalism

Rorty does not suffer this dilemma. Characterized as an 'internal constructivist realist', Rorty – who works hard to eliminate the need for such misguiding professional designation – asserts that all claims for realism must be made from a specific linguistic platform, and that language as such never actually performs the function of representing reality to the mind, but offers differing, sometimes competing, alternatives of achieving some purpose or another. The belief that the mind may adequately represent a corresponding and independent actuality is to be associated with the longing for there to be someone or something to act as the authoritative source for human knowledge, a filler of the alleged gap between our wavering, contingent existence and the necessarily stable condition of the way things are. Such longings are understandable. Nevertheless, Rorty claims, they are nostalgically attached to outmoded Enlightenment metaphors, which themselves harken back to the family of narratives that declare that an eternal arbitrator adjudicates between competing schemes of thought and ways of life, favouring those that imitate and live up to the celestial Judge's absolute norms. Rorty avers that these narratives and their Enlightenment variations no longer cohere with our contemporary circumstances, and in fact retard the development of the social hope (Rorty 1998: 306) associated with the de-mystifying secularization of philosophical thought. Then why do these outmoded views persist?

Realists cannot live without pathos, Rorty opines. Those who are theists find pathos in the alienation of the human spirit from the divine; the realists find it in the chasm that separates human thought and language from reality as it is in itself. Whether it is the urge for immortality or the desire for certainty, the ambition to transcend is at the root of these 'romantic' notions. In Rorty's opinion it turns out that Kant was in both the theist and realist camps. Rorty wishes to be in neither. Yet he claims to be a realist notwithstanding. In what sense can he make this assertion once he jettisons both theism and the realism linked to representationalism? What can realism mean detached from all external groundings for elucidation?

Warning that traditional realists 'think of anti-representationalists as anti-realists, but in doing so they confuse discarding the hard–soft distinction with preaching universal softness' (Rorty 1999b: 3) – where 'hard' refers to areas of the culture, such as religion or science, that reveal the way the world is – Rorty offers an alternative: pragmatic utility. In a move reminiscent of Sartre, Rorty maintains that the inability to extricate oneself from the 'appearances' of one's time, place, culture, etc. and escape to the 'reality' as seen from a pre-linguistic view from nowhere is, in fact, a liberation. This split, being a construct for another time and purpose, can be avoided by thoroughgoing historicists, like himself, through simply adopting a new language-game (narrative) that rejects representationalism's reality/appearance and related distinctions. Rorty's position entails that without the discovery of truth-deciding criteria or the uncovering of an extra-linguistic ground there can be no description of anything that is more or less accurate or concrete than some contrasting account. Under this new narrative, the phrases 'more accurate' and 'more concrete' may be utilized if they undergo a retooling to mean more useful for the present purpose (Rorty 1998: 294), thus allowing a ranking of the pragmatic structuring over its rivals while not succumbing to the traditional realist's temptation to lexically order the favoured approach in terms of their corresponding more or less closely to the autonomously real.

Freed from the Realist temptations, how does Rorty's anti-representational pragmatist project not fall into a self-destructive relativism?[2] Finding common ground (to a point) with Hilary Putnam, Rorty outlines their areas of agreement, as follows (1998: 43–44). Both men hold that the opinion that a convergence of views towards one big picture *is* the very essence of knowledge is absolutist dogmatism. Realists err in the attempt to view the world from nowhere. *And* in a different way so do the relativists when they carelessly argue that relativism is a universal epistemic condition. Nevertheless, humans are destined to view the world through the lens of their particular set of interests and values and to be committed to that view as better than other views. This ethnocentric destiny is not a fatal limit due to its bias, but rather it is the heart of Rortian pragmatism: the supremacy of the agent's perspective. Seated within a certain point of view, and using the conceptual system at hand to engage in a practical activity (understood broadly), an agent is involved in a way of life. Being so engaged, one ought not to construe this practical engagement as somehow divergent from or in accord with 'the way things are in themselves'. But the abandoning of this illusory kind of realism does not automatically result in relativism. There can be 'objectivity' about this practice if one accepts with Rorty that all interpretations are *fixed* in a context, *and* 'that an interpretation or an explanation is the correct one, *given* the interests which are relevant in the context'.

Thus, it is not that Rorty, as an 'anti-representationalist', doubts that the universe consists of mostly things that are *causally* independent of us, that is, that the world has causal impact on our projects. Rather, his challenge is to those such as Charles Taylor who maintain that objects have intrinsic features, features that they have 'under any and every description', so that they are 'better described by some of our terms rather than others'.[3] In short, Taylor holds that objects are *representationally* autonomous. With language thoroughly penetrating all notions of 'reality' and its objects, Rorty thinks, *pace* Taylor, that it is impossible to decide whether some descriptions of an object capture its 'intrinsic features' (how the thing is under all conditions), and others merely identify its description-relative 'extrinsic qualities' (i.e., how we depict it). Therefore, Rorty encourages us to discard the intrinsic–extrinsic distinction altogether, along with any claim that beliefs do or do not represent what is real.

Pragmatized Darwinism and Truth as Social Practice

The basis for the council to abandon the reality–appearance and the intrinsic–extrinsic distinctions is Rorty's confidence in what can be called *Pragmatized Darwinism*. He explains:

> By 'Darwinism' I mean a story about humans as animals with special organs and abilities (e.g., certain features of the human throat, hand and brain that let humans coordinate their actions by batting marks and noises back and forth). According to this story, these organs and abilities have a lot to do with who we are and what we want, but have no more of a representational relation to an intrinsic nature of things than does the anteater's snout or the bluebird's skill at weaving (Rorty 1998: 47–48).

Rejecting what Rorty considers Darwin's speculative vitalism, he attaches himself to what he terms Darwin's positivist elements.[4] In Rorty's pragmatized version of Darwinism, we humans, in what we do and who we are, should be seen as continuous with other organisms such as 'amoebas, spiders, and squirrels', save that we have the specialized adaptation of language. This adaptation, which allows us to use elaborate systems of marks and sounds to coordinate our activities with others of our species, sets us apart from other terrestrial organisms by affording us a means, in addition to sensory interaction, of controlling our surroundings, i.e., cognition. Thus, cognition is an environmental coping instrument developed to afford us increased *utility*: the maximization of pleasure and the likelihood for survival; the minimization of pain and the lessening of the chances of death. The causal impact that forms what Quine called the surface tension on a web of beliefs is itself devoid of purpose and solely functions as stimuli to which we language users respond freely and creatively to generate alternative belief (coping) systems. The creation of images of the world *via* concepts ('A concept, after all, is just the use of a word' [Rorty 1999b: 5]) as adaptive tools naturalizes human thought about the cosmos, exposing what was once thought of as representations of the world as it is to be instead of vying strategies pragmatically designed for the achievement of our current intention (Rorty 1999a: 134). How we interpret what forms that utility might take and what will count as 'objects' relevant to that utility is regulated by the creative application of language to our purpose (Rorty 1999a: xxiii) *and* the social acceptance of a proposed convention.

Yet once Kantian convergence is put aside, social agreement hinges upon the pragmatic notion of 'what works'.[5] Rorty believes that 'assent' and 'commitment' are notions that signal the acceptance into our lives of the utility of sentences about some one or other object.[6] Truth is a social practice rather than an explanation or analysis of the relation of social practice to a non-human element which gives the practice warrant or justification. And, if a social practice is conceived to be the gradual reweaving of the communal beliefs and needs in response to the causal impacts of physical happenings and the behaviours of people, then truth will follow the plait of concepts over time. What works, then, will alter along with the changes in meaning associated with current language use. 'Truth' becomes primarily a commendation or a caution to an audience, as it morphs along with the changes in what a community considers to be its goal of inquiry. The workings of truth, its explanatory power, would be keyed to the acceptances by an ever wider audience about what to do to achieve their social aims. And what leads to this acceptance is *solely* a pragmatic choice. Everything else is mere wordplay for Rorty (1999a: xxv).

Arguing against Crispin Wright's claim that there are two distinct norms for the practice of statement-making – warranted assertibility and truth (the latter of which is the marker for a matter of fact) – Rorty denies the idea that though beliefs can be justified without being true, this leads to anything besides warranted assertibility. Rorty makes the case that though fully justified to a specific audience and still not being the appropriate action does not demonstrate that there are two distinct duties: a sociological duty and a moral duty. He claims that it is simply a matter of an action being justifiable to some audiences but not others (Rorty 1998: 27). Similarly some audiences will believe that there is Truth, metaphysically speaking, as surely as some will believe stoutly that there is a creating, designing God. Another audience will not hold there to be such a God or that there is a non-human regulator of matters of fact. Neither audience can demonstrate proof for their motivation to believe as they do. Yet Rorty observes: '[w]hat norms one obeys, after all, is a matter of what norms one thinks one is obeying.'[7] Any belief becomes 'descriptively normative' once one becomes committed to some specific set of entities, but that alone cannot make such a commitment produce the *real*, extra-sociological descriptive norm about that which sits behind the description giving it ontological import. And without the employment of further criteria to discriminate between descriptions, we are left with our social commitments. That there are people with a religious, scientific or philosophical inclination who do not question God, evolving species, or the transcendental ego, that is, people who do not make a distinction between the symbolic and the existential – this fact actually supports Rorty's desire to dissolve all such dualities. It is only when pushed to justify their belief that there is a scramble to locate a supporting agency to buttress their beliefs, to give certainty to their commitments. But, whereas there are what Robert Brandom calls 'canonical designators' that map out a structured space in which singular terms can be intelligibly referenced (e.g., integers provide structured space for complex numbers; Conan Doyle's text provides for the character of Moriarty, but not for Mickey Mouse), Rorty contends there can be nothing canonical for ontological commitments, and hence no structured space is created by these commitments for there to be intelligible discourse. Rorty further notes:

> There are no acts called 'assent' or 'commitment' which we can perform that put us in a relation to an object different than that of simply talking about that object in sentences whose truth we have taken into our lives (Rorty 1999b: 10).

We are free to invent images of the world, those structured spaces that serve to realize our stated goals. Interestingly, this sort of invention equally applies to Rorty's favoured image maker, Darwin. Rorty acknowledges this fact, recognizing that Darwin's is just another competing image of the world that cannot be ontologically grounded or considered to be the image that gets reality right. Notwithstanding, in the spirit of Dewey's experimentalism, Rorty suggests that we apply the instrument of Darwin's theory to philosophy in the hope of dissolving or lessening as many philosophical problems as we can. That means that we ought to treat truth like we understand species under the descriptive influence of evolutionary theory. Truth is evolving as societies evolve in reaction to previous successes that helped and failures that hindered their progress, with progress determined within a particular community's narrative.[8] The habits of philosophical ancestors, such as Plato, Kant and Dewey (Rorty 1998: 304), either assisted in coping with a changing environment or have become liabilities, constricting options, retarding a march towards greater complexity, thwarting the development of more articulate ways to describe and control the surroundings. The current interpretation of what works is the theory of truth that has currency for us. And this theory has cash value when it avoids the unfortunate outcomes that arose from other images of the world and their epistemological claims, and opens us to a future of variety and freedom (Rorty 1998: 305) once we are free of metaphysics and the epistemology of representationalism.

Filtering Darwin (and tangentially Hegel) through a thoroughly pragmatized Dewey, as Rorty characterizes pragmatism, expediency replaces accuracy as a term of epistemic approbation. Draining the notions of 'experience' and 'consciousness' from Dewey's thought as twin distractions that threaten to reopen the breach between appearance and reality (Rorty 1998: 294–97), Rorty argues that what remains is the continuity of brutes and humans as creatures that strive for survival by productive means (growth), but by using different tools. And once we de-metaphysicalize physical and mental mutations by rejecting the claim that the current existence of a species or a culture – as the victor of some struggle for a biological or theoretical niche – has demonstrated a 'privileged relation to the way things really are', expediency is what is left, i.e., usefulness as the criterion for propagating into a better future.

But in a Darwinian world, who decides what works, what is true, what is the 'better' future? Rorty's answer is that his sort of pragmatist will

> ... have no detailed answer, any more than the first mammals could specify in what respects they were better than the dying dinosaurs. Pragmatists can only say something as vague as: Better in the sense of containing more of what we consider good and less of what we consider bad. When asked, 'And what exactly do you consider good?' pragmatists can only say, with Whitman, 'variety and freedom' or, with Dewey, 'growth' (Rorty 1999a: 27–28).

Following this line of reasoning, one cannot even appeal to evolution as the epistemic arbiter. It cannot be that evolution has fashioned our brains to get thing right about reality. That would require Nature to have discernible joints, so to speak, about which she divides herself, and, coincidentally, to have specific organisms, us humans, whose brains are synchronized to detect and offer justification according to nature's own articulation. Yet, Rorty insists, no organism is ever in greater touch with reality than any other organism, humans included. Therefore, we should drop the goal of truth as cognitive accuracy and adopt the idea that all human activity is of one, pragmatically utilitarian, piece. But how does *this* recognition of contingent functionality serve Rorty's recently noted contention that he is a pragmatic *realist* rather than a self-defeating relativist?

Davidson's Principle of Charity

For support, Rorty turns to Donald Davidson's 'principle of charity'. Under this principle an interpreter translates so as to apply some of his own standards of truth to the pattern of sentences claimed true by the speaker. As Davidson suggests, 'Charity is a matter of finding enough rationality in those we would understand to make sense of what they say and do, for unless we succeed in this, we cannot identify the contents of their words and thoughts' (2005: 319). Davidson, like Rorty, will have no truck with the concept of truth as correspondence to reality. Instead, Davidson offers the notion, beginning with his 'On the very idea of a conceptual scheme', that, charitably, most of anybody's beliefs must be true, and that this principle is forced on us as the necessary condition for there to be any workable theory of human communication. To communicate with others we must take them from our perspective to be right in most matters; 'to read our logic into the thoughts of the speaker'. Nothing more is needed for a theory of truth, Davidson asserts (1984: 197). Rorty concurs: 'To say, as Davidson does, that "belief is in its nature veridical" is not to celebrate the happy congruence of subject and object but rather to say that the pattern truth makes is the pattern that *justification to us* makes' (Rorty 1998: 25). This substantial overlapping of beliefs allows for exchange without epistemic convergence. It also allows for radical innovation of narratives without the undue drag of conformity. The 'World' might be lost, but worlds of interpretation may now flourish once the confusion over there being an immanent teleology in nature or a cosmic plan to live up to is eliminated and the job of fully justifying our beliefs to our local audience, concerning different problems that troubled the ancestral audiences, is under way.[9]

But there is difficulty brewing for Rorty with his embrace of Davidsonian Charity. The assertion made concerning justification of our beliefs in the previous paragraph would equally apply to a community which has contemporary or future practices that stand at odds with Rortian pragmatic aspirations, given that Rorty says that it is impossible to privilege our present aims and interests (Rorty 1998: 4), and furthermore states:

> . . . you should notice that it would be inconsistent with my antiessentialism to try to convince you that the Darwinian way of thinking of language − and by extension, the Deweyan, pragmatist way of thinking of truth − is the objectively true way. All I am entitled to say is that it is a useful way, useful for particular purposes (Rorty 1999a: 65).

Yet if Darwin and Dewey's use of language forms competing images of the world that cannot get reality right, and Platonic and Kantian conceptions are challenged as stale onto-theological metaphors, useful in past eras but anachronistic today, and, further, Rorty himself offers that his anti-essentialism cannot claim to be objectively true of the way the world is but only a useful way to achieve a given purpose (one that could be deemed unjustifiable by some current or future 'better' audience), then it follows that Davidson's principle of charity, from a strictly Rortian perspective, is not true *per se*, but pragmatically useful for some rationale – a rationale that might yet be decided to be lacking in purpose (utility) by a contemporary or a future audience. What this take on Davidson's Charity would mean is, if Rorty is correct, that anyone could apply his or her own standard (interpretation) of 'charity' to the understanding of Davidson's principle of charity, if they believe it may serve social utility. This leads us to either of two contrary options:

1. The principle of charity is a convention that we find useful for the pragmatic projects at hand; if the principle of charity is coherent with our language-game, then the principle will have relational value to our plans and desires without being in itself intrinsically veridical. Charity is treated as one tool, among others, that helps us realize our ends.
2. The principle of charity is a convention that is of use because it acknowledges that there is, in Davidson's words, 'a fundamentally rational pattern that must, in general outline, be shared by rational creatures' (1990a: 320), and has the same pattern truth and meaning make, so that 'belief, through its ties with meaning, is intrinsically veridical' (1990b: 136). And, conversely, any false belief would be incoherent with the fund of veridical beliefs.

Davidson appears to be suggesting that truth emerges[10] as an interpreter systematically relates propositional attitudes to one another and to various levels of phenomena. Granting that beliefs, intentions and desires are thoroughly interlocking, he thinks that we cannot grasp the nature of any particular propositional attitude by first understanding another without the formation of a vicious circle. Interpretation must be holistic, with close attention to be paid to the patterns of interrelationships therein (Rorty 1999a: 129). Using an analogy between a fallible interpreter and an omniscient one to point out that a speaker will be *objectively* consistent and correct for the most part about the world, Davidson extends the analogy to argue that fallible interpreters will be correct in general 'about the way things are'[11] if, in a dialogue, it is recognized by the participants that an authentic exchange

> ... imposes the constant burden of the interpretation on questioner and questioned, and the process of mutual interpretation can go forward only because true agreements which survive [any] elenchus carry a presumption of truth (Davidson 2005: 240).

Rorty places emphasis on Davidson's effective challenge to the scheme-content distinction: that the interpreter cannot be claiming, with any consistency, that we can achieve a God's-eye perspective about the way things are.[12] However, Rorty continues that, ultimately, Davidson's position points to his, Rorty's, conclusions about truth relative to our local patterns of justification. He thinks that any resistance by Davidson to this point is perplexing. Davidson, on the other hand, maintains that a Tarskian deflationary account (i.e., that Tarski's work on truth captures its essential aspects) is one that he does not embrace. Instead, Davidson suggests that his own view of truth helps to *identify* Tarskian patterns of truth in the behaviour of people. Even though we cannot get outside our own language and its concomitant beliefs, we can nonetheless have the ability to talk with knowledge about a public world that is not fully reducible to conventional structures of a language given that the logic of the interpreter cannot be at such variance with the speaker's own that communication between language-games is impossible (Davidson 1990b: 130). Rorty rightly observes that, *as such*, the implications of Davidsonian Charity bring us only to the conclusion that most of what is cross-interpreted among differing perspectives must be justifiable in one's worldview, but Davidson's approach cannot help us decide how to determine what in a belief is true and what is not other than by what strikes us as justified from our vantage point. And since the notion of our beliefs emerging from some neo-Kantian logical ground must involve the 'fatal' disassociation of meaning from beliefs and from what caused the belief, any attempt to return to pre-Sellars intuitionism is ill-advised.

But if option 2 above does obtain but only in the limited way Rorty suggests, then the decision in favour of option 1 comes by default. As Rorty had advised: 'there seems no occasion to look for obedience to an additional norm – the commandment to seek the truth. For . . . obedience to that commandment will produce no behavior not produced by the need to offer justification.'[13] Thus, we are left free to choose pragmatically from among the competing, coherent images of the world knowing that each must have the ring of truth, but without the possibility of assigning non-discretionary privilege to any of them. Yet with the demise of option 2, the principle of charity would be placed in jeopardy. The power of this principle hinges on Davidson's insistence that the emergence of the logical structure of argument in the behaviours of individuals allows for the confidence in what one's own set of beliefs deems objective, on the whole. And this logical structure can be trusted to significantly overlap the core beliefs, taken together, of the interpreter and a speaker under interpretative scrutiny. Of course, there is never an independent third element (regulative Truth in the Platonist sense) in the interpretative situation, in addition to the interlocutors and their language-dependent beliefs. Nevertheless, as a primitive, truth can be present as a non-reducible (emergent) property of an interpretative transaction.

Until recently, Rorty confessed that he could not see the Davidsonian concept of truth as anything more than 'a theory of justificatory behavior' (Rorty 1998: 25, n. 23). That is, Rorty took exception to Davidson's non-reducible claim that would make central the explanatory power of the concept of truth. If *we* cannot find in the noises and marks articulated by a speaker a set of inferential relationships that coheres to norms pragmatically formed by our community, there will be no patterns of expression to be detected that would qualify as rational. But it would follow that the principle of charity, like all markings on a page, is true because it currently has explanatory power relative to some language community in which it has recognized warrant, *if* we follow Rorty's lead. However, this deflationary account must treat Charity as a mere metaphor (i.e., 'charity'). It is a guiding norm as far as this principle has currency for a particular *solidarity* (a contingent grouping of like-minded persons temporarily sharing some purpose or goal). Once its utility has been cashed out, as a metaphor the principle of charity will be dead, demoted in a new context to a string of marks or sounds without relevant meaning – a museum piece of an idea.

But how could this be? The pertinent question is: How could it not be the case that the principle of charity is a historicist's construct in a Rortian world? As noted above, Rorty's ethnocentric narrative allows for the ranking of neo-pragmatic structuring over its rivals without succumbing to the temptation to lexically order the favoured approach in terms of their corresponding more or less closely to the real. It remained problematic as to how Rorty can cite Charity as useful without also endorsing it as intrinsic veridicality. For it seems that his preference for Davidsonian Charity, in order to be communicated to both supporters and critics of neo-pragmatism, requires charity to be in play *prior* to interpretative acts.

Perhaps, in keeping with Rorty's early paradigm, a solution to the current problem (i.e., the 'principle of charity' itself must be subject to Charity in order for a speaker's project – like Rorty's New Pragmatism – to have meaning) may be that the principle of charity refers, as an object of interpretation, to the frame(s) in which it is nested. The identity of an intentional object, like 'Charity', depends on practices and settings in which it is embedded. Thus any intentional object has a *meaning* in the cultural matrix that *may or may not* include for a culturally sensitive agent what its creator had intended. So in Rorty's hand, 'Charity', as one such intentional object, has meaning that is malleable to his interpretative decisions. And the meanings of those decisions, in turn, potentially are as multiple as there are interpreters of the notion as written by Rorty. 'Charity' evolves in and through the practice of interpretation.

Nevertheless, isn't the logic of Charity uncovered at the meta-linguistic level when we recognize, with Rorty, the evolutionary nature of the metaphor? Are we not led to the utility of 'Charity' by using option 2 to gain stability of the term's meaning? If not, and we revert to option 1 at this new level, then we seem to be in the snare of an infinite regress, where conventionality again and again acts as a tool aimed at some further purpose of our own making – a strategy fashioned to market one's own ever-changing preferences. Or instead, to dodge the ills of an endless regress, we are encouraged to think of 'Charity' as a freedom, the ability to freely produce and project meanings into the future without hindrance. Unfortunately, such unfettered and open-ended generation will include shades of meaning for 'Charity' that must eventually incorporate one that is diametrically opposite to the current Davidson–Rortian usage, thus undermining Rorty's neo-pragmatism.

But the reader might be thinking that such a contradictory meaning for 'Charity' would *never* have currency for thinkers like us. Yet in thinking this, would not the reader be covertly appealing to an intrinsic meaning to guide such a belief? And would the reader also be suggesting that there is a range of

meanings that are false, or logically impossible, when attached to the notion of
'Davidsonian Charity'? If so, then one would have found oneself in line with
Davidson, but at odds with Rorty who supposed that the future is not destined
and is open to all possibilities;[14] and that for all scenarios that will be found to be
possible, the outcome(s) attached to them cannot be said to be irrational any
more than, say, as a species, the rhinoceros or the arachnid is a more irrational
evolutionary outcome than is a monkey. In our paradigm 'Charity' *works*. It has
value for us. Yet, to repeat, there might be a time where 'Charity' will be
described in radically different ways in service to different purposes. Nevertheless, citing Davidson, Rorty continues, '... we can never be more arbitrary than
the world lets be' (Rorty 1999a: 33). Causal pressures will keep us from wander-
ing too far into flights of fancy. But can Rorty make this last statement without
running afoul of his Darwinian thesis? Are not causal pressures intentional
objects, i.e., the construct 'causal pressures'? And given that Rorty adamantly
rejects the 'Way the World Is' arguments, there can be no way he can appeal
to 'causal pressures' as if this description is exempt from his global critique
of representationalism. Once we concede that there are no neutral frames of
reference, and if we accept notions such as, for instance, 'racial categories'
and 'nation states' as pragmatic constructs, then 'causal pressures', as well
as 'the principle of charity', and 'evolution' are to be understood equally as
paradigm-bound conventions that we find useful for the pragmatic projects at
hand. In fact, if you will recall, Rorty already has conceded the last of our three
examples, 'Darwinian evolution', to be such a convention[15] – one among
several competing images of the world. Thus if 'Charity', 'causal pressures' and
'evolution' are examples of social constructs that have various levels of cash
value within the dominant paradigm of Western culture in the early twenty-
first century, then there is no guarantee that they will *work* for future generations or for non-Western paradigms.

Consistency demands that 'causal pressures' and 'the principle of charity'
must be understood as equivalent to that of the concept of 'evolution' within
the earlier version of Rorty's worldview, in the sense of having no special privilege than that which a society accords to them. If my reasoning has been sound,
then Rorty's claim to be a pragmatic *realist* would be seriously undermined.
Of course, Rorty can always define 'realism' to suit his purpose, but that usage
will appear less meaningful once the supporting idea of Charity has suffered a
deflation to option 1. For if Charity does not capture the intrinsic logical pattern
of truth emerging through the interplay of speaker's and interpreter's *logoi*
within the backdrop of a world – Davidson's *doctrine of triangulation* – then
Rorty's attempt to dissolve appearance–reality and intrinsic–extrinsic distinctions becomes a manipulation of sounds and symbols in service to Dewey's goal
of making philosophy 'an instrument of change rather than of conversation'
(Rorty 1998: 29), part of a foundationless cultural endeavour where 'reality'
is a value term or an object of choice. As such, pragmatic instrumentalism
forces all meaning to fall under that which the interpreting 'us' deems justified,
thoroughly eviscerating dialogue by coercing the speaker to abandon her

'barbarisms' in favour of the interpreter's lingua franca. In this sense, 'Charity' would begin and end at home, and we will have *already* found in Rorty's account an example of a definition for Charity diametrically opposed to Davidson's. So while Rorty and Davidson are in agreement that the concept of truth has its many uses and that it is but one of several concepts that form our web of belief, Davidson stresses that without knowing (a) that a belief can be objectively true or false, and (b) under what conditions that belief would be true of some things and not others, the other uses of the concepts would be impossible to grasp (Davidson 2000: 322). And it is upon this understanding that Charity becomes possible.

Ramberg, the Norm of Agency and its Implications

Bjorn Ramberg does a masterful job of elucidating Davidson's meaning relative to our discussion. Whereas Rorty, who initially did not see any philosophical difference between psychological and biological descriptions, would have deflated intentional actions by equating them to one of the many evolutionary 'gimmicks' developed for achieving the distinctive needs and desires of a species, Ramberg takes a Davidsonian position, distinguishing between a description of, and a norm-forming function of, a human community. Whereas we can arrive at an agreement about the description of intentional objects such as snow, the working of a computer or the human anatomy (each manifesting regularities or patterns open to description), when it comes to interpretations concerning the act of interpretation by agents there is a change of subject to a discussion about norms of agency, a change which Ramberg claims is inescapable. This is because:

> [t]he normativity of agency differs distinctively from the normativity of some of the functional concepts we use for the purposes of prediction and explanation in domains where we are not concerned to describe the objects or creatures as thinking beings ... [D]escriptions emerge as descriptions of any sort at all only against a taken-for-granted background of purpose – and hence normatively describable – behavior on the part of communicators involved. The point of the principle of charity in Davidson's account is that this background is *inescapable* for language users, whether (or not) we for some particular purpose are using purely descriptive predicates (Ramberg, in Brandom 2000: 362).

Ramberg offers that Davidson's account accords with Rorty's Darwinian Deweyan claim that redescriptions are useful tools to bring about the kinds of changes in our causal dispositions 'through salience-alteration'. And it is through the manipulation of language that we modify the world in which we are engaged. The pragmatic utility of redescriptions, Ramberg adds, ultimately cashes in because of the effect it has on us through the concept of error. Error arises when there is an inappropriate relation of a description as a kind of thing with a purpose, goal or end we set for ourselves. This failure is uniquely tied to the capacity for redescriptions to alter our dispositions *because* utterances become uses of language, and not some meaningless noise, when directed towards possible or actual events or circumstances. And that directedness can be self-evidently off the mark to the interpreters as well as to the speaker. Thus captured by the concept of error, missing the mark allows for a separation between the utterances and the causal patterns in the world wide enough to allow for intentionality: the system of behaviour that allows us to stand at a distance from some specific object for a specified purpose and then utilize the space to adapt our dispositions (Ramberg, in Brandom 2000: 363). Ramberg concludes that the description of language as a 'very good trick' or evolutionary gimmick in service to some predictive end of our own design cannot exhaust language as a tool for our interests. Rather, our interests extend to understanding the normative vocabulary that is employed in the very act of utilizing descriptive vocabulary. This is what makes agency a different subject than narratives of natural science; psychology does not reduce to biology because norms of rationality underpin all attempts through the use of language at explanation and control.

Davidson himself pointed to the distinctiveness of agency through attempts to interpret each other's descriptions when he wrote, 'We cannot . . . agree on the structure of sentences or thoughts we use to chart the thoughts and meanings of others, for the attempt to reach such an agreement simply sends us back to the very process of interpretation on which all agreement depends.'[16] This failure to depict others in merely descriptive terms (as utilitarian *parametrics* to use Philip Pettit's phrase) ought to alert us to the force of Charity: because description cannot be made without prescription, without being rule-governed, then all descriptive uses of language assume the agency of our interlocutors. Rorty ultimately concedes this point. Consequently, he embraces Davidson's assertion that every account of agency is *automatically* an account of truth, and vice versa (Rorty, in Brandom 2000: 371). Thus there is, according to a Rambergian understanding of Davidson, a privileged vocabulary after all, a normative vocabulary that is inescapable for language-users (Rorty, in Brandom 2000: 373).

If Davidson's doctrine of triangulation, where interplay of the speaker, the interpreter and the world determine the content of belief and speech, holds, then one would not have language, and hence belief, without being linked to a community of human beings and non-human conditions. 'There is no possibility of agreement without truth, nor of truth without agreement' (Rorty, in Brandom 2000: 16). And truth, a converted Rorty grants, cannot be reduced to the mere causal; there are relations of language to world 'which are *neither causal nor representational* . . .' (Rorty, in Brandom 2000: 374).

This concession by Rorty seems to be more than it is. While Rorty now says that most of our beliefs concerning some *thing* must be true, because truth is both intrinsically veridical *and* disputable, he, nevertheless, continues to maintain that there is no hope in getting Reality Itself right because there are no norms available to get it either right or wrong. One can say anything one cares about Reality's alleged underlying nature and 'get away with it' (Rorty, in Brandom

2000: 375). This leaves us with truth 'hovering over' (Rorty, in Brandom 2000: 376) the three corners of the process of triangulation. Still what hovers is no more real than other possible emergent schemes. No interpretation of causal patterns is any more real than any other interpretation. And its salience is determined by which one of them has more utility for human happiness, Rorty concludes.

But the community of justification that results may be one that is radically exclusive and exploitative just as easily as it may be inclusive and compassionate. Having no authority beyond the human community to which to appeal, admittedly hemmed in by the non-human node of Davidson's troika, we are left with the task of finding more useful methods of bringing relevance to ourselves from different impacting background conditions, be they understood as causal patterns or under some other description. The broadness of such a pragmatic search allows for the possibility that, through a process of persuasion, perhaps amenable to rational arguments, a community could consistently embrace, say, a religious radicalism that engages in the harming of innocent persons for the achievement of 'consecrated' ends (as has happened in recent times – only to be itself violently suppressed – in Afghanistan, Egypt and Algeria). And given the Deweyan notion, often cited by Rorty (1995: 128), that there are no intrinsic evils, only competing goods until one or the other is rejected, those 'goods' held close by a community would qualify as truths about the nature of human happiness if they could be sustained in action, over time, to an ever larger assembly of people. And Rorty himself warns that, though improbable as it might be that such an violent ideology, in fact, would be persuasive to *us* in the West in our contemporary solidarity, to impede this way-of-life's persuasive powers would be an act of intolerance (Rorty 1998: 54–55, n. 36) against a competing good. This is the principle of charity in its most politically liberal form. However, concealed behind a cloak of liberalism is the evolutionary struggle over the control of memes: such things as political slogans, moral admonitions, stereotypical icons, ad campaigns, etc. (and, of course, the talk about memes is also a meme itself). Analogizing genetic evolution to meme evolution, Rorty's claim that 'no gene or meme is closer to the purpose of evolution or to the nature of humanity than any other – for evolution has no purpose and humanity has no nature' (Rorty 1995: 128) already challenges at the meta-meme (the vocabulary–vocabulary) level, for example, the Islamic tenet that Allah is One, the source of human nature and meaning, even as he promotes tolerance at the meme (vocabulary) level.

It would seem that Rorty's new appreciation of Davidson's principle of charity and doctrine of triangulation allows for the recognition of the agency of interlocutors in a way he denied in the past. Nevertheless, Rorty's militant anti-authoritarianism associated with his anti-essentialism paradoxically undermines the agency of the other when, in asserting that evolutionary vocabulary is merely a better means to get what we currently want, he imposes a stamp of truth upon the social reality in which all meme alternatives are 'tolerantly' foregrounded. And impose Rorty must, because even when he states that his

own take on matters under discussion is contingent and provisional, he rein-
forces the veracity of the very background, the meta-meme (or meta-narrative)
neo-Darwinian paradigm that he seems to be hedging at the meme level.

Krausz's Singularism and Multiplism

To understand how Rorty's liberal agenda is at base intolerant, let us turn
briefly to Michael Krausz's work on interpretation. In Ritivoi's *Interpretation
and Its Objects*, we find Krausz presenting his controversial division of interpretation into Multiplist and Singularist camps. On one hand, Multiplists hold that
for some objects of interpretation, there is more than one ideally admissible
interpretation of it. Open to opposed, but not to contradictory, interpretations,
the Multiplist believes that there may be opposition over what counts as an
accurate interpretation without there being exclusivity as to what may be considered as valid. Yet Krausz warns that any progress made towards a 'limited
range of admissible interpretations' and the tolerating of one interpretation as
preferable does not make a Multiplist into what he terms a Singularist.

The Singularist, on the other hand, maintains that for *any* object of interpretation, there is one and only one correct (ideally admissible) interpretation.
Any other interpretation must be in contradiction to the correct one. And
whereas the *Singularists* must *deny* there can be more than one ideally admissible
interpretation, the *Multiplists* allow for the possibility of both one and more than
one interpretations. There is an asymmetry here: *Multiplism* may have appeal to
singularity of interpretation but not vice versa. Without an overarching adjudi-
cating standard to settle admissible yet incommensurate interpretations,
Krausz insists that *Multiplism* constitutes an 'ideal condition', understood pragmatically (Krausz, in Ritivoi 2003: 11–13).

Krausz's aim is to decide what distinguishes admissible and inadmissible
interpretations, and what sort of cases answer to one or more admissible interpretations. He believes his view of ideality (*Multiplism* and *Singularism*) aids in
these related tasks. Krausz writes:

> Once within the context of the pertinent practice a given object of interpret-
> ation has been fixed, it can answer to one or (exclusively) to more than one
> interpretation as so counted within that practice. That an object of interpret-
> ation is nested within a practice does not allow that both 'one' and 'more than
> one' may be admissible in an inclusive way. Either one or (exclusively) more
> than one admissible interpretation is to be found within the terms of the prac-
> tice (Krausz, in Ritivoi 2003: 319).

Applying this Krauszian claim to Rorty's neo-Darwinian thesis, one may note
that at the level of image-making meme, Rorty is a Multiplist. And it appears
that Rorty is also a Multiplist when it comes to meta-discussions about
image-making, including his own worldview with all others in the category of

contingent and revisable descriptions of 'the world' (see Rorty 2007: 27–41). Moreover, he seems to seal his association with Multiplism by allowing that future generations of thinkers, as better versions of ourselves, may come to beliefs different than ours (Rorty 1998: 54). Nevertheless, the recognition of conceptual evolution rests on a process that our present notion of rationality proscribes, which distinguishes between rational argument and coercive force. But Rorty immediately undercuts this distinction by allowing for the possibility that, say, radical Islamists or neo-Nazis may have standards of persuasion and force that differ from ours (Rorty 1998: 54, n. 35). This leads him to relativize standards of judgement, on one hand, and simultaneously to appeal to our sense of judgement to finally appreciate that he is right, universally, about the contextual-embedded nature of judgement on the other.[17] Hidden behind his Multiplist stance is a Singularist view.

At this juncture, Krausz might remind us that Multiplists have as an option an appeal to singularity of interpretation. But in this appeal the Multiplist must leave open the possibility that a set of alternative valid interpretations, incommensurate with the one currently favoured, may be operative in a future setting. In this context, Krausz cites Rorty approvingly:

> To say that *we* think we're heading in the right direction is just to say, with Kuhn, that we can, by hindsight, tell the story of the past as a story of progress. To say that we still have a long way to go, that our present views should not be cast in bronze, is too platitudinous to require support by positing limit-concepts (Rorty, in Krausz 2003: 12–13).

Krausz thinks Rorty to be a Multiplist, and not what has been termed a *critical pluralist* (one who holds that multiple interpretations are *equally* allowable). As Krausz remarks, there can be preferred interpretations even as the remaking of works proceeds:

> [F]orcing, adjusting, abbreviating, omitting, padding, inventing, falsifying, results in the production of new works (or objects of interpretation), which may in turn be interpreted. Such interpretation is like a collage . . . By remaking one work one makes another (Krausz, in Ritivoi 2003: 338).

Thus, at the level of object language an ongoing genesis of interpretation is not to be denied. Nor is the interpretation-text itself exempt from becoming the object of interpretation for some later interpretation, in the way a meta-language becomes an object-language for some succeeding higher order meta-language. However, this propagation of interpretations needs a terminus. The reason why can be seen in the following quote:

> Its [a text's] coherence is no more than the fact that somebody has found something interesting *to say* about a group of marks or noises – some way of describing those marks and noises which relates them to some of the other

things we are interested in talking about . . . This coherence is neither internal or external to anything; it is just a function of what has been *said* so far about those marks (Rorty 1999a: 138; parenthetical material added).

But is not the phrase 'to say' simply another set of marks or noises? What privileges these new utterances or scratches over the original marks and noises? Perhaps it is the current conditions and practices that cause the later expressions to resonate with meaning in the way the previous set does not any longer. Thus, the Multiplist may have her preference for that interpretation which carries meaning for her without thereby becoming a Singularist. For example, the German photographer Fiefer's works can be interpreted either as the post war glorification of the Nazi past or as the therapeutic exorcising of that past depending on one's perspective without denying the plausibility of a contrasting viewpoint. Either interpretation is opposed (contrary) but not the contradictory of the other interpretation. But in highlighting and defending this position, Krausz himself wishes the reader to accept his own interpretation of the matter at hand as an adequate (final?) interpretation. This way of arguing for Multiplism is Singularist, unless Krausz is merely expressing a preference, a meta-interpretation open to opposition, what he now calls 'ampliative reason'. But that would be absurd, for the several books and many articles he has written on interpretation would be cast as simple suggestions, informal advice, mere aesthetic sensibilities, and not the serious, tight, rational arguments for a specific position that they are. These rational arguments would be what Krausz has termed 'determinative reasons'. But if this (the mere expression of a preference or ampliative reason) is not the case for Krausz's arguments, neither is it for Rorty's despite the latter's protestations to the contrary. Rorty brings into play a terminus for thought, determinative reasons, in the meta-worldview he offers, even when those assertions are of the nature of denying the existence of such terminal worldview or an unchallengeable 'final vocabulary'. Consider this statement:

> Because every belief we have must be formulated in some language or other, and because languages are not attempts to copy what is out there, but rather tools for dealing with what is out there, there is no way to divide off 'the contribution to our knowledge by the object' from 'the contribution to our knowledge made by our subjectivity' (Rorty 1999a: xxvi–xxvii).

Here Rorty writes about an underpinning of Multiplism, but he does so in a language that is uncompromisingly Singularist. He has no choice. He *not only* suggests that his Deweyan instrumentalist perspective is one among many perspectives vying for semantic 'living-space', and *not only* argues that the neo-Darwinian evolutionist rhetoric is a linguistic 'gimmick' to help free society from the dead metaphors of Plato and Kant, and yet again states that *not only* is the Davidsonian principle of charity one such useful metaphor employed to assure any interlocutor of the reasonableness of his claim that vocabularies are irreducible to one another, and are always tailor-made for some interest often expressing incommensurate 'truths', *but* Rorty *must* also hold these three points with the singular conviction that there is, has been, and will be conditions conducive for humans to design and advance different descriptive strategies unregulated by ontological determinants or trammelled by epistemological necessities. The Rortian flux, to be understood, must be argued coherently as a unified whole. And despite Rorty's acknowledgement that his long-held doctrine of the impossibility for us humans to 'get things right' as well as the position that of the notions 'that "true of " and "refers to" are not word-world relations', must be abandoned in response to Ramberg's article (Rorty, in Brandom 2000: 375), Rorty maintains that other core doctrines – his anti-realism, anti-representationalism, and anti-authoritarianism – 'remain unaffected'. Thus his account, like any thorough Heraclitian account, paradoxically must be made with a single purpose, ironically from an all too often unspoken and unnoticed God's-eye, Parmenidean perspective.[18] To beg away from this view of Rorty's ultimate Singularism (and by implication that all argumentation is Singularist in intent) by suggesting that to write as I have just done is to evoke just one of possibly many interpretations of Rorty philosophy is to ground this Multiplist criticism in Rorty's New Pragmatism, thereby privileging, at a meta-meta- (or paradigmic) narrative level his meta-vocabulary precisely for its advancing the soundness of the historicist tactic of not privileging any idioms. Herein lies the source of what I see as Rorty's incoherence: the criticism against Kant alluded to at the beginning of this chapter can be applied to the mirror image that is Rorty's account; that is, the basis for Rorty's pragmatic realism must itself fall prey to his historicist critique in the same way that it is applied to Kantian theory *if* his writings are made as (Singularist) determinative reasons. *Otherwise*, since all objects of interpretation are under Rorty's Hesiodic narrative already intentional objects ungrounded in a normative reality – things that *seem* as x (chairs, snow, theories, Zeus, etc.) – open to any description one can 'get away with', Rorty's interpretations are ampliative reasons about Multiplism that can either be noted as aesthetic projects and easily set aside as an approach with little utility, or they are covert efforts at paternalistic Orwellian spin (Conant, in Brandom 2000: 268–341) with noteworthy psychological and precarious political implications.

The purpose of the remaining chapters of this book will be to work through in greater detail the problems with which Rorty wishes to grapple and address, and to draw the implication of this just mentioned fundamental inconsistency in Rorty's thought within the contexts of science, philosophy, politics and the self.

Chapter 2

The Foundational–Anti-foundational Debate: Its Modern Roots

Synopsis

In the previous chapter I claimed that Rorty's New Pragmatism was incoherence in that his criticism against Kant – that Kant's transcendental account of Reason, like all other descriptive accounts, was a social construct whose function was to serve a locally perceived social need – can be applied to the mirror image that is Rorty's account. That is, the basis for Rorty's pragmatic realism must itself fall prey to his historicist critique of Singularism in the same way that it is applied to Kantian theory. *Otherwise*, Rorty's interpretations are Multiplist, ampliative reasons all the way down, reasons that can either be noted as aesthetic projects and easily set aside as an approach with little utility, or they are no different than efforts at paternalistic Orwellian propaganda.

A substantial portion of the book will aim to give Rorty his due. Beginning with the next two chapters I will consider the merits of Rorty's rejection of any attempt to establish an account of how one's obligation to others is grounded in a single vision of how everything 'hangs together', while he attempts to avoid the pitfall of insignificance or the charge of illiberal manipulation. The present chapter will focus on the interplay of ideas between Kant and Rorty to expand the issues from the previous chapter. Chapter 3 will deal with the incommensurate thought of contemporary philosophers Nelson Goodman and James Harris, in order to demonstrate the *prima facie* cogency of Rorty's anti-foundational Multiplism.

Rorty's Objection to the Enlightenment's Continuance of Religious Metaphor

Rorty contends that the struggle against scepticism has been manifested throughout Western intellectual history, and has in modern times led to the belief in the ascendancy of the empirical sciences, which currently serve as our culture's paradigm for foundational beliefs. He goes as far as to say that currently science is our secular religion, implying a certain amount of dogmatism in this new sort of faith. Rorty believes that the adoption of the scientific model was a result of a wrong turn, one that has sidetracked Western thought for more than three centuries. The error lies in a continuing search for *arctetic* cause(s)[1] behind claims of empirical knowledge, rather than offering narratives for the pragmatic utility of certain cognitive tools. In taking the Enlightenment position, thinkers since Kant, either with clear intent or unconsciously, have sought internally, in 'inner space', for that which had eluded detection when the search was conceived to be external (in a mundane or supernatural sense) to the process of thought. Unable to appeal to theology for messianic guarantee, an alternative source for grounding became the personal. Yet the trick was to get beyond the (apparent) contingency and subjectivity of our own experience to a place where the question 'What and how much can understanding and reason know, independent of experience?' may be answered without a fatal return to the dogmatic speculations of the theists and their philosophical cousins, the rationalists. It appeared at the time that science itself, for reasons obvious since Hume's critique of causality, could not do the job alone. Therefore, Rorty's narrative continues (1979: 131–32), being misled by the search for the causes of empirical knowledge, the task was seen by Kant and related thinkers to require the establishment of a critical way of thought, which could be separate from yet in support of the sciences while avoiding unfounded suppositions and conjectures.

Traditionally, scientific method required the existence of an impartial distant observer, who can 'step back', so to speak, from the flux of creation and the variations of the mind to identify, gather and process pertinent data which presents itself for discernment. The goal is to fix, or justify, certain beliefs over others through the location of those propositions which are deemed essential to the areas of investigation as to force themselves upon the rational thinker. Ideally this was the fashion by which moral analysis was to be conducted as well.

The axiomatic assumptions active in the scientific approach may be gleaned from the value system as derived from Aristotle's *Nicomachean Ethics*. Alasdair MacIntyre, in *After Virtue* (1984 [1981]: 52–53), notes that Aristotle held a deeply entrenched notion of a special arena, a privileged faculty of discernment that exists and is immune to the pulls of change in nature, culture and emotion. The parallels between a virtuous person as noted by MacIntyre and a skilled scientist ought to be thought-provoking, and point strongly to the basic cultural bias embedded in the stated ideals of scientific research: a person striving to attain the ideal of rationality conducts a disinterested, methodical search for the truth about the subject under investigation in order to bring about greater knowledge about the world and those who people it, and thereby a better future for humankind. It is this sort of embedding of religious/moral values in secular pursuits that Rorty wants to dislodge in favour of a pragmatic narrative as the authentic fulfilment of the Enlightenment's divorce of the secular from the ethico-religious metaphor. And a critical step in this process is to thoroughly challenge, as a reactionary narrative, the Kantian response to Hume.

Kantian Dismissal of Heteronomous Compulsion in Favour of the Autonomous Reasoning Subject

The similarity between the virtuous person and the scientific investigator was not lost on Immanuel Kant. But rather than viewing the parallel as a cultural bias drawn from scholasticism, Kant saw the similarity as a necessary outcome of the structure of the faculty of rational judgement, and led to his development of 'Critical Philosophy', in which the philosopher rather than the scientist or moralist is the one capable of uncovering and understanding the special nature and function of the 'personal', knowing subject as that subject relates to the world and to oneself.[2]

Claiming a new 'Copernican Revolution',[3] Kant challenged the Humean scepticism by accepting as fact that our philo-scientific expectations about *cause* and *ourselves* never meet with disappointment. The reason he gives for this acceptance is based upon a currently familiar, but then novel, hypothesis regarding the relation between the mind and its objects. While agreeing with Hume that knowledge cannot be constituted simply by the receiving sense impressions, Kant rejected Hume's scepticism, promoting instead the necessity for certain fundamental conditions as the underlying basis accounting for the possibility of our very awareness of perceptual impressions, as well as for the obvious growth of the wealth of knowledge at humankind's disposal (Kant 1990: 3). In effect, Kant was arguing for the reversal of the relation between mind and its objects in the belief he could thereby dissolve altogether Hume's problem of induction.

Kant conceived that the objects of experience must conform to the understanding's operations. That is to say, the mind is not a passive receptor of sense impressions. Rather, Kant held that the mind actively contributes *something* to the manifold of impressions it encounters. Therefore, knowledge is possible if conceived as a symbiotic relationship between the knowing subject and the known object. The latter, as the manifold of experience (intuitions), is a necessary but not a sufficient source of humankind's knowledge; it is the raw material on to which the human mind projects or imposes its natural structure, or manner of knowing – the rules of logic.

Thus, Kant attempts to join the empirical and rational theories of his day into a grand synthesis. Significantly, what gets jettisoned by Kant is the phenomenally-based Lockean matter (for to know a thing is to know it necessarily as structured by the nature of the human mind, never in itself), and Cartesian innate ideas (any type of concept severed from that which is given in intuition is a vacuous idea). However, it would be a serious error to suppose that Kant merely wished to confederate the two autonomous realms of intuitions and understanding. To do this would have led to a fruitless search for privileged inner representations and, in turn, a virtual capitulation to the static Humean bifurcation of judgements into synthetic (matters of fact) and analytic (relations of ideas) sorts. Instead, Kant envisioned an indestructible union of the capacity to form concepts and that about which is given in intuition (see Hartnack 1967: 32).

With this insight, Rorty credits Kant for moving from knowledge as objects, as assumed in the positing of Cartesian clear and distinct ideas and Humean 'impressions', to their being of propositions:

> In both the Cartesian and Humean cases, one was choosing objects by which to be compelled. Kant, in rejecting both of these objects as essentially incomplete and powerless to compel unless combined with one another in 'synthesis', was the first to think of the foundation of knowledge as propositions rather than objects. Before Kant, an inquiry into 'the nature and origin of knowledge' had been a search for privileged inner representations. With Kant, it became a search for the rules which the mind had set up for itself (the 'Principles of the Pure Understanding') (Rorty 1979: 160–61).

Thus, Kantian 'experience' – the synthesis of intuition (content) through the employment of understanding (scheme) – attempts to escape the charge of subjectivism by the mind being contained or checked in accordance with the non-arbitrary laws of thought, 'rules which the mind has set up for itself'. They are the manifestations of the structure of the human mind. But 'experience' must also negotiate the difficulty of absolute containment of determinism. We are not to understand ourselves as proposition-making mechanisms. Whereas, in the Newtonian world, all things are determined by mechanistic law, Kantian understanding cannot be alienated from the reasoning subject. If an individual were to follow the laws of nature *heteronomously* – in a non-autonomous fashion under the control of irrational impulses or desires – it would be because the law does not arise from one's own nature. From a Newtonian point of view, the compulsion would be external, complete and absolute, as it is with the body's compliance to, say, the law of gravity.

From a Humean standpoint, however, where there seems to be room for options, some interest, expressed as a reason (e.g., a personal desire for immortality manifested within arguments for the trans-temporal continuity of objects and the indivisibility of substances) must be attached to the surface of the 'natural law' in order to attract the volitional matrix of an individual towards a particular desired habit of belief. It then is an inclination, a want or a desire, rather than the rational will of an individual that directs the agent's actions. Rorty would lean towards this Humean account. Yet for Kant, this thinking is seriously flawed especially when applied in the domain of scientific inquiry.

Humean emotional inclination and Newtonian physical compulsion preclude the free deliberations of the scientific understanding which Kant championed by defending the possibilities of causation and inductive inference. Scientific knowledge, properly understood, shows the scientist how the world lawfully has to be from a human perspective. It does not show merely in a descriptive fashion how the world could appear to be from divergent perspectives. Neither is it a matter of an automatic response (albeit, one unique to our species) to a stimulus. Judgements are being made freely,[4] but without arbitrariness. Deliberations of this sort are feasible only if the scientist can evade the twin dangers of the physical causal 'conatus' or drive of material determinism and the mental causal 'karma' of psychological determinism, as well as the contingent constructions of unfettered poetic imagination. And this can be done only if such laws which frame scientific judgement have an *a priori* or non-experiential, *self-referential* aspect. This is possible, Kant claims, by the human mind uniformly being a self-regulating, self-legislating, hence norm-forming reason capable of making autonomous yet consensus-forming, *objective* judgements.

By taking on the Newtonian challenge to an inadvertent secularization of theism, and the Humean objections to, coining Heidegger's phrase, the 'onto-theological tradition' at the base of Newtonian science (Rorty 1982: 140), it seemed that Kant was in a position to elevate philosophy to the position of not only *the interpreter of the sciences* but of all conceptual schemes, including religious thought. This happened by the transmutation of the problem concerning scepticism about the possibility of discovery of the nature of knowledge into an issue focusing on the possibility of knowledge as we experience it. Appealing to Berkeley's idealism while not abandoning the legalism in Newtonian thought, Kant thought he resolved the problem of the opposition of science to religion and reason to speculation by jettisoning the discredited Berkeleyan 'God' in favour of the recently mentioned 'first-person', self-regulator, self-legislator – the transcendental ego[5] (Rorty 1982: 146). The placement of science and religion under the corrective umbrella of transcendental reason consolidated these apparently incommensurable vocabularies into the idiom of the philosophical. They became, so to speak, but two dialects of one language. Thus, under the Kantian influence the philosopher's meta-narrative became the guarantor of and the arbitrator between the numerous disciplines. The philosopher is seen as the univocal voice of cultural authority; the distinct interpreter of what can be claimed as knowledge. He became the exemplar for that which was humanly possible by being the grounding force of his own opinion if and when he spoke from the position of Reason. From this standing there would be lawfulness without a distant lawgiver. Any person may attach himself to some object without thereby endangering his self-rule, *if* such attachment is accompanied by a positive freedom of attitude, a freedom for a purpose unhindered by the pulls of psychological inclinations, or push of external sociological or physical pressures. Kant claimed that in each one of us there is such a will that is subject to the same law but which is, nonetheless, the author and agent of the law – i.e., in personhood.

The argument for personhood maintains that what makes us a person is that we are rational beings all the way down, to 'strongly misread' a phrase from Rorty in favour of Kant. The persuasions of reason through the rules of logic and the imperatives of moral law are not remote from the person, but are what make the person who he or she is. The agent, as grounding Reason, compels him or herself. Thus we as people are ends in ourselves; we are autonomous persons who have, per hypothesis, the privileged relation to that which causes our construction of propositions about everything, including our world and *ourselves*.

This is due to the constituting nature of the knowing subject and our reflexive involvement in the very act of our judging rationally.

At this point it might seem that I, roughly following Rorty's reading, have been playing loose with Kant, conflating theoretical thinking with the principles of moral action, the very kind of merging that Rorty has accused Kant of and has explicitly rejected. For it is well known that Kant conceived thinking to be a tripartite activity of the mind, divisible along the lines of the faculties of the understanding, the will and the aesthetic sense. It is as a consequence of this division that Kant can assert that culture is organized into the scientific, the theologico-moral and the artistic spheres. However, this tripartite division seems too pat when it is realized that our deliberations, to be rational in the Kantian sense of this term, must be unfettered by theoretical constraints. As J. B. Schneewind comments referring to Kant:

> When we act, he says, we must take ourselves to be free. He means that whenever we deliberate or choose we are presupposing freedom ... because we cannot knowingly accept judgements determined by external sources as judgements we ourselves have made (Schneewind, in Guyer 1992: 329).

It might now be objected that while Schneewind's comment is true, nevertheless, there can be distinctively different kinds of judgements each of which are heteronomous in nature. Of course, upon the briefest of reflections it becomes obvious that this claim is itself a judgement. If, in fact, we are forced into distinctive avenues of thought, then down which avenue does the judgement in question drive? 'Philosophical understanding' is the expected Kantian answer. Yet Kant only gains awareness of the philosophical by implying it, treating it as an 'ought', from the limitations uncovered in the critical analysis of the social practices. Because of the lack of self-justification in the scientific, moral and aesthetic realms, the reasoning goes, there *ought to be* – in order to stop a slide into an infinite regress – a universal, fixed criteria to evaluate the feasibility of their competing, and often incommensurate, interpretations. This 'ought' assumes the Singularist's position of a 'hard' and a 'soft' variety.

We have been considering the hard, Kantian Singularism. Jürgen Habermas provides the soft version when he holds that the rational is manifested through and embodied in our social practices and institutions (see Chapter 4). Preserved in Habermas's minimalism is the metaphor of a unifying voice, but now whispering either here or there in the background rather than commanding from a central position in the foreground, as Kant suggests. In either case, commanding or whispering, why is this insistent, if perhaps subtle, 'ought' so defining? The (hidden?) agenda seems to be a moral-political one: the advocacy for the freedom and autonomy of the individual over and above coercions of the natural and the social. So does the 'ought' of philosophy derive from a transcendental ground,[6] or a logic immanent in all discourse, or a cultural bias for the liberal individual born from the Protestant Reformation? Thus the question at hand, stated in general terms, is: What is the nature of this meta-judgement? Is it

singular and unifying as Kant and Habermas suspect, or is it separate, and heteronomous – the Multiplist's option?

Rorty explains the thinking behind the Kantian Singularist view of knowledge is to get 'beyond argument to compulsion from the known, to a situation
in which argument would be . . . impossible, for anyone gripped by the object in
the required way will be unable to doubt or to see an alternative. To reach that
point is to reach the foundation of knowledge' (Rorty 1979: 159). The foundation of epistemological certainty rests upon the Kantian claim of the 'primacy of
practical reason' (in Kant's *Critique of Practical Reason*, 5: 119–21/124–26; see
Schneewind, in Guyer 1992: 330–33). The now familiar contention can be
restated as follows: if we do not see the limits of theoretical understanding, if
we believe ourselves to be describable in purely empirical terms, if scientific language with its deterministic stance is employed, then we will conceive of ourselves as necessarily heteronomous. However, Kant insists that to be human is
to be autonomous, albeit self-ruling with determinant limits that arise from
one's reason. Nevertheless, Kant also believed that the power of theoretical reasoning is strictly contained within the confines of experience. Thus, theoretical
reasoning has no sovereignty over moral judgements, the core of Kantian
autonomy. Therefore, our nature as moral agents (rational choosers) has juris-
diction over our constitution as rational knowers (Schneewind, in Guyer
1992: 331).[7]

To put the last point in another way, choice is a function of rational agency.
It may be exercised only by an entity that is capable of autonomous action. The
Kantian Understanding alone in its *constitutive* role cannot but accumulate
under one roof, so to speak, and classify observations fashioned from nature
or human behaviour. There must be a method to direct the inquiry of nature or
the empirical study of psychology and politics.[8] However, the Understanding
cannot achieve the necessary distance for deliberation about the goals of obser-
vational sciences themselves, locked as it is into the unifying process of synthesis
via the systematic application of the categories to intuition. Therefore, to make
the judgements about the appropriateness of the methodical applications of the
Understanding itself, there must be assumed a *regulative* role played by a judicious Reason. That is, Reason directs the Understanding to anticipate definite
kinds of regularities in its experience.

To restrain the Understanding from misunderstanding the scope of its constitutive powers and guide it to its proper field of study, Reason must set a
boundary to the former's application. Kant's limit is at the threshold of the
transcendental ideas – self, world and God (those ideas which are usually seen
as open to alternative descriptions – solipsistic, natural and supernatural – of
reality). Thus a judgement about the extent of the utilization of theoretical
ideas (a *meta-judgement* or a judgement concerning judgements about the application of the principles of empirical regularity) must take place in the free space
distinct from the faculty of empirical analysis, conferring the status of 'object' to
those items composed by the faculty of Understanding and *not* the transcendental ideas.[9]

Thus, this regulative judgement arises from the transcendental perspective removed, as it were, from the self-inferential propositional environment. Regulative judgement manifests itself as freedom to choose rationally from within the empirical environment; by reason choosing for itself, from itself, in an act of deliberation about the scheme of things at the object level. But then rational choice about the findings and limits of science and politics has wrapped within it a moral imperative to choose *rightly* about the systematic understanding of the external world and its own faculties. To do otherwise would be to choose *wrongly*, i.e., to denigrate Reason's autonomy by illicitly reassigning the legislative (lawmaking) power inherent in Reason elsewhere (as Kant claims that both Newton and Hume did in quite different ways). There is projected to be a Reason–Reality synchronicity. Though all that we may bring to our understanding is a consistent set of propositions,[10] Kant maintains that the universal consistency of logic presupposes a univocal transcendental truth. Ultimately, there is an expectation that beliefs that are transcendentally grounded are commensurate with Reason. So, empirical truth is to be understood on a moral basis – reason can never be wrong; it is the perfect arbiter, even when it is concerned with the scientific and practical understanding of the world. Rorty writes that in Kant's hand Philosophy gets to be both a science *and* morality and religion since, like science, morality and religion could now be encompassed within the bounds of reason alone (Rorty 1991a: 146).

Adequacy, Intuitive Apprehension and the Kantian Faith in Convergent Reason

The press for a physicist's clarity and precision in Kantian philosophy has at the bottom the remnants of theism, in that Kant retains in his theory the 'priestly' ability to gain a decisive view about the ultimate nature of law-abiding 'reality' and form a sacred (i.e., *privileged*) vocabulary about it. This priestly capacity was transferred into the hands of the philosopher rather than abandoned altogether, to the regret of Rorty. The transcendental idealist's stress on getting our picture of nature *right* is to carry forward the desire for 'adequacy', in the Rortian sense of the term. Granted, submission to a divine will has been transmuted by Kant into compliance with the commands of one's own Reason. Nevertheless, a struggle to express oneself involves discernment between propositions which are *adequate* in their compliance with the rules of thought and those which are not. The conclusive factor in this rational decision-making is the equivalent to a mental inkling for what is commensurable with Reason/reality. Rorty motions toward this 'intuitive grasp' when he explains this, for him illicit, point of view:

> . . . although our only *test* of truth must be the coherence of our beliefs with one another, still the *nature* of truth must be 'correspondence to reality'. It is

thought a sufficient argument for this view that Truth is One, whereas alternative equally coherent sets of beliefs are Many (Rorty 1982: 12).

Since theory guides experimentation (by theoretical ideas pointing the way for the experimenter gainfully to approach experience), and since theoretical ideas, for them to provide useful administration, must be testable in experience, then a hermetic system of relative, self-fulfilling yet mutually unjustified ends forms. The regularities chosen to study are mere arbitrary mental posits (more in this topic below). Unless, the argument continues, the posits can be extended past the closed circular loop and anchored in a foundation of *a priori* reason (or something akin to this), the claims of rational thought would devolve into a shroud of myths and superstitions (one of the alternatives available in the Kantian antimonies). However, Kantian Reason itself must be rooted ultimately in the ineffable, beyond the limits of the Understanding's power to analyse. It is mysterious at its noumenal source. What then is the critical differentiation between the shroud of myth (read *fable*) and the mantilla of the mysterious? The Kantian point is that one who understands an *a priori* proposition will *grasp* it as necessarily true. This immediate comprehension is not an add-on feature but an essential aspect of a true understanding of the *a priori* proposition. A failure to grasp the application of it in every possible world is a deficiency of discernment which would be in need of correction. Therein lies the difference for Kant. Laurence BonJour underscores this point when he says: 'To understand a proposition is to grasp the web of necessary connections with which it *is* essentially bound up' (BonJour 1985: 207).

To reframe the current point, Kant seems to believe that a well-focused judgement corroborates the noumenal roots of Reason through the apperception of the latter's endowment in the laws of thought. This logical rule of law, in turn, supports and confirms the judgement through immediate comprehension, and that this reciprocity is self-justifying and hence unconditional. Furthermore, freedom is found in the acceptance of the necessity of, and action in accordance with, the rule of law as it springs from one's own person. As one may decide to defiantly swim against, or acquiesce and swim with, the strong current of a river, the *decision to fight* the currents of Reason is no more and no less free than the *decision to submit* to its power. Nevertheless, to fight the current would be to alienate oneself from (the Singularism of) Reason and to follow the call of other (Multiplist) voices. As said before, since, as humans, we are defined as such by being rational, Reason's rules ought to be and are our rules. Thus to alienate oneself from Reason is to divorce one from one's reason, and consequently to betray oneself by submitting to the inevitable fate of determinism, or to the incessant swings of arbitrary desire, i.e., to be heteronomous, alien to oneself. In summary, to strive to embrace Reason is to make a choice for autonomy. The ethical and the rational converge, for it can be only through the respect of oneself as a person (in the Kantian sense of this term) that the reciprocity mentioned above is vindicated. The primacy of practical reason is thereby morally sanctioned. Schneewind succinctly expresses the preceding line of thought:

> Kant treats freedom as the ground of our *having* moral obligations, and our awareness of the categorical imperatives as the ground of our *knowledge* that we are free. He thus gives up the one attempt he made to support the principles of morals by appeal to something other than itself – rationality in general – and he uses our awareness of morality as a foundation from which we can extend our understanding of ourselves and our place in the universe . . . If the categorical imperative requires us to think of ourselves and the world in certain ways, then the limitations on speculative reason cannot be used to deny that we have any warrant for those beliefs. Our nature as rational agents thus dominates our nature as rational knowers (Schneewind, in Guyer 1992: 330–31).

Kant's thesis is 'By coming to know the world I begin to get better acquainted with myself'. For if it is imperative to know oneself that one think in a justified manner which will ensure the cognitive atonement (i.e., *at-one-ment* or unity) with Reason, and to act wilfully in harmony with the dictates of that Reason in order to recognize and appreciate one's own personhood, then it is imperative to get things right about the 'starry heavens above' as well. So, if autonomy means being an end for oneself, then to understand faculties of the mind and the orderly and systematic conditions in which the world is structured, it is essential to know the phenomenal environment which one constitutes, and the propositional environment which one constructs to understand the phenomenal *and* from which one gains the footing to act. Hence, as constituting and constructing agent, I react to myself in one aspect: as phenomenal – which is structured and conditioned by my spontaneous filtering of intuition through the categories. Yet, I nevertheless act for myself from the vantage point of another aspect: the noumenal – which is structured yet unconditioned by the commands of the categorical imperative. I must not mistake my reflex to react with my will to act; I must not confuse that which is constituted with the constituting agent. It would be wrong to reduce my self to a mere phenomenon,[11] not merely from an intellectual standpoint, but from a moral perspective which encompasses the Understanding (and hence its judgements about truth) while it resonates with Reason. Therefore, *pace* Rorty,[12] Kant wishes to 'hold reality and justice in a single vision', merging into his life's narrative the feeling of a numinous presence with a desire for moral justice.

Yet, an intuitive conviction in the meaning of Kant's account alone is not sufficient to lift one out of the proposition-bound phenomenal and into the noumenal. While, Schneewind asserts, the limitations on speculative reason do not apply to beliefs stemming from moral imperatives, one may still question the narrative concerning the origin and necessity of these commands. There must be either recourse to theory to support the immediacy of this grasp – BonJour offers 'it would also be nice to have an account of how intuitive apprehension works ...' (BonJour 1985: 208) – or absent such an account, there must be a covert acceptance of the mystery of it purely on faith. Rorty takes the second half of the disjunctive to be the case with Kant's and all final vocabularies as we will see in the next chapter.

The Rortian Edification of the Kantian Philosophy

An uncomfortable situation now makes itself evident. The Kantian foundation of knowledge rests upon scientific and scientific-like philosophical reasonings grounded in *a priori* ethical, intuitive apprehensions. It is a conviction or faith in the primacy of order over chaos, necessity above contingency, and ethics fundamental to science and social practice, in that order. It is a mindset which predetermines the domain of evidence. Kant makes clear his motive for the first *Critique*, thereby establishing the guiding principle for his examination of experience:

> (From what has already been said, it is evident that) even the assumption – as made on behalf of the necessary practical employment of my reason – of *God, freedom* and *immortality* is not permissible unless at the same time specula- tive reason be deprived of its pretensions to transcendent insight. For in order to arrive at such insight it must make use of principles which, in fact, extend only to objects of possible experience, and which, if also applied to what cannot be an object of experience, always really change into an appearance, thus rendering all *practical extension* of pure reason impossible. I have there- fore found it necessary to deny *knowledge*, in order to make room for *faith* (Kant 1965: 29).

To reiterate, the Kantian effort to demarcate the theoretical from practical reason has at base a purpose not opposed to theism but rather an attempt to bypass it while taking from it that which is seen to be its best – its moral outlook. Stumph notes that it was 'Kant's way of explaining the scope and power of pure theoretical reason that made possible his account of the practical reason' (Stumph 1988: 314). It may be suggested that by focusing on the eighteenth- century concern of making the world amenable for faith and morality, Kant angled his inquiry towards that local goal, skewing his investigation in the *Critique of Pure Reason* in the process. While his grasp of the human situation may be truly *a* way to go, it is far from certain that Kant's intuitive apprehension must be infallible or *singular*. As theory guides experimentation, principle guides theory. So long as the principles are grounded by intuitive grasps, there can be room for legitimate disputes about the usefulness of the narrative based on those principles (Rorty 2007: 29–30). Thus, there is room still for the Multip- list.[13] Different intuitive apprehensions can and sometimes do conflict with each other. Each one, from within their respective paradigms, could claim that the other was in error, and proceed to 'prove' this by appeal to the power, and perhaps even the self-evidence of their own basic vision based on their internal criteria for such evaluations. Nevertheless, for a Singularist, as an espouser of commensuration, a common ground must be sought. The imperative tone is assumed because of a faith that accepts unquestioningly that 'Truth is One'. The suggestion that there might be equally valid but incommensurable webs of belief – those without a common standard of interpretation necessary for a comparison to be made – cannot be taken seriously by the advocate of Singularism. Ultimately, for this advocate there must be a common voice, an ultimate common language in which all differences in beliefs arising from the limitations on human cognition can be resolved.[14]

Ironically, it was 'Kant's suggestion that using the vocabulary of *Verstand*, of science, was simply one of the good things human beings could do', which opened the way for allowing this instrumentalist insight to be reapplied to interpret the entire Kantian system in equally culturally relative terms. Thus, for Rorty, 'Kant's reduction of science to the status of a linguistic tool was the first important step in secular, nonscientific culture becoming respectable' (Rorty 1982: 149).

If, as I have suggested, Kant has manipulated science into a supporting role for morality by using the language of science as a means to assert the necessity of autonomy and hence the personhood of rational beings, and if it is granted that this moral end is rooted for Kant in an intuitive grasp of transcendental reality, and further, if the possibility of intuitive apprehensions being fallible is not ruled out,[15] then, since mistakes can and do occur in this regard, a re-evaluation is not only possible but requisite, even for the advocate of Kantian commensurability, with no guarantee of resolution of the dispute (BonJour 1985: 209). Hence, the Kantian system itself – which asserts that self-creation (spontaneity) is held in check both by the given force of the manifold of sense intuitions and the law-abiding constituting nature of the subject, in that the materials with which to work and the structures within which to build conceptions of the world are themselves beyond radical subjective orchestration (founded as they are in transcendental rules of thought) – may be called into question. As a theory concerning the nature and ultimate purpose of human beings, Kant's foundational argument could be treated (and is treated by Rorty) holistically as an edifying value, one particular to a morally-inclined German living in and being influenced by the currents of eighteenth-century intellectual culture; in short, an individual's worldview embedded in his time, place and culture. A diversity of belief systems falling out along societal lines becomes a distinct possibility under this pragmatic interpretation, in line with Rorty's understanding of Davidson's principle of charity even *after* Ramberg's correctives.[16] With the fallout comes the expectation of incommensurable meta-judgements about intuitive principles which is in line with the everyday relativism, as well as more sophisticated philosophical Multiplism.

Taking a cue from these experiences and guided by Hegelian insights, Rorty processes Kant through a historicist point of view, as well as 'the romantic sense that everything can be changed by talking in new terms . . .' (Rorty 1982: 150). And then Rorty takes it one step further. Claiming to side with Nietzsche and James, Rorty believes that the establishment of respectability for a secular but nonscientific culture is nearer completion when one accepts the premise 'that philosophy itself had only the status which Kant and Fichte had assigned to science – the creation of useful or comforting pictures' (Rorty 1982: 150). Entailed in this claim is the dissipation of the last bastion of Kant foundationalism. By dissolving the distinction of discovering over making, judging over constituting, Rorty reduces Kant's claim for scientific-moral commensuration to an ethico-political preference.[17] Pragmatic story-making, the aesthetics of narration for its own sake, topples the transcendental throne – already vacated by the forced abdication of philosophical reason – in a revolution which has as its goal the rejection of the onto-theological notion of discovering the truth (Rorty 1982: 150–51).

The story of how Rorty argues for this pragmatic turn is the topic of discussion in the later chapters of this work. For the moment, suffice it to say that Rorty wishes to complete the Enlightenment project of separation of theism from the secular narrative in order to create semantic space for a democracy of pragmatic humanism. To complete the project, however, he believes that we must go beyond the 'off-limits' signs post-Kantian thinkers had placed around the discipline of philosophy and retro-fit their critique of culture on to philosophy itself. Unleashed in the process, according to this pragmatist's vision, is the radical creativity of a self-assertive individual now unencumbered by the pressures for conformity to pre-established or traditional expectations generated by the 'onto-theological' metaphor. Following the precedent set by the liberal Western democracies separating matters theological from governmental affairs in order to open-up the culture to free discussion, Rorty proposes a parallel divorce of the foundationally-based ethico-philosophical systems from our secular (poetized) culture. In both cases – the precedent and the parallel – the intent is the same: the guarantee of a sphere of self-regard, of personal autonomy and liberty of thought made familiar by John Stuart Mill in *On Liberty*, while simultaneously acknowledging a social sphere of cooperative action beyond self-regarding actions (Rorty 2007: 30).

Chapter 3

The Contemporary Debate:
The Epistemic Regress Challenge of
Foundationalism and its Ironic Impotence

Foundationalists' Renewed Hopes and their Critics

As we have seen in the previous chapter, Kant's attempt at a systemization of reason in order to clear the ground for the possibility of a free, autonomous, morality-capable agent devolved, under the powers of redefinition of Rorty's pragmatism, into an aesthetic local preference, one coherent value-claim among several (and potentially many). The caustic attacks of anti-foundationalists such as Rorty and, as we shall see, Nelson Goodman, have led some philosophers (e.g., Laurence BonJour and James Harris) to attempt different approaches in support of foundationalism, and others (e.g., Hilary Putnam and John McDowell) to eschew foundationalism in favour of an objectivity derived from internal realism.

In spite of the looming issues related to induction (see below), incommensurability (see Chapter 2) and causality, there remains for some contemporary thinkers a firm optimism and confidence in the human ability to ground the rational thought necessary for science specifically and for objectivity in general. As the contemporary foundationalist story goes, by the proper methodical use of our reason an area of consensus can be uncovered. As noted previously, since at least the late 1700s until recently, philosophy, as a discipline set apart by Kant, had assumed the role of the most basic authority in charge of grounding (i.e., properly sorting out the subjective elements from the epistemologically 'given') all the empirical sciences (see Rorty 1979: 132–33). It is this role for philosophy as the self-appointed judge of and for the sciences, as well as the contemporary shift of judgeship to the sciences *per se*, which Rorty challenges as an unsupported attempt to gain the last and indisputable word on all matters of practice and policy.

Nevertheless, contemporary foundational philosophers still have hope that the Kantian intuitive position can be resuscitated, or at least remain the only viable view – the best of all the competing intuitions. The reason for this current optimism by contemporary foundational philosophers can be found in an argument by elimination, based on the assumption that once scepticism is seen as false there seem not to be any plausible alternatives to some form of foundationalism. Laurence BonJour has called their main tool the 'epistemic regress argument'. Briefly, the argument claims that some terminal belief (one that does not owe its warrant to other beliefs) must be necessary – epistemic justification not being possible in the infinite regress which would result in the absence of a terminus (e.g., a linear coherence system).

Thus, the quest of foundationalism, whether it be strong (basic beliefs yield knowledge which is infallibly certain, like Kant's), moderate (the same as strong but not infallibly certain) or weak (a hybrid which mixes a low degree of warrant with supporting coherence relationships), share a kinship in that all, in some fashion or another, attempt to avoid the regress trap by trying to establish a terminal basis for knowledge in justified true belief(s).

The hallmark of such a belief is 'its essential or internal relationship to the cognitive goal of truth' (BonJour 1978: 5). That is, one must have good objective reason to hold something to be true. Otherwise, in the absence of such reason one can be accused of holding positions which, while attractive in some fashion (perhaps its being an ancient, powerful allegory, or, as Rorty puts it, 'a dead metaphor'), is nevertheless neglectful of a serious pursuit of the truth (i.e., 'epistemically irresponsible'). BonJour writes:

> Why after all should an epistemically responsible inquirer prefer justified beliefs to unjustified ones, if not that the former are more likely to be true. To insist that a certain belief is epistemically justified, while confessing in the same breath that this fact about it provides no good reason to think that it is true, would be to render nugatory the whole concept of epistemic justification (BonJour 1978: 5).

Therefore, the search for a commensurable truth is the prime motive for the foundationalist because its internal logic points beyond itself. While this truth in its trans-temporal form might be illusive and debatable, it is nevertheless to be assumed. A position such as BonJour's implies that the alternative, anti-foundational positions can only be self-defeating by being involved in a linear infinite regress, or by being involved in an endless and vicious circularity, or by terminating in an arbitrary and unjustified posit or axiom. Each of the three options is self-defeating, the contemporary foundationalist claims, because each fails in its own way to allow for interpersonal concurrence, thus opening the door to charges of solipsism and scepticism (BonJour 1985: 22). If these charges can be sustained, that would leave the contemporary foundational contention as the only viable position, due to its (alleged) ability to avoid self-defeating non-foundationalist positions.

Harris, Goodman, Rorty and the Question of an Internal Paradox within Anti-foundational Preference

In *Against Relativism: A Philosophical Defense of Method*, James Harris writes to the contemporary foundationalist's main claim in his apology for their neo-foundational position (i.e., that there is reason to be confident in the claim that there is some universal notion of human understanding and a single method through which a fixation of belief is the natural outcome). His is an important position to consider here because he takes rival anti-foundational theories (some of which will be focused upon subsequently) at face value to demonstrate their inability to build from a preference for a given narrative (vocabulary, worldview, etc.) drawn from internal criteria, to the external meta-narrative position. In short, his is a clear and concise argument typical of the neo-foundational position recently sketched.

The building from a preference for criteria internal to their narrative to a meta-narrative that can make evaluative judgements of other paradigms, Harris claims, is necessary for the anti-foundationalists to make their assertion that meta-narratives are, generally, incommensurable. That is, from the anti-foundational, Multiplist perspective without a common standpoint to adequately evaluate one another's criteria for justified true belief, each theory's vocabulary hangs separate and independent from rival worldviews' competing sets of criteria. Rorty's words summarize the anti-foundational position that Harris holds suspect:

> [T]here is no such thing as epistemology and that no surrogate can be found for it in, for example, empirical psychology or the philosophy of language[;] we may be seen as saying that there is no such thing as rational agreement and disagreement. Holistic [anti-foundational] theories seem to license everyone to construct his own little whole – his own little paradigm, his own little practice, his own little language-game – and then crawl into it (Rorty 1979: 317).

Harris believes that a paradox forms for the anti-foundationalist at precisely the point where one 'crawls into' distinct language-games. Either the anti-foundationalist (e.g., Nelson Goodman's view of logic found in *Fact, Fiction and Forecast* which Rorty [1979: 321–22] endorses and recognizes to be hermeneutically immured) is trapped within the internal confines of a meta-narrative from which it is impossible to do the necessary comparisons to sustain an incommensurability claim, or he is caught in an infinite regress of meta-narrative[1] making to sustain a Multiplist stance.

What appear to be interpretations from incommensurable viewpoints from the anti-foundational perspective can be reconstructed to accommodate a level of incommensurability only at a price. As Harris insists, the anti-foundationalist must agree that the claim 'that paradigms are incommensurable can be assessed by criteria which are external to [a theory] only if paradigms are not incommensurable' (Harris 1992: 84), but share some principle, or a single set of rules or a framework in common. Of course, Rorty would unambiguously reject both conditions in favour of a non-constraining, non-confronting *hermeneutics* (a technique for interpreting texts and concepts, theories and principles therein) that allows for incommensurability without there existing a common ground for a convergent consensus (Rorty 1979: 315–16).

For Rorty holds that his anti-foundational position is virtuously circular: '*A rule is amended if it yields an inference we are willing to accept; an inference is rejected if it violates a rule we are unwilling to amend*' (Rorty 1979: 67). Nevertheless, Harris holds that his critical position of anti-foundationalism is borne out by a careful analysis of these 'hostile' anti-foundational theories themselves, from W. V. O. Quine to Thomas Kuhn and Richard Rorty (see Harris (1992: 82–85).

Harris has a deep-seated 'hope' that, given adequate amounts of information, one best account of any event, such as a crash of an airliner being caused by a bomb, a missile or catastrophic mechanical failure, would emerge after investigation. Harris challenges the Multiplist who would contend that a hope for objectivity is merely a preference for convergence; a value call – one among many possible interpretations available – rather than a unique judgement universally capable of attaining that which is true for all audiences. Harris thinks that he throws down the gauntlet by pointing out an underlying assumption that, he claims, must be at work for anti-foundationalist hermeneutical criticism to get off the ground. In answer to questions such as: 'What guarantees that method will converge toward one single theory or understanding of reality?' and 'What guarantees that our changing theories of the world are getting better rather than worse?' (Rorty 1979: 296), Harris states, in response to what he describes as Rorty's 'poignant' challenge, that it must be only in and through the context of scientific method that such questions even arise and can be intelligently understood. Harris reasserts the Kantian belief in the pre-existing objectivity necessary for the design of a well-fashioned theory or systematic interpretation of events, functioning as a focus and guide for fruitful empirical examinations. For as change can only be detected against a backdrop of stability, variations in and among interpretations must be noted over against and gauged from a location beyond the flux and by appeal to some fixed criteria. Harris believes we are led to this (as we shall see for Richard Rorty, impossible) neo-foundationalist position, by the conscious exercise of the scientific method, the use of which reveals the internal logic necessary for an interpretation to be cogent (Harris 1992: 165). To be able to say anything about the relation (either in affirmation, negation or identity) of rival theories logical rules of inference must extend beyond the flux, standing as a neutral algorithm for systematic decision-making by the objective observer or be reduced to an aesthetic experience. Harris calls this the 'criterion of progress' (Harris 1992: 192).[2]

Harris thus states what he takes to be a self-sustaining intuition concerning truth about what is real, scientifically. His argument is allegedly confirmed in the very structure of interpretative judgement used by those who oppose foundationalism by a straightforward analysis; for the anti-foundationalists are forced to use a common method of argumentation (based on logical principles grounded transcendentally) to express their belief in the incommensurability of methodological frameworks. Harris provides an ample number of cases (e.g., from W. V. O. Quine's 'holism' to Hans-Georg Gadamer's hermeneutics) as examples for the failure of what he calls their 'bootstrap method'. Two immediately relevant cases which Harris discusses involve the views of Nelson

Goodman – a view Harris considers a tamer version of relativism than Rorty's pragmatism (1992: 72) – and Thomas Kuhn. Rorty himself is discussed by Harris only briefly. However, by injecting Rorty's collaborative remarks whenever possible and appropriate, I believe an interesting foundational/anti-foundational exchange relevant to my thesis can be achieved.

For instance, Harris holds that Goodman's pluralist account of *worldmaking* is inherently flawed, a result of Goodman's insistence in there being a more and a less 'fit' way of building a radically personal system of beliefs – 'a way the world is' for oneself. In *Ways of Worldmaking* (1978), Goodman relinquishes the possibility of ever designing a procedure or set of criteria which will yield the confirmation of a theory through its correspondence to a world with an underlying 'reality'.[3] However, at the same time not wanting to fall into an abyss of unrestrained and self-defeating relativism, which would allow world descriptions containing UFOs, wizards and New Age homeopaths to stand epistemically with equal validity to descriptions of a world interpreted to have jumbo jet disasters, sceptical philosophers and skilled medical doctors, Goodman asserts a real discrimination for preferring the latter set to the former group: *entrenchment*. More will be said about entrenchment shortly. But for now, from the foundationalist perspective, his use of entrenchment works Goodman into a corner. Because he also maintains that we are all constantly involved in worldmaking in a very *literal* way. This making of 'worlds' seems to yield an infinite number of interpretations, all of which should have an equal claim on our allegiance. Nevertheless, in the debate between Singularists who believe that there is one reality with multiple versions (descriptions) of it possible, and Multiplists who argue that there are a manifold of distinct interpretations ('realities'), Goodman throws his lot with neither, insisting that the issue is beside the point, because there is no neutral way to unpack the notion of 'reality' (N. Goodman 1978: 6, 7, 94–97). Rorty concurs:

> I think that Goodman's trope of 'many worlds' is misleading and that we need not go beyond the more straightforward 'many' descriptions of the same world (provided one does not ask, 'And what world is *that?*'). But his point that there is no way to compare descriptions of the world in respect of adequacy seems to me crucial, and in the first two chapters of [*Ways of Worldmaking*] he makes it very vividly (Rorty 1982: xlvii).

With Rorty's corrective endorsement in mind we may proceed with the unpacking of Goodman's view on worldmaking.

Goodman reasons that all facts are thoroughly theory-laden. The mind is active and spontaneous, forming a myriad of predictive hypotheses from a wealth of concepts. 'Worlds' and their 'facts', that is for Goodman a certain systems of regularities, are thereby constructed out of innumerable possible sets of regularities as each individual unceasingly knits together a unique *world version* – their current, cognitive vision of what is their experience. In answer to the question: 'Can we see ourselves as never encountering reality except under a chosen description?' – as in Goodman's notion of making worlds rather than finding them – Goodman's answer is 'Yes'. Then, does not this imply that universal tolerance is in order, without the ability to separate one set of preferences from any other set? What would justify Goodman's stated discrimination of world versions into categories of 'fit' and 'unfit'? To answer this question and thereby to begin to appreciate the point of contemporary foundationalist criticism and its relevance to Rorty's anti-foundational stance, we must turn our attention briefly to Goodman's *new problem of induction* and its implications concerning the inability to discern a meaningful difference between accidental and lawlike hypotheses.

The famous Grue Paradox (Goodman 1965) allows Goodman to draw a firm distinction between the classical Humean problem of induction and his own, thus updating the challenge to foundationalist intuitions. In his argument, Goodman states that given that two different and perhaps incommensurable hypotheses (Green vs Grue) are confirmed by exactly the same sensory evidence before a certain time t, there cannot be employed anything other than personal or group preference for choosing one hypothesis over its rival. Goodman develops his paradox into a general thesis. Since any empirical observation will always warrant any inference to unobserved facts or events, even those in direct conflict with each other, there never can be established a mechanism for theory-choice which is preference neutral. Yet people tend to prefer one hypothesis above the other(s) (i.e., Green over Grue). To put it in another way, Goodman believes that Humean habits are formed about some regularities and not others. While Hume had noted that empirical experience can never justify any prediction about unobserved phenomena, Goodman suggests that the problem of induction has yet another source, the previously mentioned theory-relative 'facts'. Facts are *underdetermined*. The problem is not just that there aren't any naturally occurring regularities which the mind can positively predict (a stance with which Goodman has qualified agreement), but that out of this regulatory 'void' the mind generates a large number of possible ways to author and organize descriptions of experience. At this juncture Goodman answers the crucial question that Harris posed above: 'Why do some descriptions habitually seem valid, and others do not?'

In Goodman's answer, the ambiguous legacy of Kant can be discerned. Like Kant, Goodman holds that there is no self-defining material world 'out there', independent and ripe for discovery. And again like Kant, Goodman recognizes the creative power of the conceptual intellect. Of course, most unlike Kant and most like Rorty, Goodman unhinges his hypothesis-maker from the (supposed) twin restraints of the necessity of the manifold for the synthesis of knowledge, and of the transpersonal logic of spontaneity which epistemologically grounds and unifies experience. This disconnection, of 'general' lawlike statements from a specific individual accidental hypothesis associated with a specific time and place (based on the rejection – as impossibility tangled and ambiguous – of the traditional bifurcation of hypotheses into non-spatial and non-temporal), grants Goodman's worldmakers considerable latitude for *projecting* – advancing as locally true – hypotheses. (Note this line of reasoning accords well with

Rorty's view concerning the formations of solidarities around historical-cultural language-games that will be an important focus of Chapter 4).

However, one should recall that according to neo-foundationalist philosophers, the general anti-foundational strategy being espoused in Goodman's *Ways of Worldmaking* (as amended by Rorty) starts adherents down the slippery slope of radical relativism, and ultimately to scepticism. Their strategy only confirms Harris's suspicion that arguments of this type will always lead to a fatal infinite regress, a destructive circular self-contradiction, or terminate in arbitrariness.

In anticipation of the form of criticism posed by Harris, Goodman employs the concept of *entrenchment*. In Goodman's analogy, because the Grue Paradox leaves both hypotheses (Green and Grue's) 'actually projectable', it threatens to make relative all actual projections, irrevocably blurring lines between law-like and accidental hypotheses (N. Goodman, in Margolis 1968: 458). Goodman reckons that there must be found a procedure to preserve this useful distinction from within the preference structure of a given group or society. As with legal precedent, entrenchment appeals to historical decisions made by a community.[4] The projection with the greater number of linguistic decisions made persistently in its favour 'entrenches' or grants to it the appearance of valid, lawlike inductive references, and relegates other projections to the status of the invalid. Hence, truth – meaning the generally accepted *interpretation in a community* – would be a function of linguistic convention, involved as it is in pragmatic rhetorical decisions about what has worked for a given community. For Goodman, entrenchment has everything to do with the preferred choice of predicates, and nothing to do with a predicate's supposed correspondence to a natural (non-linguistically bound) fact. Preference itself is impacted by the language already in place or entrenched. This manner of thinking corresponds with Rorty's way of thinking when he writes:

> We can get [commensuration] not because we have discovered something about 'the nature of human knowledge' but simply because when a practice has continued long enough the conventions which make it possible – and which permit a consensus on how to divide it into parts – are relatively easy to isolate. Nelson Goodman has said of inductive and deductive inference that we discover its rules by discovering what inferences we habitually accept, so it is with epistemology generally (Rorty 1979: 321).

As it will become even more evident in Chapter 4, Goodman's view of entrenchment anticipates and supports Rorty's understanding of the sociological nature of truth (see Rorty 1982: xxxvii and Brandom 2000: 89). Thus any criticism of the former may have serious implications for the latter.

Harris wishes to break what must seem to any committed foundationalist to be a self-contradictory claim. Because Goodman's position cannot allow a given projection as ontologically superior to any one frame of reference, *not even his own*, he seems guilty of the charge of being committed to a thorough-going relativism which must devolve into flagrant scepticism (Goodman's comment 'outline of facts concerning the fabrication of facts is of course itself a fabrication' [1978: 107] seems to support the criticism). Goodman's posturing for nonproliferation of world versions by means of the Darwinian notion of fitness, or 'fit for practice', leaves foundationalists dubious. Any appeal Goodman makes for a criteria of rightness, according to Harris, must lead to arbitrary categorizations and a logical self-contradiction common to relativism (e.g., the claim made by a relativist that there are no universals, of course, is a universal assertion), or to a stealthy appeal to what I will call a 'meta-meta-narrative' or paradigmic (Singularist) standard. For a foundationalist there can be no other valid opinions. Even a retreat away from an 'everything goes' relativism to Goodman's dictum for restraint on world versions to only those which are fit, and hence locally 'right', highlights a relativism on the meta-theory level. Goodman's observations at this elevated level must be rule-free if consistency within his programme is to be preserved (i.e., Krausz's ampliative reason). But this allows the reader the radical liberty to take or leave his observations at will; to consider this anti-foundationalist locally 'right' or locally 'wrong' (Harris 1992: 71).

This last point concerning the self-limiting and circular nature of the radical liberty of interpretation has the appearance of a serious charge, one that must be addressed. Rorty recognizes the challenge. He embraces the criticism, and thereby uses the force of Harris's attack for his own purpose. Rorty has acknowledged the circularity like that of Goodman's and asserts that this is a virtuous and not a vicious circle, a circle in which, in fact, all thinking is involved (hence his promotion of hermeneutics). Rorty believes that he stops the view's backslide into self-contradictory relativism by embedding all hermeneutical circles ethnocentrically in the time and place of a particular culture, while embracing Heraclitean-style contingency of all textual claims.

More on his ethnocentrism in Chapter 4. But for now it is worthwhile to note that Rorty holds the circular flow of foundationalist thinking itself. And if Rorty is correct about the embeddedness and circularity of all thought, is not Harris's analysis of Goodman's version of worldmaking itself biased and circular in some way? For example, Harris 'elevates' Goodman's new problem of induction out of the arena of induction and into a discussion about *abduction*: a reference to the element of Peirce's tripartite division of logic which contains the formation of hypotheses as distinct from deduction and induction:

> If we adopt Peirce's distinction, then the new riddle of induction is properly viewed as a riddle of abduction, a *meta-scientific* riddle . . . For Hume's problem [of induction] to arise, the hypothesis must already be in place. Goodman's new riddle of induction is clearly a problem concerning how a hypothesis gets selected for confirmation (Harris 1992: 60–61).

To appeal to a separate category of reasoning in this fashion has the hallmarks of foundational inclinations deeply carved in the discrimination. There is already in place the belief that a self-destructive epistemic regress must ensue if there is an attempt to bypass the grounding of confirmation theory in a universally comprehensive, meta-theoretical structure. We seem to have returned to the anti-foundationalist point that was made earlier against Kant. That is, for Harris to apply Peirce's bifurcation of confirmation theory from hypothesis formation is to beg the question. What is up for discussion is precisely the issue if it is the case that lawlike, theory-formation is of a logically different kind than confirmation theory. Of course, from within the neo-foundationalist viewpoint, where the scope of the search for the truth is circumscribed by the criteria manifesting preordained principles, there is a foregone conclusion that beliefs which are ungrounded (in a manner defined by neo-foundationalists) are irrational because of their contingent (read *arbitrary*) status.

Furthermore, Goodman makes a good case against syntactical and, as noted above, semantic supports for lawlikeness (Goodman, in Margolis 1968: 456–58), thus laying the groundwork for Rorty's own anti-foundational stance. Goodman strikes at the core of the Kantian assumption about lawfulness by bringing under scrutiny assumptions therein about regularity's purity and uniqueness in a way well-suited for a pragmatic criticism. The well-known conjoining of *a priori* rules or conditions with necessity is supposed to contribute the fruits of scientific explanation and prediction by exempting these rules from contingencies and vagrancies of location in time and/or space (or as Rorty puts it, to allow for the projection of rules 'from the conditioned to the unconditioned – from all imagined audiences to all possible audiences', Rorty in Brandom 2000: 32). Even if the rules held in this fashion, and we ought not concede that they do at this moment, the application of them to any given situation, or to any association with manners of linguistic expression, is still a judgement call made from within a particular meta-narrative. It is still a construction of a system of regularity imposed upon the subject matter. Unless an indisputable foundation can be unearthed which has the power to overwhelm dissent – and as we have seen earlier, an overwhelming extrinsic force precludes self-asserting autonomy and, hence, self-control – then a sceptical question is never far off. Until then, the rules are wide open for radical interpretation, and hence revision or even replacement, given that there seems to be no evidence suggesting an irresistible elemental, empirical given, or constraining logical force to compel assent, once the basic intuition (Rorty's *final-vocabulary*) for them is disputed by an evaluator. Justification appears to turn local and individual, even for the foundational language-game. Thus whether Goodman's new riddle of induction is understood as part of the traditional controversy associated with confirmation theory or as belonging to the debate over the existence and nature of abduction, the basic issue of the difficulty of epistemological choice – the relative, but perhaps not limitless, freedom an individual has to exercise that choice in judgements independent from external constraints or internal compulsions – which Charles Taylor has termed 'self-determining freedom' (Taylor 1991: 27) – is still alive. Or as Goodman writes: 'My outline of the facts concerning the fabrication of fact is of course itself a fabrication; but as I have cautioned more than once, recognition of multiple alternative world-versions betokens no policy of laissez-faire' (N. Goodman 1978: 107).

Conversation over Confrontation: Rorty's Rejection of Commensurable Debate

Nevertheless, as was said in the previous section, a foundationalist does not have to prove that his view must hold to maintain a basic faith in his position. All that must be shown is that the anti-foundational Multiplist position is untenably self-defeating. Thus we turn our attention briefly to Harris's critique of the work of Thomas Kuhn, always with an eye on how the dispute impacts on Rorty's narrative.

Harris argues in a similar fashion to his critique of Goodman that at the metanarrative level, Kuhn's theory, as espoused in *Structure of Scientific Revolutions*, cannot be supported by its own internal logic alone and must lead, when properly understood, beyond itself to a grounding reason. That is, if we turn Kuhn's argument back on itself, either there is no objective reason to prefer and adopt Kuhn's theory over another (it is simply a matter of arbitrary preference[5]), *or* if one is 'converted' by Kuhn's engaging and comprehensive narrative and adopts the theory in an inspired moment there arises no opportunity to question this choice. The freedom critically to evaluate the choice of paradigm is forfeited by the act of being won over by his alternative narrative. Debate is closed at the moment of conversion; rational evaluation, and consequently the ground for meaningful exchange of opinions about the choice, have already been ruled out by the exclusive power of the paradigm change (see Rorty 1999b, *passim*). For any foundationalist aware of the importance of freedom for Kant, this outcome is unacceptable. From their viewpoint the 'bootstrap method' fails once our liberty to make a fair, impartial and reasoned judgement in favour of or against, say, Kuhn's theory, has been undermined by the internal logic of that selfsame theory. The freedom of self-determination, which Romantically inspired anti-foundationalists laud, is paradoxically eliminated with the disqualifying of convergent rational evaluation. The personal motive to adopt a Kuhnian view, *sans* Kantian Reason, devolves to blind chance, mere happenstance, or, ironically, *external* verbal persuasion. The neo-foundationalists assert that the loss of the ability objectively to ground theory in such a way as to eliminate the contingencies of time, place and (counter-)cultural bias renders anti-foundationalism epistemologically impotent. Once again, neo-foundationalists argue, this leaves as the only plausible alternative some version (perhaps yet to be formulated) of scientifically reasoned inquiry, due to this generally being the only objectively, self-correcting, reliable and non-contradictory method for grounding theory. Harris concludes:

> Not only is science the only method within which it even makes sense to talk of mistakes, it is, additionally the only method which purifies itself by eliminating those mistakes. Science is the only method of fixing beliefs where the very practice of the method itself does not give rise to doubts about the method (Harris 1992: 167).

However, Harris's criticism underscores a pattern of debate which Strawson finds, at best, misguided, and which reveals the assumption behind the arguments of the neo-foundationalists, most specifically when they deal with a Rortian-style anti-foundational approach. Strawson observes:

> So there arises the demand for a justification, not of this or that particular belief which goes beyond what is entailed by our evidence, but a justification of induction in general. And when the demand arises in this way it is, in effect, the demand that induction shall be shown to be really a kind of deduction; for nothing less will satisfy the doubter when this is the route to his doubts . . . Of course, inductive arguments are not deductively valid; if they were, they would be deductive arguments. Inductive reasoning must be assessed, for soundness, by inductive standards. Nevertheless, fantastic as the wish for induction to be deduction may seem, it is only in terms of it that we can understand some of the attempts that have been made to justify induction (Strawson, in Margolis 1968: 445).

But, Harris insists, it would be epistemologically foolhardy to attempt to address the specific issue of induction, old or new, or more generally, to take part in the debate between neo-foundationalist and anti-foundationalist, without first ensuring a common vocabulary for communication by grounding the discussion within some fundamental logical principle(s). This move, of course, frames the wider debate in the way Strawson objects to in the narrower issue (see note 4). The anti-foundationalist, to make his case about the ultimate contingency of theory choice, must either sacrifice his entire project by engaging the neo-foundationalist within the latter's language-game – a deductive enterprise which has but one outcome, that of a QED in some transcendental, determining source – or break off the debate at the point where the theist-inspired notion of truth by compulsion resurrects itself in the appearance of the infinite regress argument. As Rorty states, a concept is 'just the use of a word'. And well-loved words or phrases are not abandoned when confronted by 'would-be knock-down arguments' (1999b: 4–5), because 'classic philosophical stand-offs are not susceptible of resolution by means of more careful and exacting ways of drawing out meaning' (1999b: 13). It is, therefore, no wonder that Rorty wishes to change the subject by dropping the pretensions of a philosophical debate where the expectation is that there will be one and only one winner of this trial by intellectual ordeal.[6] Rather he would prefer to open a conversation among distinctive narratives, where the aim is to exchange life-stories in a non-competitive, edifying manner.[7] Here the reader ought to be reminded that Rorty wished the foundationalist to engage in a conversation within his, Rorty's, own paradigm. If there is no neutral ground from which to compare intuitions against stable and universal criteria, as Rorty believes, then at least he is consistent in his position, even if the yearning for a consensus converging upon a unifying narrative is thereby frustrated. Rorty contends that the trade off is worth it: a liberal and inclusively tolerant democratic community. (I will take up Rorty's contention in this book's Part III.)

Rorty holds that the guarantee for creative and humane conversation rests in the isolation of the poetic, self-assertive imagination to the sphere of the private while arranging for the possibility for free, unrestrained public dialogue. This can be accomplished, he argues, by minimizing coercive language associated with the encouragement of the pain of physical cruelty and psychological humiliation, and through the solidarity formed around liberal-democratic institutions designed to ensure tolerance and non-malfeasance. In dividing the public and the private in what I will call his 'Jeffersonian Strategy', Rorty believes he can prevent the onto-theological, imperious use of language while ensuring the unrestricted and uncontained exercise of one's creative imagination. In this way he holds that the domination of the theistic-influenced Kantian metaphor can be finally and fully set aside, opening the way for a liberal, tolerant expression of multiple, incommensurate views (Rorty 2007: 35). Thus, it is no surprise that for Rorty interpretative Multiplism is thoroughly aligned with the historicist camp. As D. P. Chattopadhyaya has put it, there can be no grand scheme of universal epistemology or methodology. Rather, an austere relativism currently prevails, with a concomitant multiplicity of interpretations of what is 'really there'. He continues in close agreement with Rorty: 'our ways of knowing the world, manifest or scientific, are unavoidably interwoven with our habits and actions and means of coping with the same' (Chattopadhyaya, in Ritivoi 2003: 229).

Rorty would take exception with Chattopadhyaya's friendly use of 'relativism' as he would with Harris's foundationalist challenge. Rorty's version of pragmatism eschews the relative-absolutist distinction that has dominated much of philosophical discourse. He does so by rejecting the idea that the justification of our beliefs to each other makes it likely that our beliefs are true for all audiences, past, present and future. In 'Is Truth a Goal of Inquiry: Donald Davidson vs. Crispin Wright' (in Rorty 1998), Rorty argues that there is no reason to believe that justification will guarantee the possibility of universal truth. To assert justificatory universalism is to assume that representationalism is a defensible position. But as already argued, Rorty believes that there is no way to know *THE* truth about things in themselves. Therefore, truth should be understood in its cautionary mode. That is, the use of the term 'truth' is a warning against making unconditional assertions in the face of unpredictable situations that are bound to arise in the future. And when a narrative appeals to more and more people, there is a corresponding lessening of the danger of rebuttal, and hence less need for vigilance. Nevertheless, there is never a moment when caution is terminated in one final, unconditional vocabulary. (Issues of induction merge with our experiences in justifying our beliefs to an audience.)

Thus Rorty's anti-foundationalism seems to sidestep Harris's charge of an infinite regress as well as the charge of aiding scepticism. If he argued otherwise, Rorty would be admitting that the space of reason is finite and structured. Reality would then function as a given that shrugs aside inaccurate representations of itself, opening the field of thought to more and more accurate imaging of what is by denying what isn't. In refusing to play the foundationalist's representational language-game, Rorty presents a view that aims to *persuade* readers of the utility of the intellectual tool he is employing. His use of this tool is pragmatic and not epistemic.[8] By proposing a novel way to understand our social environment, Rorty offers us an intellectual adaptation that, if it works, will meet our current needs. It will not expose or conceal an underlying reality that structures the social world any more than Kant's intellectual tools did.

That does not mean that contextuality slips into a self-defeating relativism. To think differently, Rorty continues, would be to presume the possibility of a non-contingent, universal justification; that this tool now being used is a tool that will be of equal use in all contexts and under all conditions, suggesting its utility has to do with its close fit to what is. Such a presumption would be like claiming that a hammer is not only a good tool for hitting nails but a good tool for every purpose. Therefore, justification cannot converge on some universally grounding principle, just as a particular tool cannot be useful in all situations. As Rorty asserts, there is 'no area of culture, and no period of history, gets Reality more right than any other'. Nevertheless, echoing Goodman's notion of entrenchment, this does not prevent the advancement of a social solidarity which one finds to be serious (as opposed to frivolous and arbitrary) by being in accord with one's personal sentiments.

For instance, as Rorty often argues, if there is no practical difference between convincing one's peers to accept your perspective and having your perspective taken to be true, then to claim otherwise is to fall victim to what Sellars termed 'The Myth of the Given': the idea of a clear and incorrigible presence of a fact, truth or entity impressed upon one's mind. And the claim that there is some non-human authority that specifically determines truth from falsehood is merely a preference for a narrative tool that no more and no less gets at what is real than any other language-game one may employ (Sellars 1991: 140–41). And unless the neo-foundationalist can demonstrate a difference that makes a difference, then their final language should be recognized for what it is: one among many approaches to the puzzles of life. Their persistent claim that the foundationalist narrative is justified by the conditions of the world, or is a better bet because the Goodman–Rorty view is a self-defeating circular argument, is in the same way logically circular. Thus the neo-foundationalist view is in danger of being deemed as a self-defeating argument under neo-foundationalist criteria.

Rorty's Rejection of Putnam's Internal Realism

We appear to be confronted by a philosophical stand-off. This impasse might yet be avoided if Rorty's argument would only move towards a position called 'internal realism'. This position accepts that it is impossible to settle which interpretation is adequate to the way the world is. Nevertheless, it is possible for universal truth to emerge from the persistent dialogue between narratives using the social conventions at hand. Hilary Putnam is an advocate of this type of realism,[9] in part because he finds, like Harris, Rorty's standard notion of justification to be self-contradictory. But Putnam takes a different tact on this charge than Harris. Putnam's critique centres on Rorty's claim that justification is both a sociological question and a basis for reform. Putnam's puzzlement stems from his difficulty in understanding how any of a private dissenter's beliefs could ever achieve warrant if justification rests with the majority of his peers. Putnam wonders:

> How does 'Maybe a majority can be wrong' cohere with [Rorty's other] claim that what is and is not a warrant for asserting something is a sociological question? Can a sociologist, qua sociologist, determine that a majority is wrong? How? (Putnam, in Brandom 2000: 84).

If it is admissible for a sociologist or someone else to assert warrant apart from the majority's current judgement, then reform of the majority's beliefs is possible because '[t]here can be better and worse norms and standards' (Putnam, in Brandom 2000: 85). And Putnam has a point because this sort of reform is implied, as we shall see, in Rorty's Jeffersonian Strategy, when the poetic impulse challenges the entrenched metaphors of her contemporary society. Reform, Putnam observes, is logically independent of whether or not people take it to be a reform, and that this understanding is internal to his and Rorty's shared sense of 'reform'. To oppose Putnam on this point would leave Rorty's sense of 'reform' as a mere 'compliment' given to whoever enacts the sort of change Rorty endorses.

And what justifies Rorty's practice of pragmatically justifying our beliefs? Nothing. Putnam charges that to be consistent with his claim that justification is sociological, Rorty ought to invest effort in empirical research of the actual norms and practices alive in the current Western culture. But Rorty's anti-representational position prevents him from embracing a scientific approach. This leaves him with only a story about Western cultural practices – his poeticized story. Putman reminds us that, for Rorty, stories

> ... cannot represent accurately or fail to represent accurately; they can only enable us (that is, enable Rorty himself, when he is the one telling the story) to 'cope' or fail to enable us to 'cope' with the flux that bombards our surface neurons (except that for Rorty, even speaking of 'surface neurons' is already telling a story ... one which Rorty, unlike Quine, does not wish to privilege) (Putnam, in Brandom 2000: 86).

Rorty's tact also makes 'sociologists' characters of Rorty's narrative; fictionalized agents of judgement in the story Rorty is constructing. Putnam echoes Harris's allegation that anti-foundationalists such as Goodman and Rorty are trapped in solipsism. Putnam refuses, however, to join Harris in the foundationalist camp. Rather Putnam opts for what he terms internal realism. He resists the idea that we must transcend our subjectivity to achieve an objective standpoint. Putnam (and, as we will see, John McDowell) insists that while situated in the world we can reach agreement about the facts of that world: that is, the norms of inquiry reach beyond solidarity and converge on factual truth through the active exchange of interpretations. The conditions for the objectivity about the world can be analysed only in concert with the conditions for the intersubjectivity of a mutual *understanding* of what is being said by a speaker and heard by an interlocutor.

Rorty, however, refuses to embrace the entirety of Putnam's internalist arguments, because he considers that talk about such things as intersubjective agreement is locally embedded and unavoidably transitory (Rorty 1998: 46). Furthermore, Rorty rejects what he sees as the subtle scientism in Putnam's recent writings. The use by Putnam of phrases like 'just a story' and 'just conversation' causes Rorty to believe that Putnam is still entrapped in the onto-theological outlook that depends on Kantian-like attempts to find something ahistorical in the causal flux of life to shepherd diverse voices into tight consensus. Putnam's recent adaptation is for Rorty an unfortunate regression to the representationalist story-line that has played out its effectiveness in the contemporary world, even in its repackaged internal realist form.

Rorty thus claims to remain a Multiplist all the way down. How, with the rejection of internal realism, Rorty can still maintain his Multiplist stance without slipping into destructive relativism or, alternatively, running afoul of the Heideggerian critique of pragmatism as itself being the unfortunate culmination of the onto-theological tradition's will to power, especially in the light of some Rortian comments, will be the topic of the next chapter.

Part II

Chapter 4

The Denial of Scientism and Performative Contradiction: The Aesthetics of Pragmatic Narratives

The Contingency of Language and Scientific Essentialism Synthesis

The implications of Rorty's philosophy are as devastating as they are liberating. To bring on new worlds of fresh ideas, the belief in transcendence must be bleached out of philosophical, scientific, moral and political judgements – even when cast as intersubjective meaning running through diverse interpretations (as internal realists wish) – and the material re-dyed in ethnocentric multicolours of synthetic origin. Sociological agreement becomes the only method for the advancement of local or 'tribal' norms. This means that Multiplism must also extend to logic. From the anti-foundational, Multiplist point of view logic is no more or no less a form of poetic narrative than the stream-of-consciousness writings of James Joyce. Rorty says as much in 'Response to Hartshorne' when he discounts the possibility of an ideal language in favour of the proliferation of contingent language forms (Rorty, in Saatkamp 1995: 30, 32–33 and 35–36).

But is Rorty's vision of western rationality a democratic revolution driven by and allowing for aesthetic creativity as Rorty claims it is, or a paternalistic solidarity that introduces antinomianism and the rule of power in place of a hierarchy of reasoned methods and their institutions? What does Rorty offer which will avoid the Pandora's Box of capricious and cruel invention, warned against by Heidegger, once the poetic language replaces the narrative of structured authority founded in either external metaphysical or internal interpersonal constraints? Can Rorty's advocacy of an unconditionally licensed productivity of the poet be adequately balanced by a historicist's sense of a principle of tolerance in social practice without tipping over into either self-indulgent subjectivism or cultural imperialism?

In order to establish his 'democratic utopia', Rorty recognizes the need to contain radical self-assertiveness when it manifests itself in the practice of public cruelty and humiliation. However, his brand of pragmatism prevents him from appealing to a unique human nature as the basis for self-control in public situations. This presents Rorty with the responsibility of distinguishing radical creativity from fanatical resourcefulness without recourse to transcendental solutions available to Kant (see Chapters 2 and 5) or twentieth-century philosophers such as Harris, Carnap and Hartshorne (see 'Wittgenstein, Heidegger, and the Reification of Language', in Rorty 1991b: 53–54), or Putnam's internal realist alternative.

As it was previously noted, standards are local and ethnocentric for the Rortian pragmatist. Thus, what counts as radically creative or fanatically over-the-edge expression is relative to the group to which we think it is necessary to justify ourselves – to the cadre of shared believers that determines the reference of the word 'we'. For such a pragmatist, justifiability to a community that would entail a transpersonal truth is 'simply irrelevant' (Rorty 1991a: 176–77).

To Rorty's critics, his dismissal of convergent consensus around truth seems ad hoc and potentially a dangerous development in the light of world events since the Holocaust. If the Kantian option is truly blocked and foundationalism flounders, and internal realism slips towards representationalism, then philosophical realists must seek an alternative route to counter Rorty's attack upon the contemporary definitions of rationality and truth. What seems to be needed is some theory that allows for a non-privileged,[1] contingent choice of language – in line with Rorty's view of languages as artifacts of human use which are wholly pliable to our pragmatic intentions – that also fixes upon (1) those parts of our experience (e.g., our interaction with the physical world) that can be shown to be identical in all possible redescriptions of the worldly encounter or (2) the communicative rationality that links truth with justification from within a given language. Such attempts may be found, respectively, through the use of modal logic in Saul Kripke's theory of reference and Jürgen Habermas's notion of unconditional validity. In an attempt to amplify and focus points made in the previous chapter, we turn now to these thinkers.

Habermas offers a version of 'internal realism' that extends Putnam's version by directly challenging Rorty's ethnocentrism even while it avoids commitment to representationalism. And while Kripke's theory, put forward in *Naming, Necessity, and Natural Kinds*, is itself largely outside the theme of our current discussion, his attempt to insist on a correspondence theory of knowledge while maintaining the contingency of language offers us bridging insights into the issue of justification and truth in what I believe is a significant manner. Thus, I will present Kripke's views first and then consider Habermas as a pragmatically based supplement to Putnam's internal realist argument.

Kripkean Scientism

The Kripkean concept of a 'rigid designator' refers to the same object or individual across the spectrum of possible worlds in which that object or individual would exist.[2] The reference is not to be confused with Lockean nominal essences. For unlike the 'scientists' of Locke's time who could not reconcile in an orderly fashion the variety of radically different qualities, resulting in a haphazardly gathered collection under the same term (e.g., the psychologically traumatized and the epileptic under the category of 'insane'), modern science has a distinct advantage over its predecessors. With modern science's power to identify (with relative accuracy) entities in the world through orderly empirical observation and analysis based on inductive inference, it is believed by advocates of scientific realism that the employment of this scientific method is crucial for the discovery of the fundamental, underlying structures of the universe. The method has had the happy consequence of dispelling myths, superstitions and misconceptions about the world and its contents, while simultaneously empowering experts in the field with the ability to penetrate to what is actual and not merely skim at the level of the phenomenal or merely engage in effect-oriented, creative linguistic projects.

However, any attempt to account for this power of insight must confront and explain the fact that the terms used concerning 'natural kinds' – objects which have their essence in common (e.g., the atomic number 79 defines what is essential among all lumps of gold) – had their origin in pre-scientific language use. Prior to modern science the only way to ascertain if the 'stuff' in question belonged to a particular kind was by sociological justification; the practice of comparison of said 'stuff' to the description, or concept popularly accepted in that culture, to ascertain if there was a fit. If successful, then the 'stuff' was proclaimed to be of that certain kind. A major problem with this method for the scientifically inclined (but of course not for anti-essentialists like Rorty) is that descriptions, as well as the details of the general definition of the 'stuff' singled out, could vary from person to person and by community. This diversity of opinion would leave anyone who was concerned at arriving at a convergent consensus about the common nature of, say, gold, epilepsy, or the like, in a quandary as to the boundaries and limitations of a kind. Furthermore, another concern for convergence realists is the perceived need to maintain the separation of theory-formation from political and social practices. For once the socio-political aspects of inquiry moves from the background into the foreground, the issues associated with various values, interests and cultural perspectives enter and would contaminate the reflective process. Therefore, the attainment of knowledge requires the radical separation of theory and practice, reason and emotions, science and culture.[3]

Kripke maintains that sociologically derived definition descriptions are handy, albeit limited, means of locating things of a certain kind named by a speaker. These referential descriptions do not in any way determine what it is to be of that kind. For Kripke the properties of a thing, that which a thing truly has or is, is ultimately a matter of nature and not of language.

What was done by the primitive speaker was, coining Putnam's term, 'to baptize' or to make an initial use of what is taken to be a good example of some naturally occurring substance, such as gold, and then invent the term 'gold' to subsequently refer to whatever has the same set of appearances or qualities as the precedent-setting sample. Kripke further held that the speaker need not have knowledge of the real essence of the object. The designator, by use of their senses only, need be aware of the surface qualities associated with that object. Yet, as noted, this sociologically based method is highly inexact (for example, the confusion involved in identifying the accurate categorization of fool's gold or of the marsupial mouse,[4] and at worst it can be dangerously misleading (e.g., the close appearance between edible mushrooms and poisonous toadstools).

Kripke, encouraged no doubt by such historical examples, argues against the beliefs that what occurs in a case like the marsupial mouse was not that the new discovery was merely a conventional (contingent, *a posteriori*) replacement of the ad hoc non-scientific label with the more defined scientific idiom. Nor does he hold that an expansion of the analytic definition of 'marsupial' was enacted to include this mouse-appearing animal. Rather, Kripke believes that something more basic happened. He claims that, if true at all, the discovery was an uncovering of the necessary physical essence of that creature, and that this disclosure was an integral part – the last link in the causal chain – of the original enterprise initiated by the 'baptism' made by, as it were, British colonists in Australia (Kripke, in Schwartz 1977: 93). Kripke postulates the possibility of an *a posteriori* necessity.

Kripke's causal theory has a name refer rigidly in all possible worlds, regardless of any particular facts about the bearer. A name or a term will refer to some entity rigidly even if some, most or all of the qualities associated with its traditional or baptized description do not obtain in some possible world. Hence, what Kripke maintains as important are the properties (identified by labels such as atomic number 79, H_2O, etc.) that do hold under all possible descriptions of the worlds in which the entity in question could exist; that is, across all 'worlds' Goodman could 'make'. It is these trans-world properties, discovered empirically, which would be considered essential or necessary to the entity. All other properties or qualities discoverable *a posteriori* would be considered contingent – obtaining in some but not in other worlds[5] (Rorty 1982: xxiii).

Kripke holds that it is uniquely science's task to uncover precisely what that 'stuff' is in all possible worlds where it may exist. An analytic list of properties logically implied in an initial baptism would be superfluous to whether the term obtains in a given case, except perhaps for the list to function as a cluster of markers which help the hearer or reader to spot and interpret what the speaker or writer had in mind, and thereby initiate the process of scientific inquiry.[6] Rorty, referring to Kripke as one of the 'technical realists', puts it this way:

> The question 'Is "X is Ø" *true*?' is thus to be answered by discovering what – as a matter of physical fact, not of anybody's intentions – 'X' refers to, and then discovering whether that particular or kind is Ø. Only by such a 'physicalistic' theory of reference, technical realists say, can the notion of 'truth as correspondence to reality' be preserved (Rorty 1982: xxiii).

The assertion that there can be necessary *a posteriori* discoveries is a tenable position from Kripke's point of view due to the distinctions which he makes between the epistemological from the metaphysical, and both from the notion of the analytic.[7]

Kripke first notes that the term *a priori* is an epistemological notion meaning knowable independent of the phenomenal realm, while the linguistic conception of *analyticity* means tautologically true. Then he remarks further that the metaphysical idea of *necessity* as being true in all possible worlds (a modal notion) could accommodate *a priori* and analytic concepts. This is nothing new. However, he continues by claiming that synthetic scientific propositions arrived at by empirical discovery can be necessary as well – if and only if what is discovered is the essence of the 'stuff' (marked by rigid designators) which is under investigation.[8] Thus, the claim is that 'scientific essentialism', as it is called, is a method that escapes the surface or merely linguistic identification of objects, and arrives at an appreciation of a core reality. And it arrives at the essential, it is claimed, without appeal to Kantian transcendental notions, or slipping into cultural nominalism. Scientific essentialists, such as Kripke (and early Putnam),[9] reason that since natural kinds are uncovered by methodological scientific investigation, and since such discoveries are seen to be empirical yet necessary truths, scientists must be the investigators capable of peering directly into the underlying structures of kinds, be they chemical, biological, or of physics. As such, the scientists are said to be the final arbiters of what is real apart from the merely sociological and psychological; linguistic usage being a mere catalyst in the process of trans-linguistic correspondence of rigid designators to natural kinds. As Rorty also notes in the introduction to his *Consequences of Pragmatism*, the early Putnam asserted:

> The trouble is that for a strong antirealist [e.g., a pragmatist] truth makes no sense except as an intra-theoretic notion. The antirealist can use truth intra-theoretically in the sense of a 'redundancy theory' [i.e., a theory according to which 'S is true' means exactly, only, what 'S' means] but he does not have the notion of truth and reference available extra-theoretically. But extension [reference] is tied to the notion of truth. The extension of a term is just what the term is true of (Putnam, in Rorty 1982: xxiv).

The early Putnam illustrates his point when he admits that he has no knowledge that could distinguish elm trees from beech trees. He has precisely the same concept of one as of the other: 'a deciduous tree growing in North America'. Yet when Putnam makes a statement containing the word 'elm', we take him to be referring successfully to elms. If he makes a claim about a property of elm trees, it will be considered true or false, depending upon whether that property applies to those trees which are in fact elms. There is nothing 'in the head' that could fix his reference; rather, he concluded, his linguistic community, containing some speakers who did know the difference between the two trees, ensured that when he said 'elm', he referred to elms. Putnam refers to this feature of language as 'the division of linguistic labor', a division that privileges the expert with the authority to rigidly designate or fix scientific meanings. This interpretative authority is at the heart of Kripke's theory.

Organism-Environment Interface:
The Discarding of the Cartesian Mind

Nevertheless, there is a difficulty with Kripke's approach to truth. Donald Davidson refers to the Kripkean position as the 'building block' approach to reference, paving a causal avenue leading from object to individual speech-acts. But this form of causal connection is problematic. Rorty notes that Kripke's approach can be susceptible to errors in the establishment and determination of exactly what there is. The referential avenues may be, in fact, wrong-headed or dead ends. Thus with Rorty, we focus on one implication of Davidson's warnings about the scheme-content split, as follows: '... [one] may never know to what [one is] referring. This allows the possibility of a wholesale divorce between referent and intentional object ...' (Rorty 1991a: 134).

Applying Davidson's denial of the scheme-content distinction developed previously in Chapter 1, along with his slogan that causation (unlike explanation) is not under a description – properly understood,[10] if we take Kripke's theory at face value then it seems possible that a relation between the world of causal events and a set of beliefs can vary or 'slip' to the point of complete severance – be false, despite all else remaining as it is, that is, even if the causal links between objects and individual speech acts are unaltered. Rorty charges:

> This approach leaves open the possibility that speakers may get these path-ways wrong (e.g., by being largely wrong about what there is) and thus that they may never know to what they are referring (Rorty 1991a: 134).

Why must this be so? If, as Rorty suggests, the initial use of language is like any other use of language (i.e., the product of cultural manufacture) then all 'baptisms' are *fully* sociological. Kripke accepts this condition, but continues that as familiarity with a given nominal designation is shared and passed on throughout a given linguistic community, the extra-lingual referent is carried along (in a causal chain), but remains fully shrouded within its definite description. Not until the scientific community establishes a firm word–world relationship (e.g., 'water' is necessarily H_2O) which resists subjective schematization or local linguistic convention, that is, they rigidly link the specific set of noises or marks to a natural kind, is the shroud lifted to reveal reality. But this claim for a non-conventional causal hook-up between word and world misses its mark. Rorty elaborates on the issues involved in the underdetermination of theory:

> [O]ur ability to give a causal account (e.g., an evolutionary account) of how we came to use the words we do and to assert the propositions we assert shows nothing whatever about whether we are representing reality accurately. *Any* community with a reasonably complete language and a reasonably imaginative scientific world-story will be able to give such an account of how it came to speak and believe as it does (Rorty 1982: 133).

Rorty contends that in spite of Kripke's reliance upon it, the term 'corresponds' ceases to be helpful because of the 'world' being underdetermined. When there is allowed to be a gap between designator and referent, there is driven a wedge between referent and intentional object with all content being washed from the referent. This opens the way for incommensurable descriptions that may have equal cash value in that they both give us functioning pragmatic accounts capable of achieving that which we aim for. And it is the ethnocentric nature of knowledge claims that cause conceptualizations of the 'facts of the matter' to be in the context of some convention or language-game. For, according to Rorty, any causal transaction can be exemplified non-rigidly by many 'conventions of representations' depending on the practical needs of a particular group. This permits Rorty to say that there is getting meanings right, not *representing* meanings correctly (Rorty 1998: 37). Therefore, the use of the terminology of 'representing accurately' is not propitious in demarcating discourses one from the other, and, in fact, interferes with the constructive flow of conversation among discourses by designating one language game as epistemically privileged over all other discourses. Rorty can hold that Kripke's ridged designations are not necessary *a posteriori* placeholders that accurately refer to natural kinds; they are socially constructed tools to achieve certain practical ends.

Furthermore, Rorty's stance against Kripke's *Scientism* does not affect Rorty's credentials as a realist. To assert that there is a reality that is the cause of our account of it is not to say that the description one has currently built up is the only one that is accurate and, hence, exhaustive of the ways in which the causal environment can be described. The scientific idiom is a particularly successful narrative approach to the achievement of practical ends, but this does not suggest that *lingua sciencia* is the singular means of escape from the constraints of an entrenched language to one that has more utility. There is nothing that privileges scientific vocabulary to allow for it to rigidly determine terms in a way that other disciplines cannot. As already suggested, the causal world is underdetermined. There will be alternate, systematic descriptions or designations of the causal environment that will account for any body of observations.

With this pragmatic reading of designation it can be inferred that there can be no 'slippage' in the causal relation between the organism and the environment. Rorty contends that judgement and reality are linked to the point of never being out of phase with each other (Rorty 1991a: 10–11).[11] The Rortian socially-embedded sense of judgement is limited to Humean 'habits of action'. Included in this are the marks and noises which are usually characterized as human (public) communication. Judgements are not representational in this sense. Asserted in the Quine–Davidson–Rorty argument, meanings and beliefs are inalienably intertwined. Rorty likens natural essences to 'lumps' and states that '. . . both Kripke and his opponents are too preoccupied with the distinctive lumpishness of lumps'. Rorty suggests that rather than attempting to capture sameness in either words (texts) or world (lumps), we think of them as points within the 'transitory webs of relationships' (Rorty 1991a: 89). Therefore, with no possibility for a Kripkean-style abstraction of the essence of reality from the way it seems to us, and thus our believing and speaking about it, there can be only 'better and worse nominal essences' (Rorty 1991a: 86). This is as it should be, given Rorty's 'Jeffersonian program' (Rorty 2007: 30–31) to exorcise what may be termed the 'ghost of the Will of God', which must be in force to inspirit the 'intentionality' of natural kinds (Hall 1994: 91). The rigidity of science melts into a fluid form of literature once we question scientific essentialism from a neo-pragmatic perspective.

From another angle, the 'slippage' of which Kripke is accused stems from and is connected to the familiar Rortian charge that there is the misguided need by some to impose an observing intermediary (i.e., a rational mind) between an organism and its environment that is able to realize and isolate the sense (meaning) discovered from the appropriate physical fix between word and world. Hence, if we are not cautious, by reifying linguistic acumen we again fall prey to the scheme-content dilemma which leads to the erstwhile realist's hierarchical ranking of alternative conceptual schemes in terms of metaphysical adequacy. Rorty asserts that if we remove the representational supposition of the observing 'I', the 'fatal temptation' to hold on to the distinction between 'in itself' and 'for us', then the difficulty of determining which of these schemes is precise in its designation of the real is easily removed. There is nothing further to seek than that which we already know about the causal transactions between the organism and the environment. We can deal with the coherent patterns of noises and marks made by that organism and shared with others in the community in response to the surroundings without positing an observing subject that is immune to the contingent and the transitory. The shifting environmental pressures and our collective actions and reactions to them form the historico-sociological differences among patterns of justification. What is propitious, then, is what works in the present context, not what is materially fixed by a privileged subject.

Following Davidson's appeal to Charity and his concomitant rejection of a building-block atomistic approach in favour of a holistic semantic, we must take those responses made by socially embedded speakers to environmental pressures to be mostly true. To impose an intermediary of a Cartesian mind with its 'inner representation of the environment' is for Davidson a category mistake that makes the truth to be as if an object to be grasped and tested against a 'fixed goal' beyond linguistic utterances. Rorty agrees with Davidson. To Rorty's way of thinking, the idea of goal fixing implies a metaphysical picture that rests upon an archaic understanding of truth and meaning; a reified metaphor of the Mind's Eye that is past its prime.

In summary, to judge is not to discover, whether transcendentally, by an independent standard, or by an essence which 'makes true' the judgement. Nor is it through the Kripkean use of a contingent vocabulary which serves to delimit an area of study until the time in which a science can confirm, by the use of a rigid designator, the underlying universal modality of a natural kind. To be 'true' is simply, for Rorty, to cohere in a linguistic pattern which 'hangs together' well, or 'works' pragmatically as an explanation relative to an interaction between an organism and its environment. Hopes for a theory-independent, language-marking, matter-of-fact relationship such as Kripke proposes must be abandoned, along with the contrast noted previously by Davidson between the world and the world as we know it. Thus the neutral distance underwriting the power of scientific discovery, and hence scientism, is an illusion. It is because of this chimera that objectivity and its dialectic opposite, subjectivity, dissolve for Rorty. There is no way to be simultaneously inside and outside a language-game. Rationality must become local rationalizations (i.e., opinions based on solidarity – politics – and not an epistemology of convergent and fixed truths). Correspondingly, the free-standing discerning self fades away in the face of this pragmatism of Rorty's – supported by selected arguments of Davidson.

Normal Language and the Creative Challenge of Ironic Innovation

If Rorty's critique of Kripke is compelling, a question arises as to how the misguided conception of an 'inner' and an 'outer' reality initially takes hold and dominates human dialogue. If we, as organisms, cannot be 'out of phase' with our environment, how then did previous organisms (most notably, philosophers) ever fall (in an almost biblical sense) into the original errors of traditional notions of objectivism, foundationalism, scientism, and the illusion of a substantial (free-standing) self? Any historical appeal to an earlier manifestation of the error (e.g., the needed projection of the gods of mythology to explain that which was beyond the comprehension of the ancients) merely delays the ultimate posing of the selfsame question.

Rorty could manoeuvre beyond this problem by an appeal to a transformation reminiscent of Kohlberg's.[12] The contingencies of one age are not those of the present era. What worked in the Enlightenment no longer works today. Yet people cling to past conventions, as if sacred dogma, and miss the change of circumstance that beckons an alteration in convention. This holdfast attitude might be likened to a person of adult age who clings to adolescent behaviour despite the adjustment towards responsibility a spouse and child demand.[13] In addition, given that for Rorty the vocabulary associated with causation and rationalization ought to be strongly distinguished one from another,[14] it is implied that a fissure between the causally interacting public 'self' and the creative, judgemental private 'self' must run all the way through the individual as well. Hence, while organisms *per se* cannot be environmentally out of phase, for human persons, at least, their reified account of circumstances can be at odds with other contemporary accounts more in tune with evolving conditions.

If we accept the pragmatic position that all language-games are equal (i.e., none more privileged than any other as accounts of reality), being contingent artifacts which are more or less tailored to organism-environmental interplay, then no language-game is epistemologically superior to another. It follows that the Rortian language-game is not automatically superior to that of, say, the Enlightenment's or ancient Greece's. Still, the contingencies of the present time, culture and material circumstance may favour his pragmatic vocabulary rather than that of Descartes, Kant or Plato. But this in itself is a judgement made from within Rorty's language-game; this was the sense of Putnam's charge quoted at the end of the last chapter. So why should the reader choose Rorty's narrative account of our interface with the causal world? Because Rorty's pragmatic take on things works for a contemporary audience? This too is a judgement, also from within Rorty's narrative. Are we left with smoke and mirrors when it comes to the judgement of pragmatic utility? Not if we accept the further judgement about the contingency of the self and ethnocentricity that is the basis of any theory, as Rorty suggests we do.

To insist on context-independence would be to endow reason with causal powers that enable a particular descriptive vocabulary to resist refutation regardless of time, place and social conditions. If reason is not so endowed, one may conceive of an ideal audience with the collective ability to speak a privileged vocabulary that allows its constituent speakers to escape human limits and achieve a God-like grasp of the totality of possibility. But Rorty insists that there is neither such an audience, nor a privileged vocabulary that provides, *a priori*, a language of justification with the potential to draw all mundane audiences into universal consensus. There are only diverse linguistic communities, each of which has their own final vocabulary, their shared context-embedded perspective on reality, a 'reality' that is always and already interpreted from that standpoint.

Since, in the Rortian narrative, the reality-appearance distinction is a remnant of our authoritarian onto-theological tradition – the transmutation of the extrinsic, non-human power (that must be submitted to) into the secularized intrinsic nature of reality that still carries with it all the authoritarian drawbacks inherent in the tradition's outdated metaphor – then the secularized metaphor of power/submission ought to be discarded along with the remnants of its religious origin in favour of an ongoing conversation among individuals and solidarities. And Rorty believes that his narrative is able to accomplish this aim.

To Rorty's mind, a natural order of reason is one more 'relic' of the idea that truth consists of correspondence to the intrinsic nature of things. Absent an ahistorical standpoint from which to judge the intrinsic nature of reality, there is no such thing as a proposition being justified without qualification or an argument which will better approximate the truth *per se*. For Rorty, there is no context-independent reason which somehow indicates and underlies all descriptive vocabulary. He considers the idea of context-independence truth a misguided effort to hypostatize the adjective 'true'. Such hypostatization leads one to believe that there is a goal of inquiry beyond justification to relevant contemporary audiences. Rorty often states that all reasons are rationales for a particular people, constrained by spatial, temporal and social conditions. When we have justified our beliefs to an audience we consider pertinent, we need not make any further claims, universal or otherwise. This goes for the argument Rorty now makes for his own perspective. To 'ground' his views, Rorty embraces Western values.

It is obvious that by encouraging open-ended conversations, Rorty does not want to throw out entirely the fruits of Western culture. To the contrary, he says that he is 'lucky' to have been raised within this cultural tradition, especially because of its complementary tendencies for critical analysis and tolerance. Still, he does not hold that his luck of being raised in a tradition of liberal tolerance is any different from that felt by Germans who considered themselves fortunate to enrol in the Hitler Youth in service to the Führer. It's simply a chance matter as to in which society one is born, and what set of beliefs have come to be valued therein and inculcated into its children.

Carrying forward his naturalistic, Darwinian views into education, Rorty sees us humans as creatures whose beliefs and desires, for the most part, are formed by a process of acculturation. With no non-relative criteria or standards for telling real justifications from merely apparent ones, it follows that there can be no teleological mechanism independent of specific social narratives to determine the socio-ethical superiority of one solidarity over another. Furthermore, if we all acquire our moral identity and obligations from our native culture (the niche in which we find ourselves), and there is no way to elevate one social narrative above the rest, then why not embrace our own social virtues and theoretical contentions as valid and try to redefine the world in terms of them? This is Rorty's Protagorian argument for ethnocentrism: there is only ourselves nested in the habits of action evolving over time into the current, provisional societal solidarities we find useful for achieving our purposes. To look beyond our ethnographic conditions to a view from nowhere is impossible; to take on habits of action alien to Western understanding and practice is the folly of giving up the historical ground for our poetic licence and replacing it with alien ideas, values and goals.

Once we do accept (if we do) Rorty's ethnocentric model as a way to avoid Heidegger's criticism of pragmatism as the ultimate fruit of the onto-theological mindset, the question of 'Why Liberal tolerance?' ceases to be a philosophical inquiry concerned with uncovering knowledge of the truth inherent in Liberalism and becomes a political notion focused on achieving the practical outcomes that such a notion renders possible (more will be said on this shift to the political in Chapter 7). But it seems then that the only feasible line of defence left for us against cruelty and humiliation of, say, slavery or genocide, in the face of pragmatic tolerance of free poetic invention, is to boldly assert the solidarity of liberal democrats. As Rorty, in an optimistic mood, hopes in 'Philosophy and the Future':

In politics there will be only *one tradition*: that of constant vigilance against the predictable attempts by the rich and strong to take advantage of the poor and

weak. Cultural tradition will never be permitted to override Rawls' 'difference principle', never permitted to excuse inequality of opportunity (Rorty,
in Saatkamp 1995: 204; emphasis added).

Obviously, in a contingent world these future pragmatic utopians will have to
be blessed with the perennial luck of having persuasive speakers among their
ranks so that the judgements upon which the principles of liberal rights are
based are never out of vogue, and the cry of 'Never Again' is in no way silenced.
As noted in Chapter 3, Rorty adamantly states that the triumph of any final
vocabulary is never possible.[15] Then a 'hope against all hopes' must be made
that future vocabulary shifts will be only in the direction of a deepening commitment to the bourgeois freedoms Rorty and other 'wet liberals' favour. For as
we previously observed, there is no guarantee for what they deem as a fortunate
trend – for progress in the Deweyan sense – beyond chance and struggle in the
universe of contingency.

Even if we, in a less critical mood, join Rorty to optimistically embrace this
constantly threatened task of sustaining liberal solidarities, there still remains a
lingering doubt: to maintain, along with Rorty, that to state something to be
impossible is to claim that it is not to be believed by any audience. From his
perspective this claim aptly applies to the theories of Kant and Kripke. Then
the alternative offered by Rorty is presented as plausible – a.k.a., believable
by at least contemporary audiences. However, if we consider the position of
Charles Taylor when he writes, '. . . to believe something is to hold it true; and
indeed, one cannot consciously manipulate one's beliefs for motives other than
their seeming true to us' (Taylor, in Malachowski 1990: 258), we might ask if
Rorty plays fast and loose with a phrase like 'true to us', claiming that it is historically embedded when convenient to his theory-building, and forgetting this
limit when trying to be a persuasive and creative narrator. I believe that, in
fact, he equivocates in this matter, and that this equivocation directly affects
his ability to argue coherently for his thorough-going Multiplism. And this
inability in turn will impact on his rationale for separating public vocabularies
from the private ones with detrimental implications for his entire New Pragmatism project.

Yet, for the moment, if we grant to Rorty that the dividing line between
objectivity and subjectivity has been blurred to the point of non-relevance,
and if we accept that Rorty's anti-foundational arguments correctly challenge
the onto-theological claims running through scientism, as well as Kantian and
internal realist thought, while allowing his arguments to escape being painted
by the same onto-theological brush, then the force of Rorty's critique of these
claims must be a matter of aesthetic preference. This conclusion Rorty recognizes and embraces. Absent metaphysical and foundational grounding, Rorty
argues that 'the right sort of theoretical glue' naturally binding together the
social organism and the private person is never available. At best, all that is
at hand to bind societies and individuals are the twin adhesives of common
vocabularies and shared hopes.

These shared hopes would be expressed in the public rhetoric in a nominalist and historicist manner. Derived from a local, conditional common sense, rather than a studied, theoretical convergence on one truth, this solidarity is based on a common vocabulary of shared future longings associated with the pre-linguistic impulse to avoid pain and seek happiness (pleasure). This we share with the animal kingdom. How a local community understands life's pangs and mobilizes to avoid present discomforts and injustices so as to garner a modicum of satisfaction is a matter of trial-and-error adaptation. And language is the tool that creates the necessary opening for the alteration of our common condition – in line with the cultural preferences we inherit – which in turn enables the projection of future hopes to alleviate a present tormenting state of affairs.

Simultaneously, language use makes possible a unique form of pain for those individuals who are out of step with common practice, namely a punitive vocabulary of humiliation and condemnation designed to reinforce public sentiment (understood as common in intolerant Singularisms of the onto-theological ilk). This is where liberal (Multiplist) tolerance enters the Rortian narrative. A forbearance of differences is a counter to this tendency to use language to shame into silence the poetically free spirits. Noting that tolerance has been the device that has greatly contributed to the flourishing of innovative ideas among Western cultures in recent centuries, Rorty, in his ethnocentric mode, sees no reason not to recommend it to the rest of the world. And recent history has shown the pragmatic worth of this narrative. It is a value that has extended, beyond societies where this liberal tradition began, to far-flung lands and societies that are without a history of liberal open-mindedness. Finding a niche in different cultural soils, liberalism has been adapted to distinct social environments as it spreads, while at the same time changing the local social climate to one more hospitable to its prospective adoption. But unlike a natural species, liberalism's existence can never be wholly a matter of random selection, even while its survival is never guaranteed. As we have seen, for Rorty, there can be no assurance that the preference for liberal democratic principles will be sustained in a future social environment; just as there is no guarantee that the human race will maintain its present biological status in a changing natural environment. Nevertheless, a conscious manipulation of language raises the chances of liberalism's survival above mere chance; liberal democracy may be realized, when it is, only intentionally and wilfully.

A convincing story, Rorty's narrative has a hypnotically persuasive effect. While drawing the reader into his account about the contingency and historicity of all narratives, Rorty's own storyline, linked as it is to neo-Darwinian interpretation, ironically takes on the air of descriptive factuality that Kripke wishes to claim for science. It is easy to forget that Rorty readily admits to be writing as a creative poet who offers a pattern of marks that signify his web of beliefs, a central strand of which maintains that there is no privileged vocabulary, no *a priori* language of justification that allows for a universal consensus. We'd also do well to remember that Rorty holds that there exist only diverse linguistic communities with their own final vocabulary, and their shared context-embedded perspective on a 'reality' that is interpreted from that stand-point. Thus, Rorty presents us with an Escher-like loop, a hermeneutical circle that turns on the assertion of the compelling cogency of his meta-narrative as he lobbies for his narrative's justification in a Darwinian social context devoid of privileged standpoints. What is left unsaid by Rorty and often unnoticed by his critics is that his meta-meta-narrative or alleged new paradigm describing a universe of communities with multiple, incommensurate final vocabularies is a Singularist claim that either, *pace* Rorty, must necessarily justify itself to all audiences to remain credible, or is itself an embedded perspective susceptible to future deconstructions. If the former is the case, then at this higher narrative level Rorty is open to Habermas's charge of performative contradiction. If the latter holds, then an inexorable proliferation of meta-narrative levels develops, leading to an infinite regress that makes it impossible to sustain meaning at any narrative level, as BonJour and Harris have predicted.[16] In short, either Rorty's project is not cogent or it is semantically empty. Let us now consider each case in its turn and Rorty's response.

Habermas's Performative Contradiction Critique

The motivation for the continued attempt to fix judgement among persons and across cultures is stated succinctly in Crispin Wright's *Truth and Objectivity*. Wright expresses a concern that if there is no 'fact of the matter' to ground meaning of sentences rigidly, then

> ... there are no substantial facts about whether or not they are true. Thus irrealism about meaning must enjoin an irrealism about truth, whenever the notion is applied. And irrealism about truth, whenever the notion is applied, is irrealism about all assertoric discourse (Wright, in Rorty 1998: 36).

It is the inflation of the relativity of judgement and the failure of externalists' attempt to ground truth in transcendence that inspires Jürgen Habermas to locate a universal justification within language.

Habermas writes in 'Richard Rorty's Pragmatic Turn': 'In forfeiting the binding power of its judgements, metaphysics also loses its substance' (Habermas, in Brandom 2000: 33). With the loss of judgement's binding power, philosophy can be rescued from its drift towards irrelevance only by a post-metaphysics 'metaphysics'. According to Habermas, this is what Rorty is attempting to do. In Rorty's hands, philosophy must become more than academic; it must become relevant in a practical way. Recasting Heidegger in post-analytic terms, Rorty see the deflationary trends in contemporary philosophy as leading to their own negation if left unchecked by edifying creativity. These trends form a pattern that can lead to their own extinction if there is not new life breathed into old metaphors by restating them stripped of their corrupting Platonic metaphysical prejudice. Central to this bias, according to Habermas's understanding of Rorty, is the Platonic distinction between 'convincing' and 'persuading'. Rorty wishes to replace the representational model of knowledge based on the knowledge/opinion distinction with a communication model that discards objectivity for intersubjective solidarity. Doing so would eliminate the antiquated and elitist distinction between convincing and persuading, clearing the way for an unbiased, open-ended conversation among equals who actively participate in the identification and pursuit of valued practices, so Rorty hopes.

Nevertheless, Habermas contends that the Deweyan vocabulary which Rorty uses obscures an important and necessary line between participant and observer. By assimilating interpersonal relationships into adaptive, instrumental behaviours, Rorty cannot distinguish between the use of language directed towards successful actions and its use oriented towards achieving understanding. Without a conceptual marker to distinguish argumentation from persuasive manipulation, 'between learning and indoctrination', Habermas thinks that Rorty's project is lacking critical standards that make a real difference in our everyday practices. Habermas concludes that Rorty fails to realize the nature of intersubjectivity demanded by his project, an intersubjectivity that presupposes an interplay of conflicting interpretations that opens to the possibility of error relative to beliefs currently deemed justified by a particular audience. Self-awareness of the possibility of error in normal (embedded) language use undermines dogmatic convictions in an individual's now problematized beliefs, allowing for the distinction between believing and knowing that encourages the individual to explore other interpretations, other discourses.

Habermas employs the term 'lifeworld' as the dimension where one's discourse projects against and (potentially) overlies other ways of life in the public space of intersubjective communication. Communication is understood by Habermas as a cooperative enterprise where discourse and practice interplay as interlocutors speak and act upon each other. And while it is true that we never leap to a 'place' beyond our situated humanity to achieve transcendent objectivity, nevertheless Habermas holds that to focus exclusively on truth as a tool for pragmatic action (attempts at coping or adapting that renders the concept of 'truth' superfluous) causes someone like Rorty to miss the necessity for integrating rational discourses (attempts at knowing the truth as such) into the communicative model. In Habermas's words:

> Only the entwining of the two different pragmatic roles played by the Janus-faced concept of truth in action-context and in rational discourse respectively can explain why a justification successful in a local context points in favor of the context-independent truth of justified belief (Habermas, in Brandom 2000: 48).

Usually, lifeworld actors accept funded beliefs as unconditioned reality as a matter of practical necessity. To live is to live with and in a vision of the world. This pragmatized vision is reflected in the normalized language associated with and informing this vision expressed as truth-claims about this reality. However, the injection of the possibility of error (i.e., of epistemic humility) causes a 'shake-up' of dogmatic justifications, and the solidarity formed around these justifications, leading beyond the contextualized belief-driven practices towards the supposition of ideal justificatory conditions. Habermas continues:

> For this reason, the process of justification can be guided by a notion of truth that *transcends justification* although it is *always already operatively effective in the realm of action* . . . This need for justification, which sets in train the transformation of shaken-up behavioral certainties into problematized validity claims, can be satisfied only by a translation of discursively justified beliefs back into behavioral truths (Habermas, in Brandom 2000: 49).

This socialization of knowledge differs from Rorty's solidarities in that Habermas thinks that we are not entrapped within a context of justification, 'escaping' only by a conversion to an alternate context to better cope with the world. Otherwise, knowing is subsumed into practice, yielding a field of unrelated Rortian ethnocentric interpretations competing one against all for the attention of an ever larger audience. It is a type of persuasion that inculcates new ways of speaking like the evolution of new species, which struggle for survival competitively in lieu of intersubjective communication.

According to Habermas, Rorty's approach to justification leaves him paradoxically in the tradition of 'subjectivity', the 'pertinacious' philosophical custom of modernity that champions subjective self-emancipation in the form of a reconciling self-knowledge, the self-containing secular equivalent for religion's unifying power: Faith in the containment in God's 'hands'.

Over the last century the door has been steadily closed to any appeal to a metaphysical grounding of language (as it was to an appeal to religion before: see the appeal to *logos* in the Gospel according to John in the Christian New Testament). Habermas, of course, understands this closure as a welcomed event. It marked the end of an overly subjectivized era initiated by Kant and Hegel. But it also began an unfortunate slide to postmodern relativity, which involves a 'totalizing self-critique of reason' that is entangled in a *performative contradiction*. This sort of contradiction involves the critic's use of the very cognitive tools that he places under attack as authoritarian means to attain power within the conversation in which he is engaged. Paradoxically, a critique of reason must involve the use of reason in its deconstruction, or risk being considered merely sounds and marks expressing emotive reactions to causal stimuli.

To escape the charge of performative contradiction and the equally unappealing alternative of meaninglessness, and as an alternative interpretation of Habermas's view of justification, Rorty must level every discipline to the status of a 'language-creating', aesthetic interpretation. Each interpretation had its period of fluidity and semantic dynamism. Equally true is that every interpretation has already passed, or will pass at some future time, into a rigid state of encrusted meaning. These stagnant interpretations are deemed by those married to a Kuhnian worldview to be the exclusive representation of reality and are taken to be the 'normal' language. In the period where challenges are rare, agreements on interpretation are seen as stable, based on truths about what is that are (mis)taken to be immutable. However, in periods of intensive dispute, when rival interpretations are in constant interplay, creatively distinct 'abnormal', or revolutionary, uses of language emerge. These novel vocabularies surface to challenge status quo interpretations; everything is in flux, with old words being given new senses and new idioms being crafted to cover fresh ways of experiencing life. But this revolutionary-renovative process, what Habermas terms a 'linguistic world-disclosure', lacks an objective testing process that balances and checks poetic licence. Habermas writes in *The Philosophical Discourse of Modernity*:

> The 'Yes' and 'No' of communicatively acting agents is so prejudiced and rhetorically overdetermined by their linguistic contexts that the anomalies that start to arise during the phases of exhaustion are taken to represent only symptoms of waning vitality, or aging processes analogous to processes of nature and not seen as the result of *deficient* solutions to problems and *invalid* answers (Habermas 1992: 206).

In response, Rorty acknowledges only the poetic aspect of linguistic use while dividing its expression into distinct areas of public (normal) vocabularies and private (abnormal) linguistic innovations. Following Peirce, Rorty considers beliefs to be habits of action, and rational discourse to be a special case of acquiring habits of action by the comparison or contrasting of other persons' habits of action to one's own (Rorty, in Brandom 2000: 57). Thus, there will be only stylistic (non-discursive) differences between sentences such as 'That is why I think my assertion true' and 'That is why my assertion is true' (Rorty, in Brandom 2000: 56).

The expected Habermasian counterpoint would be that Rorty's argument for merely aesthetic differences between preference statements and truth claims is at core an instance of a performative contradiction. If we take Rorty's assertion at face value then his claim for the validity of his Peircean position must itself be a stylistic choice, a habit of action, what Krausz has called an ampliative reason: an explication of one's preferences without demonstrative reasons offered as to why one holds this position or why others should abandon their view in favour of one's own. This non-confrontational statement of one's worldview appears tolerant, and it may well be if it is taken as simply an emotive expression for a meta-narrative preference. But even if we allow Rorty to merely state or amplify his meta-narrative to ever larger audiences, there seems to ride behind the statement the promotion of a position designed to win over the crowd, not only with rhetoric akin to Shakespearian prose but with demonstrative arguments to the effect that we should accept, paradoxically, that all argument is stylistic. If this understanding holds, then the very act of world-disclosing is a tacit advocacy of this way of life as one that ought to be lived by everyone. Rorty's argument for (and from) ethnocentricity is then a demonstrative argument meant to promote

Multiplism as a specific meta-narrative to all audiences in all times. It is an ungrounded Singularist contention concealed behind the Multiplist's aesthetic narrative of liberal tolerance.

Habermas gives the impression that he could support my contention that behind all Multiplist claims there resides a Singularist claim (Habermas, in Brandom 2000: 48). He states that the mode of world-disclosing creativity cannot eliminate the need for a genuine problem-solving function in ordinary language. Habermas insists that there is a special status for a world-disclosing literature, separate from problem-solving critical philosophy. The artistically beautiful and the propositionally true are to be found in distinct modes of knowledge (action-context and rational discourse, respectively). Accordingly, Habermas contends that within critical thought based on good reason there exists an internal connection between justification and truth that is defendable in all possible contexts. Thus, while he agrees with Rorty that semantic (scientific) externalism fails to achieve its objective of grounding linguistically the real by an appeal to rigid designators, Habermas disagrees with Rorty when the latter places all narratives, *qua* narrative, on a par with each other aesthetically by understanding them as creative projections of the poetic construction. Habermas refuses to allow for the notion that narratives may differ aesthetically but cannot contradict or act as logical contraries (the relation by which two statements are not both true, while it remains possible their being both false). That is, he denies that the normative character of reason ought to be appreciated as another preference of Western culture, one coloured by an insinuating Platonism. Habermas directly challenges Rorty's pragmatism on this point:

> The program of a rational revision of deeply rooted Platonic prejudices pre-
> sumes we are capable of a learning process that not only can take place within
> a given vocabulary and according to the standards prevailing in a given con-
> text but that seizes hold of the vocabulary and standards themselves. This
> reason alone requires Rorty to provide a suitable equivalent for an orienta-
> tion toward truth that aims beyond the prevailing context of justification
> (Habermas, in Brandom 2000: 50).

The seeking agreement with an ever wider audience, numerically and in diversity, beyond the confines of one's solidarity, takes Rorty beyond 'preaching to the choir' to evangelizing the unconverted. Without normative orientation, truth becomes 'a context-dependent epistemic validity-for-us' offer that is pitched to unsuspecting markets of language users. The acceptance of this persuasive presentation creates a growing monopoly on memes in the marketplace of ideas that, according to Rorty, gives us decreasing reason to think that we will be refuted any time soon. However, any attempt to lessen the possibility for competing memes to arise seems to contradict Rorty's stated desire for as much intersubjective agreement as possible, unless the agreement referred to is to be understood as a discouraging of aesthetically displeasing expressions to advance those the individual or solidarity favours, in other words, agreement through manipulative persuasion.

Rorty answers that there can never be made a justification that is unconditional. (For the moment, let us pass by the obvious paradoxical need to justify this claim unconditionally.) He continues that to believe the opposite claim would be tacitly to make an utterly baseless 'empirical prediction about what would happen in a potentially infinite number of justificatory contexts before a potentially infinitely diverse set of audiences' (Rorty, in Brandom 2000: 56). Furthermore, there would be no special distinction to be made between the non-rational, non-linguistic part of one's environment and that part which is human and language-using, save in the inescapable prescriptive vocabulary of normality. Rorty admits that seeing humans as 'fellow-obeyers of norms' is a recognition of the species as a community of tool-users. No community, no toolkit; but equally, no toolkit, no community. So, while humans, as norm creators/followers, are different from other elements of the environment by the human act of creating linguistic standards, nonetheless, '[t]he passage from the one action-context to the other raises no philosophical problems which could be solved by a better understanding of the concept of truth' (Rorty, in Brandom 2000: 57). Truth, like all other concepts, can only be understood by its various uses. Rorty suggests that at best we can use 'truth' in its endorsing – and as we have seen, its cautionary – modes, that is, respectively, to advocate or demonstrate a particular use of the term, and to warn that at some future time in front of some different audience, what was now held definitively accurate may, by new empirical evidence or better explanatory hypotheses, be revised in part or entirely rejected as false.

Acutely aware of the common sense usage as well as criticism such as Habermas's, Rorty recognizes that there is something unconditional about the term 'truth' in its disquotational use. But it is not its normative justificatory function, as the following quote attests:

> [T]he unconditionality in question does not provide a *reason* for the fact that the cautionary use of 'true' is always apropos. To say that the truth is eternal and unchangeable is just a picturesque way of *restating* this fact about our linguistic practices. The whole pragmatic force of the claim that truth is not conditional is to *express* willingness to change one's mind if circumstances alter, not to explain or justify this willingness. We are not contritely fallible because we are in awe of the unconditionality of truth. Rather, to speak of truth as being unconditional is just one more way of expressing our sense of contrite fallibility (or, more robustly put, our sense of the desirability of comparing one's habits of actions with those of others in order to see whether one might develop some more effective habits) (Rorty, in Brandom 2000: 57).

Yet only a few pages on, Rorty makes what for him seems to be an extraordinary claim against the alleged intrinsic property of truth. He writes just as whoever gets sick could not be said to be healthy, 'What is refuted was never true'

(Rorty, in Brandom 2000: 58–59). What makes this claim a surprise is that it is said without caution, implying a disquotational use of the concept of 'true'. While Rorty notes from the pragmatic perspective the vacuity of the proposition 'Truth cannot lose in a free and open encounter', he fails to see the universal validity of the term 'true' in his counterexample concerning truth's refutation. From the pragmatic perspective what can be asserted is: what is refuted has never been true (justified) for some contemporary audience. To say more than this is to hold that an opinion missed an objective mark or standard, one that can be appreciated by all audiences.

Rorty recaptures this cautionary sense of true a few lines later in a discussion about 'the better argument'. 'Betterness' is 'relative to the range of arguments at our disposal, just as our criterion for betterness of tool are relative to the technology at our disposal' (Rorty, in Brandom 2000: 59). But he immediately follows this claim with a further statement: 'Arguments no more have a context-independent property of betterness than propositions have a context-independent resistance to refutation' (Rorty, in Brandom 2000: 59). We should ask if this claim about 'betterness' can be consistently maintained as a disquotational claim, or is it the better argument only if we accept that which works pragmatically for Rorty; as an endorsement from Rorty. It seems that Rorty is caught in the web of his own critique. On one hand he cannot advance the position he endorses without also employing the cautionary use of what he holds as true, if he wishes to be self-consistent. On the other hand, if we follow Rorty with appropriate caution, then we must look with a critical eye at his employment of what, in common usage, is understood as a universal justification, or objectively true, disquotational claim. How else can we appreciate Rorty's criticism that Habermas is making 'an unfortunate effort to hypostatize the adjective "true"'? Is it always wrong under all conditions and in every environment to create 'the impression that there is a goal of inquiry other than justification to relevant contemporary audiences' (Rorty, in Brandom 2000: 58)? If so, then Rorty must be in agreement with Habermas's statement that 'true propositions are resistant to spatially, socially and temporally unconstrained attempts to refute them' whenever Rorty offers his negative assertions as true. Otherwise Rorty must be expressing an aesthetic disinclination, with which one may agree if one has the taste for Rorty's kind of literary parry and thrust.

In short, Rorty must be in a performative contradiction, or be expressing an ampliative reason – which ought not to be confused with discursive reason. If it is an ampliative reason it must either stand isolated from interpersonal dialogue as a bald assertion or engage in conversational exchanges to reinforce its preference by campaigns designed to form an expanding audience base through an endlessly regressing justification for its aesthetic legitimacy.

But, Rorty retorts, the later Putnam-inspired insight that notions such as 'reference' and 'truth' are internal to our worldview has undermined the representationalist notion of objectivity by allowing the 'innocent' use of semantical notions within a worldview, while denying the possibility of transcendent notions external to a worldview. The innocent internal uses function solely as 'empty compliments', remarks of emotive endorsement of some current practice. The employment of such compliments occurs equally in pro- and anti-representational worldviews. The suggestion here is that critics like Habermas are making their own emotive statements that rest on nothing more than the endorsing and cautionary use of 'true'. That is, Rorty claims that at the meta-narrative level of discourse there is a plurality of incommensurable preferences that clash without the hope of resolving into the *one truth*.

In an Internet paper entitled 'A Pragmatist View of Contemporary Analytic Philosophy' (1999b), Rorty states that 'classical philosophical stand-offs are not susceptible of resolution by means of more careful and exacting ways of drawing out meanings'. This statement, along with his thought from Thesis Six that there isn't 'any method shared by Kripke and Davidson, or by Nagel and Dennett, that is more peculiarly philosophical than ordinary argumentative give-and-take – the kind of conversational exchange which is as frequent outside disciplinary matrices as within them' (1999b: Thesis Six/15), lends to the idea that what is constantly under consideration are the ampliative reasons of interlocutors that do not so much bridge a gap between opposing intellectual camps as gradually reweave 'individual or communal beliefs and desires under the pressure of causal impacts made by the behavior of people and things' (1999b: Thesis Ten/17). And it is in the reweaving that the hope for one whose human imagination 'flares up' to recommend 'a way of speaking which we had not thought of before' is anticipated (1999b: Thesis Sixteen/18). Rorty concludes that:

> Just as intellectuals cannot live without pathos, they cannot live without gurus. But they can live without priests. They do not need the sort of guru who explains that his or her authority comes from a special relation to something non-human, a relation gained by having found the correct track across an abyss (1999b: 18–19).

Therefore, conversation is strictly a catalyst for paradigm change. Convergent consensus among incommensurable worldviews is an illusion. There is only an eristic struggle for the semantic high ground in a Rortian universe where Nietzschean gurus shake us into the realization that we've been captivated by a picturesque objectivist metaphor of the intermingling of distinct and incompatible interpretations hoped for by Habermas.

Perhaps, then, after Rorty's creative reweaving, the only acceptable dogmatism is that of the iconoclastic sort. But this understanding of the place of the cautionary in conversation provokes a further question: Why should the style preferences of a private narrator such as Rorty get incorporated into the public sphere? What is the aesthetics of his position that should be more attractive to our present time than the several rival meta-narratives also in play? Furthermore, if the public truths of society to which Rorty belongs ought to remain distinct from the private sphere even after the objective-subjective distinction is discarded, why buy into and endorse his personal meta-vision of utopia as our political visions? And how do we distinguish a utopia of hope from a dystopian 'reign of terror' in a non-foundational, essence-free world?

In the next four chapters we will assess Rorty's political vision as expressed in his 'Jeffersonian Strategy' to see if, by his own standard, it 'hangs together well' as a narrative of hope for our time, and how the strategy impacts on the notion of self and the alleged freedoms it engenders.

Chapter 5

Rorty's Jeffersonian Strategy: The Privatization of the Philosophical

... that the impious presumptions of legislators and rulers, civil as well as ecclesiastical, who, being themselves but fallible and uninspired men have assumed dominion over the faith of others, setting up their own opinions and modes of thinking as the only true and infallible, and as such endeavoring to impose them on others ...

... that our civil rights have no dependence on our religious opinions, more than our opinions in physics or geometry; that therefore, the proscribing any citizen as unworthy the public confidence by laying upon him an incapacity of being called to the offices of trust and emolument, unless he profess or renounce this or that religious opinion, is depriving him injuriously of those privileges and advantages to which in common with his fellow citizens he has a natural right ...

Be it therefore enacted by the General Assembly, That no man shall be compelled to frequent or support any religious worship, place or ministry whatsoever, nor shall be enforced, restrained, molested, or burdened in his body or goods, no shall otherwise suffer on account of his religious opinions or belief; but that all men shall be free to profess, and by argument to maintain, their opinions in matters of religion, and that the same shall in nowise diminish, enlarge, or affect their civil capacities (Thomas Jefferson, *An Act of Establishing Religious Freedom* [1786]).[1]

Rorty's Jeffersonian Strategy

Rorty has argued that just as Thomas Jefferson reasoned successfully for a privatization of religious beliefs by divorcing them from secular politics in order to guarantee intellectual (and ultimately political) liberty, so too must we now cut away the foundationally-based philosophical systems from our secular (poetic) culture (Rorty 1991a: 175ff) in order to complete the reforms begun in the Enlightenment. It should be remembered that a major reason for Rorty's antifoundationalism is that foundational systems are contemporary parallels of religious doctrine that likewise dogmatically confine, in the modern instance as in the past, human creative freedoms (Rorty 1989: 52), freedoms that are the backbone of a liberal democracy. In this critique Rorty follows Heidegger, who has made the case that intellectual submission to a higher power has dominated Western culture since the time of Plato. It was the leaven for the rise of the Christian narrative, based upon the Augustinian notion of volition with its prescription in his doctrine of the 'Two Wills' (Augustine 1960: Bk 8, Ch. 9), for the transformation the human will from a tool of self-service into an instrument for the will of God.[2] Embedded herein is the assumption that in the clash of incompatible wills, so to speak, a trial by ordeal ensues, the outcome of which reveals the lawful and true structure of reality; in Judeo-Christian terms, God's Will. However, as William of Ockham observed (*I Sentences*, 42, 1, G),[3] there would be no divine 'sin', nor any contradiction, if God caused a human to act in hatred to God Himself. The reason for this circumstance is the unfettered liberty of God's Will. That is, divine omnipotence implies the unlimited capability for the production of effects, even without a secondary cause (e.g., in the case of miracles). Thus, for example, empirical causal relations are seen as radically contingent. God, by fiat, could produce effect 'B' without employment of the secondary cause 'A'.[4] At precisely this point there enters a moral arbitrariness into divine volition. Whatever God wills is, by definition, that which is 'good' and thus requiring human submission. God cannot sin because He can never be in a position to oppose His own will, even if it meant changing the rules of His 'game' from, say, Thou Shall *Not* Steal to Thou Shall Steal from the Rich to Give to the Poor or even to Thou *Shall* Steal. God's constancy in perfection is supposed to preclude any wilfully cruel and arbitrary change. From the human perspective, however, this theodicy leaves our will adrift, severed from its rational moorings, due to the extremely contingent conditions introduced into man's physical and moral life by the unfathomable will of an almighty yet unknowable deity, and to the imperfections inherent in human cognition. A fundamental and unconditional surrender of the powers of reason and self-assertion seem to be the only option short of risking self-destructive folly captured in the biblical story of the Tower of Babel.

In America, this line of thought was expressed through the Puritan interpretation of Calvinist theology. A predestining God knows and justly wills the elect and the damned in advance. Through no earned merit, but only through the radically free dispensing or withholding of grace by God alone, is each group duly designated. Conformity to a 'saintly life', as described by scripture, circumstance and the characterizing sermons of the Puritan ministry, was an outward sign of a salvation that was never guaranteed while on this side of heaven. Thus, power to define oneself was mediated through the interpretative judgements of the frontier Puritan community and its moral agents, the clergy. In a way strongly paralleling their tenuous toehold to physical life on the North American continent in the seventeenth century, this submission to the prevailing theological narrative was one of insecure posturing, as much as it was active conviction. Those who deemed themselves to be the chosen few were militant perfectionists, with little toleration for the common foibles of humankind. The muscularity of their claimed unassailability as the blessed ones functioned to conceal their fears concerning the contingency and precariousness of their beliefs about their personal spiritual status and physical circumstance. As such the line between public proclamation and the private description was submerged. What resulted was an assertive ethnocentric group-will, crafted through the biblical interpretations of the ministers, which suppressed contrary individual volitions (consider the plights of Roger Williams in 1636, Anne Hutchinson in 1639, as well as the Salem Witch Trials of 1692). It was in opposition to the repressive elitist outcome of the Augustinian-Puritan/Calvinist narrative that Jefferson, influenced by Enlightenment ideals, sought a separation of submission from expression.

The Jeffersonian delineation (as quoted in the chapter opener above) initiated a type of self-assertion which sought its justification from within one's experience through acts of self-grounding (that were later codified as the right of freedom of belief and expression in the First Amendment of the United States' Bill of Rights). Then, as in contemporary American society, a growing multiplicity of competing values vied for supremacy in the marketplace of ideas, threatening secular antinomianism. Common opinion had it that this trend towards what is perceived as anarchy can be checked only by tempering political pressure for intellectual free enterprise by appeals to methods of adjudication modelled upon Enlightenment scientific objectivity (Hall 1994: 27).

At the root of this view of objectivity is the belief that reason as exemplified in modern science adequately serves as the paradigm for unbiased rational thought. Unhinged as Western intellectual culture was from the securities of a deistic guarantor (ultimately and ironically by the thoughts initiated by Descartes[5]) and challenged by Hume's sceptical arguments which emphasized the contingency of experience by attacking the grounding powers of inductive inference, a firm platform for rational decision-making was sought by a turn inwards toward the subjective. Begun by Descartes' grounding of self-assertion in indubitable self-consciousness, extended to the material world via his methodological development of analytic geometry, and subsequently supported, as some have suggested, through Kant's Copernican Revolution, the 'sovereignty of self-foundation' was established. Its kingdom was the realm of philosophy. Rorty offers his take:

> Kant put philosophy 'on the secure path of a science' by putting outer space inside inner space (the space of the constituting activity of the transcendental ego) and then claiming Cartesian certainty about the inner for the laws of what had previously been thought outer. He thus reconciled the Cartesian claim that we can have certainty about our ideas with the fact that we already had certainty − a priori knowledge − about what seemed not to be ideas (Rorty 1979: 137).

As mentioned in a previous chapter, Kant, through his critique of science, aesthetics and morality, demarcated the cultural spheres for each mode of knowing. In doing so, he set philosophy, taken to be the overarching study of the underlying structural components of our beliefs, as the final arbiter of which the various discipline's claims were, in fact, rationally justifiable. His intent was to deduce the formal conditions of their knowledge claims, establish their necessity, and to render them mutually compatible through the offices of philosophy (see Rorty 1982: 85–86). Thus the modern discipline of epistemology was born as a way to reconcile subjective autonomy and lawful objectivity. *Logos*, the foundation of hierarchical thought, was viewed as the normative mode by which we understand and ground these other areas of study through rational explication. Thus, in the subsequent Kantian-influenced era of epistemological dominance, 'Philosophy' was conceived as the *logos* or conceptual ground for culture ('because culture is an assemblage of claims to knowledge'). Jefferson accepted as compatible the principles of self-determination and the rule of law, incorporating them into *An Act of Establishing Religious Freedom* and later in the United States' Declaration of Independence.

In Rorty's estimation, epistemology, unfortunately, has become the surrogate for our primordial theistic impulses (see Rorty 1979: 3–4).[6] As such, if I may borrow a term from Joseph Campbell (1968: 15, 337), it can be seen as the 'holdfast': the father-tyrant, the keeper of the status quo, who is, reapplying Jefferson's phrasing, 'setting up [his] own opinions and modes of thinking as the only true and infallible, and as such endeavoring to impose them on others'. The error lies, according to Rorty, in the very demarcation of modern thought into competing spheres by this one overseeing discipline – Philosophy (Rorty 1982: 86).

Hence, if one follows Rorty, the special and privileged role that epistemology is alleged to play in the organization of meaning should be reevaluated and ultimately put aside, along with scientism, as a relic of the onto-theological paradigm. Just as with Jeffersonian religious toleration (Rorty 2007: 30), there is *no need* in post-Philosophical (so called by Rorty; also known by him as 'revolutionary') cultures to refute the systems of other thinkers in order to assert one's own intellectual/poetic freedom. All that it takes to realize his 'Jeffersonian' programme, according to Rorty, is the abandonment of the dependence on an all-encompassing system as the legitimizer for every other discipline[7] (Rorty 1979: 6, 367 and 1999a: xxv), an abandonment only partially achieved by Jefferson himself due to his acceptance of the absolutist's notion of the rule of law. Rorty suggests that philosophers such as William James, John Dewey, the earlier thoughts of Heidegger and the later philosophy of Wittgenstein, have kept in play

> ... the historicist sense that this century's 'superstition' was the last century's triumph of reason, as well as the relativist sense that the latest vocabulary, borrowed from the latest scientific achievement, may not express privileged representations of essences or nature, but be just another of the potential infinity of vocabularies in which the world can be described' (Rorty 1979: 367).

When unencumbered by the weight of 'systematic philosophy' and its insistence on a convergent consensus, old onto-theological views may be shed and new vistas, anticipated by Jefferson, should open at the 'periphery' to the human imagination. 'Edifying philosophers' – Rorty's term for those who recognize the contingency of all vocabularies, that is the ungrounded, pragmatic invention of language-games in free response to changing conditions and circumstances – intentionally stand outside the mainstream so as to be in a position to de-construct the so-called permanent ahistorical systems in a generational push for a place for their own 'revolutionary' thoughts, for their own time and cultural moment.

It is in this spirit of intellectual freedom that Rorty wishes to pare away theoretical philosophy tradition from the inventiveness of poetic self-assertion, a separation that I previously termed the 'Jeffersonian Strategy'.[8] His aim is to recognize the *prima fascia* parity for all narratives by the removal of impingements by the public sector (i.e., ingrained or 'normal philosophy', and entrenched or 'normal science') on the impulses of 'edifying' self-creativity. Thus, by levelling the playing field in an attempt to undermine authoritarian academic systemization in favour of an unrestricted, democratic conversation among equals, Rorty (developing a lead he gleaned from Thomas Kuhn[9] (see Kuhn 1970: 2) brings into serious question the bedrock of contemporary confidence in the foundational objectivity: the belief in a privileged status of philosophico-scientific rationality,[10] that there is a study of the subject matter called knowledge itself over and above particular social practices. To reduce this institutionalized, and supposedly advantaged, grounding vocabulary to just another voice in a conversation, however, it must be demonstrated that this school of hierarchical rational thought can never successfully posit the epistemological and metaphysical supports for its claim of universal commensuration, thus neutralizing the BonJour–Harris critique of anti-foundationalism. As Rorty asserts:

> A liberal society is one which is content to call 'true' (or 'right' or 'just') whatever the outcome of undistorted communication happens to be, whatever view wins in a free and open encounter. This substitution amounts to dropping the image of a preestablished harmony between the human subject and the object of knowledge, and thus to dropping the traditional epistemological-metaphysical problematic (Rorty 1989: 67).

Otherwise, without the elimination of the epistemological-metaphysical problematic, with the pronouncements of the ministers of *logos* (e.g., Kripke and Habermas) holding sway, Rorty's Multiplist project cannot go through as one of several compelling, albeit incommensurate, voices in the conversation among human communities. There would be no room at the meta-rule level for 'abnormal' approaches, whose central contention is precisely that there is no one set of eternal solutions in which novel vocabularies fit current conditions for better or for ill. Abnormal voices would be silenced, and from the pragmatist's perspective thrown out of court as non-philosophical by the tribunal of epistemological arbiters.[11] In fact, Rorty goes as far as regretting the very use of the terms 'epistemology' and 'metaphysics' in his writing due to their biasing the reader towards hierarchical thought. Rorty would rather recast his pragmatic narrative in terms of an ongoing critique of 'dominant metaphors and images' (Rorty, in Brandom 2000: 214) in the hope that by doing so he can help usher in an era of liberal social practices tolerant of poetic licence.

The Personalization and Liberation of Creative Thought

Rorty goes about his purported liberation of creative thought from social conformity by aligning with those who lay siege to the belief that there is a clear and
firm distinction between knowledge claims and mere opinions (e.g., Habermas). This distinction (along with those made between logic and poetry, reality
and appearance, moral truth and prudence) is, for Rorty, no longer an appropriate use of language. Those boundary lines were originally an outgrowth of
Plato's idea that the variations in human *nomoi* is a symptom of our alleged
separation from the Really Real (Rorty, in Brandom 2000: 123), as well as
Kant's critique of pure reason,[12] insofar as speculative metaphysics assertions
about reality are dismissed as non-sense, that is, having no basis in phenomenal
experience, and turning instead to epistemological certainty through the lawfulness of appearance.

Rorty, following closely the challenge to epistemology of Quine's critique of
the analytic/synthetic distinction, takes the central demarcations between
objective-subjective and knowledge and opinion to be not firm but 'fuzzy'
(Rorty 1991a: 38), and ultimately detrimental. That is, as derived from
Dewey and James,[13] all knowledge claims are open to redescription in pragmatic language in terms of a distinction between agreements which are easy
(e.g., mathematics and formal logic) and those which are hard to reach
(Rorty, in Brandom 2000: 23). Hence, all claims of objective knowledge are
not based upon or grounded in ahistorical, transpersonal truths, as many philosophers have held since Plato. Rather, Rorty opines, they are no more and
no less than local conceptual claims (contingent value proposals) rooted in
the historical nexus of events, which has achieved a widespread adoption due
to the culture's perception that they are useful (see Goodman on *entrenchment* in
Chapter 3).

For example, Euclidean geometry, under Rortian redescription, becomes
naturalized by jettisoning its Pythagorean 'mystical' assumptions; geometry as
a tool to be considered simply as a pragmatic way for the ancient Greek society,
fond of abstraction, to decisively solve vexing property-line disputes. The added
assertion that geometry is an ahistorical system of truths served to reinforce and
encode this abstraction as a conclusive legal instrument. Following this understanding of geometry's social purpose, Rorty is in a position to insist that all
claims of an uncovering of universal and necessary truths ought to be appreciated similarly, as a tool useful for social cohesion and function, and that their
ahistorical pretence ought to be abandoned in favour of a local pragmatist narrative lodged in a moment of history.

This demystification of would-be ahistorical universals is, for Rorty, only
the first of two moves necessary to de-theologize human thought. The critical
process which originated with the ancient Greek thinkers who, from Thales
to Aristotle, gradually combed out the cultural apparatus of the Olympian
gods in favour of the notion of a supreme philosophical principle and cause
(i.e., Aristotle's Prime Mover),[14] now must continue with the winnowing of

the theistically-laden chafe of foundational-rationalist construction rooted in Cartesian apodictic mentality from the wheat of ironic redefinition. Again, poetic self-expression ought to be liberated from the impositions of entrenched societal expectations in this next step through the separation of the private sphere of creativity from the public realm of social entrenchment to ensure a space for free expression, a cornerstone of democratic liberalism. This would be accomplished when we discard all pretences to knowledge as representation of a non-human reality in the medium of the mind and take the power and responsibility for inventive responses to the natural and cultural environments into our own hands (see Rorty, in Brandom 2000: 216).

It might be objected that this alleged demystification adds up to nothing more than philosophical infighting directed against the Platonic-Kantian position by the promoters of Pragmatic Philosophy. This would be incorrect. This type of academic dispute would not engage Rorty, because to participate in strategies of refutation would draw Rorty directly into the theoretical debate structured by Kantian assumptions about the nature of rationality; a debate Rorty wishes to avoid as a dead-end use of language given the several hundred years that there has been no substantial progress making sense concerning notions drawn from epistemological theory, and as ultimately beside the point. Since the possible outcomes of this style of engagement lead to an acquiescence to a governance by Kantian rules (Rorty 1991a: 83), a thrust towards Hegel's dialectical idealism (Rorty 1979: 135) or a drift into scepticism (Rorty 1979: 139–40), Rorty wishes to avoid those paths which lead only to the closing of conversation (Rorty 1979: 113–14), opting instead for a historical narrative which, like *Proust in the Past Recaptured*, redescribes the past and those in it, but never finalizes it or them in one encompassing theory/narrative (Rorty 1989: 105). Rorty accuses the proponent of the epistemological narrative of the mind as the mirror of nature of providing no room to further the conversation:

> He wants to make clear that because the realm of possibility is now exhausted, nobody can rise above him in the way in which he has risen above everyone else. There is, so to speak, no dialectical space left through which to rise; this is as far as thinking can go (Rorty 1989: 104).

Rorty maintains that there is no naturally (or logically, or supernaturally) occurring limit imposed upon human thought. Thus, Rorty suspects that the epistemological theorist intent is intimately linked to his psychological urge to control future intellectual vistas. Rorty expresses a wish to alter the focus away from the hegemony associated with Singularist claims of a universality of reality towards the liberating diversity of contingent personal and cultural visions in an effort to forestall the antinomianism of the sceptic and to advance creative invention. He desires to change the subject because he thinks that whether through the ahistoric (e.g., Plato and Kant), or through decisive historical events (e.g., Nietzsche and later Heidegger), those who are motivated to have the last and eternally deciding word are attempting to be immortal *via* the avoidance of future redescription of their final vocabularies by other poetic minds. This is the moment of their inauthenticity, their betrayal of the principle of creativity in an effort to have their creative endeavours saved from time and chance through being identified with permanence and immortality. They aspire to shut down the future avenues of communication and inventiveness, and paternalistically impose their 'unsurpassed wisdom' upon all future generations to avoid confronting contingency inherent in all conceptual constructs. Their *faux pas* is in the attempt to synthesize into a universal, and hence inerrant, *public* expression for all audiences, that which can only be realized in *private*, or at most local, belief. The hope to express a Singularist final vocabulary, to achieve the sublime in and through an eternal system of symbols, is to cheat future generations by dogmatizing imaginative invention (Rorty 1989: 120). It is to claim as a trans-human experience, by way of a transcendental or teleological source, that which, because it is without conclusive proof, can safely be said to be temporary and indigenous. It is illicitly to assert the superiority of timeless understanding over contingent and temporal imagination. It is to mirror the tendency found in most of the world's religions to restrict the expansive possibilities by unquestioned beliefs. This kind of non-democratic semantic hegemony is what Rorty contends non-pragmatic thought covertly intends. This is why, despite there being no way of grounding one's paradigm choice, even Rorty's, one should opt for his New Pragmatism as an antidote to the paternalistic Singularism of onto-theological vocabularies.

Solidarity, Self and the Primacy of the Contingent

But why does Rorty wish to abandon theories of universal truths rather than merely tolerate them as simply another voice in the conversation of humankind? Is there not a place in an aestheticized world for both the claims for objective understanding and the assertions for imaginative creativity in human life, even when they seem diametrically opposed to each other? Why should Singularism be the lone exception and be excluded from an unrestricted conversation of humankind? Doesn't Ockham's Razor demand that knowledge claims and opinions shuffle into a level set of competing constructs once a plausible argument is found to simplify matters to the point of eliminating alternative, hierarchical systems at the meta-narrative level? If the answer is 'Yes' then a shift away from a search for the definitive causes of phenomenal knowledge to a plurality of cultural explanations for empirical beliefs, which Rorty advocates for his liberalism, would be in order the moment it can be asserted with confidence that the Singularist Parmenidean-Aristotelian point of view, as the original basis for the discipline of Philosophy, is merely one of many alternative means of coping with life. Since it still seems plausible (and for Krausz, not inherently illogical) to pursue a singular interpretation within Multiplism, this leaves open the possibility that a foundational position that seeks a standard that transcends (externally grounded), or is teleologically immanent (but not part and parcel of the world), or is somehow embedded in the uniqueness of human psyche, soul or mind ('self-moving' cognitive givenness), might be allowable in a Multiplist universe without abandoning the Multiplist agenda.

Nevertheless, the reformist Rorty considers the search for enduring objective certainty is wrongheaded, like holding on to a belief in astrology or phrenology, where these latter 'disciplines' lack the cohesive narrative, justifiable to current audiences. Therefore, at the meta-narrative level there seems to be a need for criteria for aesthetic discrimination which sets apart justifiable from implausible narratives, narratives that would be akin to the Puritanical intolerance that Jefferson combated, without Rorty's version of Multiplism becoming another imperious construct designed for the establishment of its own exclusive hierarchy (i.e., Multiplist theories over Singularist theories).

Perhaps Rorty would offer that, unlike the pragmatic Multiplist, to locate their durable standards Singularists of all stripes must claim to already be in the very vantage point which is being sought, that is, somehow to have a perspective already beyond the flux of time, culture and circumstance allowing her to know reality in-itself. This circle of reasoning appears close and vicious unless someone can provide an epistemological escape route out of cultural embeddedness from which this notion springs. The best opportunity for escape, it could be argued, was some derivative of the Kantian transcendental argument (see Chapter 2). But, as Rorty has argued, Kantian strategies have failed to establish the unchallenged, universal, *a priori* necessity of that interpretation (see below). Hence, if Rorty is to be believed, there appears to be no way currently available, including Habermas's (or McDowell, in Brandom 2000: 109–23), to argue for Singularism without 'assuming the consequent', i.e., that an objective point of view capable of capturing reality *objectively* exists. As we have seen, this is exactly what Kant's Copernican Revolution assumed. From an aesthetic point of view this is an unsatisfactory and flawed story-line.

> The Copernican revolution was based on the notion that we can only know about objects a priori if we 'constitute' them, and Kant was never troubled by the question of how we could have apodictic knowledge of these 'constituting activities' for Cartesian privileged access was supposed to take care of that (Rorty 1979: 137).

and

> How do I tell a world constituted by linguistic practices from a world constituted by facts – facts which somehow (despite the sentence-like appearance) are not themselves 'constituted' by any such practices? I have no idea (Rorty, in Brandom 2000: 126).

Rorty believes the claim that an objective point of view capable of capturing reality *objectively* exists to be an example of the too frequent and erroneous attempts philosophers have made at 'self-foundation', the grounding of the meaning of the self upon some absolute principle, entity or substance. And for a system of thought, especially internal realism, that must stay within the confines of moment, place and species while locating a truth that is not merely a well-fitted piece in a linguistic practice, but a transpersonal truth, this result seems to be a fatal trap that undermines this family of narratives.

Rorty suggests that the trap originated with Descartes who conflated the first-person experience and third-person analysis of the self, thereby greatly overextending, and mislabelling as objective, the arena of certitude available to an individual. This is the very snare – conflating objectivity with the self's own subjectivity – in which Kant was enmeshed (see Chapter 2). If this trap is truly fatal, and it seems to be even for the weak position of foundationalism which allows for supporting coherent systems (see BonJour 1978: 4–5), then assuming the success of Rorty's dismissal of *a priori* truths (as universal and necessary) in *Philosophy and the Mirror of Nature* (1979: 148–55, 160–61) and 'World Well Lost' Rorty (1982: 3–18), and the demise of the hoped-for discovery of any naturally-occurring standards (see Chapter 4), there appears to be no possibility of speaking about an idea as being objectively real, or intersubjectively certain in areas as diverse as the self and politics.

The distinctions between knowledge claims and opinions disappear as the belief that humankind has the ability to stand back to view and judge reality fades into a flawed flight of the imagination. Neither made nor discovered, so-called objective facts merge with putative subjective values so that what is seen to be an essential fact and what is thought to be an accident of opinion blend into that which is derived wholly from the contingencies of one's cultural traditions and expectations therein; an aesthetic preference. Therefore, following the Quine-Davidsonian lead, with this blending of the entire objective/subjective, fact/value, rule-governed/playful behaviour, fixed schemes fuzz into non-relevance as they open to redescriptions better suited for the times (see Rorty 1991a: 83).

Thus, a communal consensus, in the sense of a convergent agreement formed around a central and objective truth, is, for Rorty, out of the question (see below). It requires a background schema (see below), which Rorty asserts can never be philosophically substantiated. In the place of consensus, expectations of 'solidarity' among members of a socio-historical community should prevail (Rorty 1991a: 21). Solidarity is founded upon the accumulated wisdom of a specific culture. The preference for this group's themes is not a matter of discovered eternal truths about nature or humanity. As previously noted, nature and humanity are radically contingent notions from Rorty's perspective. Hence, becoming involved in the uncovering, discovering or fixing of truth(s) is to miss the point (Rorty 1989: 5), as Rorty's critique of Kripke and Habermas suggests. To use the term 'truth' (or even 'truths'), as in 'We hold these truths . . .', is to merely apply a term of commendation for the preferred set of beliefs that have been of useful value in the experience of one's group.[15] It follows from Rorty's views on truth and consensus that solidarity should be viewed as a contingent agreement made over time (as long as it works) by those who freely enter into it. Solidarity is fluid because it is based on invention, a cultural artefact, and not a static result of an adherence to an eternal philosophical principle, 'externally' or 'internally' given:

'[P]hilosophy' is not a name for a discipline which confronts permanent issues, and, unfortunately keeps misstating them, or attacking them with clumsy dialectical instruments. Rather, it is a cultural genre, a 'voice in the conversation of mankind' . . . Interesting philosophical change . . . occurs not when a new way is found to deal with an old problem but when a new set of problems emerges and old ones begin to fade away (Rorty 1979: 264).

In sum, what ultimately is being challenged by Rorty (1991a: 22) is an aesthetic preference masked as the sole truth, for a universe involving objects (substances, entities, 'I-know-not-what' matter, etc.), ways of coming to know these things (exclusively through scientific, objective reasoning, for example), and entities (e.g., human beings) capable of securing knowledge about ontologically real objects, *via* a special faculty (i.e., the Cartesian–Kantian autonomous reason). Rorty aims his arrows of derision at those who inauthentically wish to ground solidarity in objectivity. Thus Rorty claims to offer an alternative perspective, an alternative rationalization, which encourages the redescriptions of our experience and the 'dedivinized' philosophy and science, making room for the interplay of democratic and free thought, without the tangle of metaphysical and epistemological dogmatic pretensions that smother creativity, stifle conversation and disrupt the democratic process.

While Rorty's 'Jeffersonian' challenge – important because his ideas are a live option as abnormal discourse in the contemporary philosophic debate – has serious consequences for objectivism and foundationalism, these metaphysical and epistemological positions are but two legs of the tripod upon which rests the 'intolerant' philosophico-scientific assumptions of our age and culture. The third leg is the concept of a human nature as a substantial self at the centre of personal experience. This conception is borrowed from modern thinkers in the Cartesian-Kantian mainstream, and, of course, has its implications in metaphysics, epistemology, morality and politics.

To have a self, an entity which is the central essence to, and of, our personal experience seems to most observers to be a given. Yet indications in several fields of study, such as anthropology, suggest that this view of core individuality might be associated with a Western cultural bias against the primacy of group identification. And in the face of such indications, thinkers may be open to alternative views about nature and the self, even to the possibility that the Western, traditional outlook concerning the substantial mind is simply another gloss, which may have power of coherence, but not the force of a grounded and unquestionable, singular truth.

The Adverbial Theory, Self and the Fluidity of 'Truth'

Rorty asserts that just as foundationalist communal consensus must give way to social solidarity, the view complementing communal consensus of the mind as inner space capable of holding representations of reality ought to be replaced by a demystified notion of mind.

An important approach in opposition to the traditional act/object ontological theory is offered by the proponents of the Adverbial Theory. This alternative offering suggests that the grammatical structure of sentences, resulting from the linguistic generation of complex expressions designed to account for the vast contents of experience, are responsible for the misleading appearance of a corresponding relationship between a putative free-standing object and its purported representation in the mind. No one, it is argued, other than an out-and-out Platonist, would seriously argue that a stutter or a limp has an existence independent of the person whose speech or gait is so modified. Yet, when applied to the thought process, the majority of past and contemporary philosophers readily embrace the tradition which isolates social practices from the selves that engage in them. The questions of why this distinction is made between the physical and the mental properties of a person, and why it should not be approached in a radically different fashion, seems to be at the heart of Rorty's stated alliance with Donald Davidson concerning the identification of 'truth' with social practices.

No longer confined to the analysis of perceptual experience, through the work of Wilfrid Sellars and Michael Tye, the Adverbial Theory has come to be applied to an analysis of belief and desire discourse – matters of believing in a certain way (Kim and Sosa 1995: 8). For, just as after-images, hallucinations, etc. cannot exist without a sensing person but are rather modes in which a person senses, so too beliefs, desires, etc. are not objects of possession. Rather, they are semantic modes of thought.

The Adverbial Theory is linked to Rorty's way of thinking through his desire to demystify the fable of the mind apart (Rorty 1982: 14). No longer must we formulate in the usual intricate fashions our beliefs and practices in relation to something not ourselves. Rorty consistently believes that this epistemological route has been often tried in the efforts to avoid scepticism in the public or private sphere, but each attempt will lead to a dead end (Rorty 1991a: 154). Better, philosophical explanation can and should be reduced to descriptions of our practices concerning practical reasoning alone. Discarded is the anchor of the representationalist, i.e., the view from a distance, in Jonathan Bennett's phrase, 'with the eye of a stranger'. What Rorty embraces in its stead is the already mentioned Davidsonian triangularity. A view that 'true' is explained in terms of the language the mind comes to know through the community in solidarity as it copes with the world. Echoing Kim and Sosa (1995), it is a way we *are*, a way of life which confers meaning as one's linguistic community wrestles with the ongoing process of causal interaction, rather than something we *have* epistemologically independent of that intra-communal life. Rorty restates the Davidsonian point as follows:

So the thing to do is to marry truth and meaning to nothing and nobody but each other. The resultant marriage will be so intimate a relationship that a theory of truth will *be* a theory of meaning, and conversely. But that theory will be of no use to a representationalist epistemology, nor any other sort of epistemology. It will be an explanation of what people *do*, rather than a non-causal, representing, relation in which they stand to non-human entities (Kim and Sosa 1995: 154).

Truth will be as true (accurate) as we believe it to be true (justified by contemporary audiences to themselves), and we may believe it is true if it works (lets us get what we want, desire, or find aesthetically satisfying) as it relates to the natural and social environments. Again, for Rorty, since there is no access to a standardizing thing-in-itself to be employed as an assessment tool to grade social practice, we cannot become a stranger to ourselves, or radically estrange ourselves from our socio-cultural roots in order to 'get at' the knowledge of the way things are, including our 'selves'.

What it means for members of a given society to be part of a culture is also the current truth about that culture. What is true about that culture is described through widely accepted metaphors, alive in the current social model, as conveyers of the meaning of a contingent historical situation as a community struggles with its environment. All theories in society, be they scientific, moral, political or creative, are to be appreciated as one aesthetically appreciates art or poetry, that is, as the mental exercise of metaphorical adjustments (i.e., linguistic descriptions and redescriptions) to 'the practices of real live human beings engaged in causal interaction with the rest of nature' (Kim and Sosa 1995: 157). Therefore, the creative self emerges from the environment-community interface rather than it being the independent judge of the demarcations of disciplines.

Rorty wishes us to move with him and to see that there is no metaphysical centre upon which empirical and other epistemological fragments may adhere. This ties in with his overall redescription of the modernist worldview into pragmatic language.

In his essay, 'The Contingency of Selfhood' (in Rorty 1989: 23–43), Rorty defends the contingencies and discontinuities of the 'I' against the pre-Nietzschean school of realist thought, which held that 'the particular contingencies of individual lives' were superfluous (Rorty 1989: 26). One apparent motivation of this 'school' is fear of death and personal limits (echoing Foundationalist motivations for a conclusive final vocabulary); that is, if we consider the human circumstances as radically limited to a contingent spatio-temporal matrix, we reduce its status to that of a dying animal, a level at which humanity would be incapable of encompassing transcendental truths. And it was this often unexpressed emotional fear which, perhaps, prodded some (in the spirit of Plato's *Phaedo*) to posit a central essence for humankind. This is a 'divinization' of the self, and by Rorty's gloss, a canonization which is as arbitrary as it is unwarranted. For it merely reflects the God-fearing urge to establish a shrine to a powerful force, processed through Kantian epistemology, and relocated within the 'breast' of each and every human. Another manufactured projection, a mental tool designed to cope with the contingent of life, the 'self' is exposed as an invention intended to associate the authoritative power of the divine with our cognitive functions. Uncovered as a metaphor for the web of beliefs and desires, Rorty subjects the 'self' to the same kind of unfettered redescription that he applied to the notion of 'world', opening novel and unrestricted conceptions for and about the 'poeticized' individual.

Kantian Autonomy, *Sensus Communis* and the Ambiguity of Agreement

Given Rorty's constructivist view of the poetic self, this pragmatic stance must now avoid a collapse into an 'anything goes' redescription (to avoid the parallel charge levelled by James Harris against Nelson Goodman, mentioned above in Chapter 3). And if one accepts Onora O'Neill's article on Kant, 'Vindicating Reason', in *The Companion to Kant*, then Rorty's task becomes somewhat more difficult. The difficulty is due to O'Neill's analysis of Kantian Reason which notes a constraining element (missing in Rorty's account), an element that offers protection against relativism that threatens to harm or demean the individual if an account of the self such as Rorty's is accepted.

O'Neill argues for a view of Kantian reason that 'constrains' (O'Neill, in Guyer 1992: 298), one that supports Habermas's contention for demonstrative reason apart from world-constructing. While allowing for a variety of manners of thought and ways of life, reason is seen to constrain in three ways or through three maxims. First, it rejects all submissions to 'alien' capacities and authorities, that is, those which are wholly speculative and thus arbitrary. To bow to these 'outside' influences (erstwhile lawgivers) would be an unreasonable and groundless imposition upon reason's autonomy. This rejection accords well with the previously mentioned 'Jeffersonian' element in Rorty's thought in that the poeticized self can introduce iconoclastic abnormal vocabulary that may challenge established norms.

Second, Kant makes the case for a 'consistency restoring review' in order for the autonomous reason to ensure against the future creep of heteronomous thought. Thus, O'Neill continues, the aim of Kant would be to assert a 'plurality-without-preestablished-harmony' which would be in line with Rorty's 'Jeffersonian' views concerning emerging solidarities of tolerance and the role of the ironic poet within that society. However, according to O'Neill's interpretation, there is a third maxim which would seem to set Rorty and Kant in diametrical opposition, radically changing the central meaning of the first two protective constraints. Before we look into this third constraining element of Kantian reason, let us turn to a more detailed rejection of the labels of 'scepticism' and 'relativism' for Rorty's form of pragmatism in order to evaluate better this possible Kantian–Rortian opposition.

As we have seen, rather than endorsing a self-refuting scepticism, or a thorough individualistic relativism which would make dialogue almost impossible,

Rorty accepts the ethnocentricity which comes with being radically situated in one's own culture (Rorty 1991a: 203). His view of the role of ethnocentricity consolidates several key points. Thus, instead of this being a disadvantage, he believes one's embeddedness in one's ethos to be the only viable view to take. In a foundationless world, it makes sense to commit to the way of life which one finds familiar and of value. Once one becomes aware that the human condition is wholly the fruit of one's socio-historical view which has been inculcated since birth, and once one assumes, again using the phrase Putnam coined, 'a God's-eye standpoint' – a spectator view of reality (Rorty 1991a: 6, 13) – is an unfortunate remnant of the ancient theistic metaphor, the individual's rootedness in one particular culture is inescapable. Every step back, so to speak, to gain perspective on an object of study carries with it all the cultural adaptations that are assumed to be left behind by such attempts at detachment. Hence, the epistemological study of the free-standing real (metaphysical, transcendental, or transpersonal) is impossible. And with it goes the 'skyhook' necessary to lift one out of one's situation to a privileged position from which to observe objectively, and thus gain pure knowledge about one's phenomenal world and phenomenal self. What becomes 'real', as with what is considered 'true', about the 'world' and the 'self' is the best description(s) of experience currently available in and through one's culture. Any other claim in favour of a world or a self as objectively necessary conditions for the synthesis of our experience appears to be self-aggrandizing group bias masquerading as a universal truth. Descriptions from other groups become available only at the areas tangential to places where there is a possible coincidence of meaning (which Davidson and Stroud claim to be considerable). Where there is no coincidence, conversation is not possible, leaving only local and rival interpretations or, at best, the possibility for conversion from one rival paradigm to another (Rorty 1999b: Thesis One/13).

Fortunately, coincidence is enough. Despite the fact that Rorty holds the belief that there cannot be a universal culture, due to his contention that there is no fundamental language-game, nor any grounding *a priori* condition, in common among the various human communities where a meeting of the minds can take place under that single aegis, Rorty does not rule out intercultural (or intracultural) 'translation' that may yield mutually beneficial, practical outcomes, allowing the formation of solidarities. If I understand Rorty correctly, translations of this sort suggest a version of Ethical Egoism, in that each party to interpersonal interactions maintains the power to redescribe the interlocutor's meaning for the benefit of solidarity, only so long as the translations work for both of them. If not, and conversion of the interlocutor to one's interpretation proves impossible, the conversation ends to be replaced by rival antinomian assertions. This account helps to harmonize statements by Rorty that seem to claim interpersonal communication is both the ideal of his New Pragmatism and an impossibility among those speakers with differing first principles.

Now it is possible to rejoin O'Neill's analysis of Kantian reason. The third maxim, crucial for our discussion of Rorty's Jeffersonian Strategy, is also designed to avoid a collapse into solipsistic antinomianism and social anarchy to which ethical egoism is prone. Kant's antidote to anarchy and isolation is to base an agent's thinking on principles open to others (O'Neill, in Guyer 1992: 301). In this way Kant claims that a universal lawfulness is maintained while the rejection of alien lawgivers is sustained. Thus, reason's autonomy is not law-less self-assertion; there is containment. But at the same time this containment cannot be the product of outside restraining forces either, whether they be part of, for example, Platonic speculative metaphysics, European theism, or (one could safely project) a Rortian-style cultural embeddedness. Reflexively self-grounding – yet universally available among all those involved in *unforced* dialogue – law-giving/abiding reason, as detailed by Kant, must therefore be non-polemic at its core. In this context, 'polemic' means a forced victory for one side; in short, a form of 'war' (see Chapter 7 for a linkage to my discussion of Hobbes). O'Neill cites Kant's *Critique of Judgement* (21, 5:239) to underscore this point, as follows: 'We assume a common sense as a necessary condition of the universal communicability of our knowledge, which is presupposed in every logic and every principle of knowledge that is not one of scepticism' (O'Neill, in Guyer 1992: 300). Hence, a general understanding or agreement, a *sensus communis*, is forever impossible in a polemicized environment. Even if the issue is localized to language-sharing communities, the proposed solution 'once more subjects thought and action to some arbitrary, if less arbitrary, power' (O'Neill, in Guyer 1992: 294). What is demanded to maintain autonomy and discipline is a rejection of such momentary ways of thought, and in its place must necessarily be an abiding principle arising from reason itself that can be recognized, understood and followed by any rational being in a non-eristic dia-logue with all other rational beings.

Rorty's retort has been already suggested. Since the voice of another might be forceful enough to drown out one's own voice, there is always the danger of conceptual imperialism in public discussions where convergent consensus is expected. This point follows currently from the application of the first maxim against the third. Rorty aggressively defends his position by insisting that Kant is himself guilty of imposing unvindicated speculation with regard to axiomatic assertions about the reality of a supreme and universal principle of reason as a necessary condition for communication. Kant's arguments for a law-abiding autonomous reason are sustainable only by reflexive (circular) rea-soning, that is, through 'cognitive reason'. This kind of argument which depends upon descriptive grounding suffers because it must also function beyond the relation of self-referral. It must act simultaneously as a final vocabu-lary which is presentable to others in a persuasive manner in order to 'woo' the consent of everyone else. The aim is to bring about an ever-expanding men-tality for disinterested, 'pure' spectators through 'reflective judgement' to the point of achieving the *sensus communis*. Once accomplished, the end of all discus-sion on the topic at hand would ensue at the moment each particular judging agent engages their cognitive reason in self-justification. Yet anything that necessarily must be the case epistemologically, through an internally consistent logic, does not automatically serve to establish its being the case with quasi-metaphysical universality, even when the topic is reflexive reason, and even if useful information results.

Hegel made a similar observation – recasting Ockham's comments concerning an omnipotent God – when he stated that, in principle, *a priori* concepts, even if we accept them as Kant did to be the determiner of our experience, might have been different. Thus, it might be said that the way things are experienced is, at its core, as arbitrary as divine volition is under the Augustinian notion of the Will of God. This last point can be applied against the Kantian assumptions about the metaphysical status of a pure and disinterested judge with its implied distinction from the world as thing-in-itself, as Rorty in fact does with (apparently) devastating effect. The result is that reason functions to offer us nothing more than a systematic unity for some (any) coherent point of view (including that of, say, a consistent Nazi) once, with Rorty, we ignore all unsubstantiated appeals to a reified representation of reason. Thus the possibility for further conversation remains open and free, even for those who like O'Neill see value in the third of Kant's constraining maxims and danger in its absence. For now it legitimately may be asked of any agreement among individuals: Was the perceived convergence a result of persuasive argument (the making of 'abnormal' discourse 'normal'), or of a rational disclosure leading to some transhistorical truth applied across disassociated points of view? Further, and to the point, how does one judge the difference between the two (respectively, solidarity and convergent consensus) when their alternative outcomes appear identical for one who is truly convinced about the agreement reached? Obviously, an infinite regress threatens the Kant–Habermas–O'Neill position, as we are called to make a new judgement of discernment now at the meta-critical level. Any escape from this regress appears to be more a matter of belief akin to a religious faith or aesthetic preference than a rational given. That is to say, one's preferred method or discipline would be applied as personal consistency demanded. As O'Neill observes, Kant's

> insistence that 'reason is no dictator' reiterates the thought that there is no algorithm that fully determines the content of reasoned thought or action ... Reason offers only necessary conditions for thought and action [A 795/ B 823 ff.; *Groundwork*, 4:424] (O'Neill, in Guyer 1992: 296).

However, if the Hegelian point is valid, then the necessity of *a priori* concepts could be partitioned into distinct conceptual systems (perhaps culturally grounded). Thus cocooned, and accepting the Kantian distinction between receptivity and spontaneity, each conceptual system would individually process the unsynthesized intuitions into their own unique version of experience: '... to change one's concepts would be to change what one experiences, to change one's "phenomenal world"' (Rorty 1982: 4). In principle the cocooning could be endless in its scope, only to be limited by the powers of invention within the field of distinct conceptual judgements. And, upon reflection, the containment function of a faculty of receptivity will not obtain for the reason – just alluded to – that a judgement must be present in all meaningful explanations. In his article 'World Well Lost', Rorty states that

> [i]nsofar as a Kantian intuition is effable, it is just a perceptual judgement, and thus not merely 'intuitive'. Insofar as it is ineffable, it is incapable of having an explanatory function. This dilemma . . . casts doubt on the notion of the faculty of 'receptivity' (Rorty 1982: 4).

If this observation remains unchallenged, then, as Rorty suspects, all receptivity to 'independent reality' drops out and radical spontaneity rules, rendering communications impossible among incommensurable conceptual frameworks – those that do not share a common vocabulary. And, once again, Rorty can invite us to evaluate which of all the ungrounded theories plays well for us lovers of democratic freedom. Nevertheless, the possibility of relativity and the threat of scepticism seem imminent where the correspondence theorist's view that 'the Truth is One' fails and a belief in multiplicity of valid coherent 'worlds' takes its place (e.g., N. Goodman's *Ways of Worldmaking*). Rorty does not believe that either of these possibilities is a necessary condition, nor should they be.

If one closely follows the move made by Kant to initiate his Copernican Revolution, that is, his building his system of reason analogous to Copernicus' re-centring of our astronomical viewpoint to the helios, it becomes apparent that there is a loophole large enough for Rorty's pragmatism to fit through. As with the Einsteinian view in which Copernicus is seen to have made a clever adjustment of viewpoint which wrested increased understanding about the universe, and which even contributed developmentally to the Theory of Relativity, without thereby establishing the sun's astronomically absolute centrality in the cosmos or even in our planetary system, from a Rortian view Kant is in a similar Copernican position regarding Kant's claim for the absolute centrality of cognitive reason. Consider: empirical reality would remain the same for the human observer under the Lockean hypothesis that objects come to be known to us through conformity of the mind to the object, as well as under the Kantian hypothesis that objects are objects of knowledge to us only by conforming to the necessary structures of the human mind. Clearly, the fact that Kant provides an explanation of synthetic *a priori* knowledge, where empirical accounts do not, is an achievement of human creativity and imagination. It also furthers our understanding of the capacities of the human intellect. Nevertheless, as with its analogous counterpart, Kantian Critical Philosophy has tremendous utility if not overstated and dogmatized. For if we can and do move smoothly between the poetic and the meteorological importance of a sunrise, as well as the astronomical import of a solar system, without the necessity for competitive comparison and without a loss of meaning for the former two by (when judged to be important to do so) being covered under the explanatory powers of the latter, then might we not glide, guided by our purposes, as easily among the various and incompatible philosophical theories, even those in contradiction to, say, Kant's?[16] After all, in both cases, the original Copernican Theory and the Kantian Copernican Revolution, it still seems to be a matter of pragmatic judgement as to which of their several disciplines it would be more advantageous to employ. Just as the medieval theological dictum – 'Believe and you will understand' – was replaced by its Enlightenment alternative – 'Understand in order to believe' – the latter in its turn is being displaced, so the argument goes, by the pragmatic suggestion that understanding and belief are alternative, and at times incommensurable, coherent uses of language which are employed to get a handle on, and to manipulate towards one's purposes, life's causal impacts. Rorty asserts that the arts, the sciences and the political institutions of society are each distinct attempts to solve problems, that is 'to modify our beliefs and desires and activities in ways that will bring us greater happiness than we have now' (Rorty 1982: 16). Thus, it could be argued that very little would be lost, while gaining the renewable liberty of intellectual creativity, if we adopt Rorty's 'Jeffersonian' assumptions about philosophical social tolerance of diverse 'poeticized' projects in place of 'Philosophically' sanctioned metaphysical and epistemological projects which search for foundational grounding for the various disciplines. In this way Rorty may avoid the charge that he is a covert Singularist.

But can he maintain, as a liberal must, that meaningful conversation is possible among individuals holding divergent worldviews without pre-establishing a Singularist view of a pluralist world at the paradigm or meta-meta-narrative level? Rorty has already suggested that conversation ceases when interpretations do not overlap. Unless Rorty can provide a substantial (non-Singularist) ground for conversation there cannot be the meaningful exchange necessary for a democratic solidarity. Therefore, it is critical for Rorty to establish an alternative way to communicate that preserves his Multiplist stance about society and the 'selves' that populate it.

Rorty has cited the work of Davidson which challenges the whole notion of the dichotomy of scheme and content (which gives rise to the assumption of competing conceptual frameworks) to call into question the 'obsessive' need (Rorty 1982: 13) to ground in some fashion our beliefs in some sort of foundational conceptual base. This criticism revolves around the previously mentioned (Chapter 1) Davidson's notion of 'Charity' in 'radical interpretation'. As we recall, in order to commence communication between oneself and the members of another language group (or as with Creole, linguistic sub-grouping within one language, i.e., French) there must be supposed a substantial number of background beliefs between the subject and the interpreter. This follows from the claim that 'knowledge of beliefs comes only with the ability to interpret words', and from a reasonable conviction based upon evolutionary theory that, as a member of a surviving linguistic community, the majority of any one of its members' beliefs could not be false.[17] Hence, it is only possible to assume a widespread accord exists among beliefs taken as a whole between would-be communicants. As Davidson observed:

> Charity is forced on us; whether we like it or not, if we want to understand
> others, we must count them right in most matters. If we can produce a
> theory that reconciles charity and the formal conditions for a theory, we
> have done all that could be done to ensure communications. Nothing more
> is possible, and nothing more is needed (Davidson 1984: 196–97).

Thus, neither the posit of the 'world' as an independent thing-in-itself nor the
hypothesis of a common conceptual matrix (*sensus communis*) necessary for
the guarantee of rational autonomy and universality is needed. The containment of wildly alternative frameworks is thereby eliminated as well, with the
view that takes differences among language-games as relatively minor adjustments to the rather large set of common beliefs currently being held. Correspondence theories drop out in favour of coherent rationales.[18] Therefore, the
spectre of relativism is not realized, according to Rorty, due to the benign
restraint of the Principle of Charity.[19] By adopting the Davidsonian position,
Rorty, in saying that 'only the world determines truth', is suggesting that we
take this sentence fragment in the liberal Deweyan sense of a 'funded experience' – those beliefs which are not being challenged at this moment – while
steadfastly maintaining that there is no distinction between scheme and content.[20] To do otherwise, to label 'the world' as the given 'sense-data', 'the sensual manifold' or 'stimuli', which stands over and against the manner in which
these are received and spontaneously organized and represented, is to move
well within some specific epistemological theory, even as one moves out of the
realm of the transcendental metaphysics. We again find ourselves dislodged
from the illusory role of independent arbiter of truth and thoroughly planted
within a given cultural paradigm. Yet we are not drawn into 'anything-goes'
scepticism, for while representationalism is abandoned, Rorty maintains his
belief in beneficial ethnocentrism: that there is truth, in a Davidsonian sense,
within the chosen vocabulary of a given community (see Rorty 1982: 15).
But is his ethnocentric Jeffersonian Strategy truly sufficient to preserve his
Multiplist stance? Can Rortian pragmatism walk the line between relativism
and representationalism without falling in with Singularists on the meta-meta-
narrative level?

Chapter 6

The Hermeneutical Approach and its Implications for Rorty's Jeffersonian Strategy

Rorty, Gadamer and the Reach of Hermeneutics

To begin this chapter, it would be helpful to briefly summarize Rorty's Jeffersonian Strategy. What must disappear from our conversation concerning the public or private sphere are any petitions for transcultural rationality, as well as any appeal for consensus through convergence within a society or among cultures. Traditions and the solidarities built up around them gives the force of conviction to the group's beliefs. They are not founded on anything more than a cherishing of one way of life and the wish to promulgate it. Thus, these same esteemed beliefs are open to revision and radical redescriptions (i.e., to be made and unmade: see Rorty 1999a: xxii) by individual 'poets' when there is a significant shift in the social environment. Rorty aims through 'Jeffersonian' tolerance of open conversation among creative 'poets' to keep fresh the practice of liberalism while simultaneously appealing to the Jeffersonian democratic tradition to achieve restraint of the poetic excesses of cruelty and humiliation.

However, under this description, the neo-pragmatic position might itself seem to be guilty of circular reasoning. Rorty does not shy away from this, as he believes there is no contradiction here. The circle is hermeneutical (Rorty 1979: 364–65). That is, it is interpretative rather than descriptive. He believes that interpretative exchanges take on a flavour of an ironic Socratic discourse – where, just as when the background and foreground shift in a perspective drawing, the original meaning of an idea or value gives way to a previously disparaged or unexpected meaning – without sliding over into the expectation of a pre-existing common ground to be reached. Hermeneutics allows a sensitivity to narratives or texts that does not involve 'neutrality' to content or an extinction of one's point of view. There is no corporate view in Platonic–Kantian sense. Since we always are situating a narrator's meaning, with charity, in relation to the whole of our web of belief or, conversely, our point of view in relation to the narrator's text or voice, there is no escaping one's historical embeddedness, one's ethnocentric prejudice. We, as humans, must project out from our socio-historical bias. Hence, there must be legitimate prejudices: authentic ways of life found in actual practices of peoples and cultures. This is acceptable in hermeneutics, and it is implied throughout Rorty's thought.

To reiterate a key question raised in Chapter 1 and again in the previous chapter: Ought the Multiplist thesis assumed in Rortian hermeneutics be accepted, and if so, then can one's interpretative understanding be extended, and in what manner, beyond the personal to the interpersonal (public), and if so can it be shared at the meta-narrative level without begging Singularism at the meta-meta-narrative or paradigmatic level?

There seem to be at least two opinions about the scope and extent of hermeneutical meaning. For example, in *Truth and Method*, Hans-Georg Gadamer gives us a developmental view of hermeneutics. He claims that there is a chance for a true playful interpenetration; we are not completely enveloped by our uniqueness, isolated within our solitary 'horizon' – 'the range of vision that includes everything that can be seen from a particular vantage point' (Gadamer 1994: 302), as the Hegelian In-Itself must be. He believes that a person who is trying to understand is always in the process of projecting a meaning upon a narration which she encounters. However, this biased expectation, this 'fore-projection' (Gadamer 1994: 267) is in need of constant revision as she encounters challenges to her pre-judgements. In the following passage Gadamer, while writing specifically about the hermeneutical work necessary to understand a text, is intending to speak broadly about all avenues of understanding, including the understanding involved in the interplay of conversation:

> [A] person trying to understand a text is prepared for it to tell him something. That is why a hermeneutically trained consciousness must be, from the start, sensitive to the text's alterity. But this kind of sensitivity involves neither 'neutrality' with respect to content nor the extinction of one's self, but the foregrounding and appropriation of one's own fore-meaning and prejudice. The important thing is to be aware of one's own bias, so that the text can present itself in all its otherness and thus assert its own truth against one's own fore-meaning (Gadamer 1994: 269).

Every revision of one's fore-meaning is capable of projecting before itself. In a dialectic fashion, a new projection of meaning, that which emerges from the interplay with the interlocutor's text or narration and one's funded beliefs, causes one to form new understandings and new interpretations to replace less suitable ones (Gadamer 1994: 267) in an act of 'fusion'.

> This is the reason why understanding is always more than merely re-creating someone else's meaning. Questioning opens up possibilities of meaning, and thus what is meaningful passes into one's own thinking on the subject (Gadamer 1994: 375).

But more than this, the act of questioning, if done appropriately, yields personal insight. As Richard Bernstein observes in *Beyond Objectivity and Relativism*, the inability to establish a common, nonpartisan platform for the comparative analysis and hierarchical arrangement of one life-form against another, or in brief, the incommensurability of different forms of life, 'always presents a challenge that requires learning to ask the right questions and drawing on the resources of our own linguistic horizons in order to understand that which is alien to our interpretative matrix. In Gadamerian terms, it is not a dead metaphor to liken the fusion of horizons – that which is the constant task of effective-historical consciousness – to an ongoing and open dialogue or conversation' (Bernstein 1991: 144). As Gadamer believes, it is only through a dialectic encounter with others that we can gain insights and true knowledge of ourselves. This was the aim of the process of Socratic dialogues – i.e., to come to know oneself better. And in the process a rational account *emerges*.

> The maieutic productivity of the Socratic dialogue, the art of using words as a midwife, is certainly directed toward the people who are the partners in the dialogue, but it is concerned merely with the opinions they express, the immanent logic of the subject matter that is unfolded in the dialogue. What emerges in its truth is the logos, which is neither mine nor yours and hence so far transcends the interlocutors' subjective opinions that even the person leading the conversation knows that he does not know. As the art of conducting a conversation, dialectic is also the art of seeing things in the unity of an aspect (*sunoran eis hen eidos*) – i.e., it is the art of forming concepts through the working out the common meaning (Gadamer 1994: 368).

For Gadamer, hermeneutics is primarily an interpersonal practice of *Bildung*, or self-formation through the medium of *logos*. In the to-and-fro play of conversation, one is 'thrown' beyond the subject/object, the interpreter/narration split into dynamic fusion of horizons, a kind of emergent *sensus communis*.

In sharp contrast, Rorty regards Gadamer's take on hermeneutics, at best, as merely another attempt at achieving the 'comfort of consensus'; at worst, 'a form of mystification' (Bernstein 1991: 199). Rorty thinks that all efforts such as Gadamer's are wrongheaded because we are embedded into our language-game and cannot emerge from it piecemeal. Nor can we merge with other language-games incommensurate with our own; we are always in radical projection without the possibility of Gadamerian 'playful' interpenetration. Solidarities might form due to a coincidence of interests constituting a grouping labelled 'us', but never a gradual process of expanding 'horizons' to meld into an intimately shared perspective. Given this extreme subjectivist (for individuals) and ethnocentric (for groups) position, a Rortian 'conversation' between incommensurable vocabularies has the appearance to a Gadamerian of lectures delivered at cross purposes, with collective pronouns such as 'we' and 'us' functioning not as inclusive terms but as boundary markers demarcating the part of the 'conversation' which fits one's particular bias from the part which does not. This introverted emphasis may be seen in Rorty's definition of 'edification'.

In a telling passage, Rorty discards Gadamer's term *Bildung* as 'too foreign' while offhandedly setting aside the translated English word 'education' as 'too flat'. In doing this he creates the need for the replacement term – 'edification' – which he supplies. This allows Rorty the freedom to customize its meaning as follows:

I shall use 'edification' to stand for this project of finding new, better, more interesting, more fruitful ways of speaking. The attempt to edify (ourselves or others) may consist in the hermeneutic activity of making connections between our own culture and some exotic culture or historical period, or between our own discipline and another discipline which seems to pursue incommensurable aims in an incommensurable vocabulary. But it may instead consist in the 'poetic' activity of thinking up such new aims, new words, or new disciplines, followed by, so to speak, the inverse of hermeneutics: *the attempt to reinterpret our familiar surroundings in the unfamiliar terms of our new inventions.* In either case, the activity is ... edifying without being constructive – at least if 'constructive' means the sort of cooperation in the accomplishment of research programs which takes place in normal discourse. For edifying discourse is *supposed* to be abnormal, *to take us out of our old selves by the power of strangeness, to aid us in becoming new beings* (Rorty 1979: 360; emphasis added, except for 'supposed').

The italicized sections of this passage suggest a subtle but significant alteration of the purpose of interpretation. Rorty marries hermeneutics with the self-assertive, rendering any adaptation to the unexpected a matter of poetic licence in service to one's drive for practical satisfaction. Conceived in this manner, hermeneutic understanding remains idiosyncratic even as participants move into contiguous semantic spaces (i.e., into solidarity). Thus for Rorty, the only possible way of fully achieving a Gadamerian inclusive agreement is for one side of the alleged 'conversation' to abandon its original language-game while simultaneously undergoing a Kuhnian conversion to the alternative vocabulary at a particularly critical moment in that individual's act of coping.

In brief, Gadamer's developmental hermeneutics stands in substantial contrast to Rorty's revolutionary hermeneutics at precisely the point where the reach of horizontal projection is at issue. It remains to be seen if Rorty's understanding of hermeneutics can be sustained successfully within his radical Multiplism without tripping into postmodern relativism or compromising his Multiplist principles. We shall take up this thread in the concluding chapters. But for now it is instructive to note that Rorty holds hermeneutic understanding to be less like a traditional mathematico-logical demonstration and more like encountering a stranger. Consistent with what was said above, apparently the deep reason for his position on hermeneutics seems to be related to Rorty's view, noted earlier (Chapter 4), that logic itself must be idiosyncratic, thoroughly contingent and plastic, rather than statically objective (Rorty 1979: 181). Furthermore, implied in this revisionist view is the instrumentalist's appreciation of all strategies for coping, including logic, which is captured in the following extract:

Strong poetry, commonsense morality, revolutionary morality, normal science, revolutionary science, and the sort of fantasy which is intelligible to only one person, are all, from a Freudian point of view, different ways of dealing with the blind impresses – or, more precisely, ways of dealing with different blind impresses: impresses which may be unique to an individual or common to the members of some historically conditioned community. None of these strategies is privileged over the others in the sense of expressing human nature better. No such strategy is more or less human than any other, any more than the pen is more truly a tool than the butcher's knife, or a hybridized orchid less a flower than the wild rose (Rorty 1989: 37–38).

It follows that logic in general and the logic of hermeneutics in particular is a pragmatic tool in Rorty's toolbox, which, *pace* Gadamer, may be used when and how the creative thinker (the poet) sees fit to achieve her ends. And by claiming to be building upon Freud's insights concerning different methods of adaptation (Rorty 1989: 33), Rorty can conceive that this idiosyncratic streak runs through the individual, with nothing left over – neither from logic *per se*, nor from scientific method, nor the hermeneutic melding of minds within a common horizon.

At this point the charge of antinomianism could be revived; self-assertion could take on a Romantic flavour, reminiscent of idealization of the unbounded Nietschean *obermensch*. It is not a difficult move to make between the notion of an unfettered deistic will of Augustinian origins and a similar volitional freedom now associated in a creative *anima*. Nevertheless, the idiosyncratic 'poetic genius' must also be tempered. Romanticism has made a 'god' of the affective self, who through his artistic endeavours is able to reach the ineffable or the sublime. Rorty sees the need to de-divinize this notion as well – another holdover from the Enlightenment optimism – by burning away the dross of the 'self-foundational', now introduced from the side of the mystical, leaving 'self-assertion', the creative expression of one's beliefs and desires, as the treasured existential gold. Yet the question remains open concerning the issue of containment once the theistic and the Kantian restraints have been removed from the autonomous, albeit contingent, creator. In Chapter 8 we will consider the possibility, drawn from Rorty's Freud–Davidson thesis, of competing sets of incompatible beliefs 'within' an individual as a self-restraining device. But at this present time, we must return to Rorty's Jeffersonian Strategy, its concomitant 'external' programme for controlling domineering idiosyncratic impulses and, in the light of Rorty's understanding of hermeneutics, the Strategy's attendant difficulties.

Rorty's Jeffersonian Strategy: The Basis for Tolerance or an Opportunity for Intolerance?

As we have seen, in the opinion of Rorty any claim to transcultural foundations has outlived their usefulness in a free-flowing conversation that characterizes an egalitarian solidarity. Our coherent beliefs, entwined with our historical and cultural settings, are open to the democracy of contingent alliances of utility as

we continually interpret and redefine our idiosyncratic life-story. If one wishes
to remain a dogmatic Kantian, for example, this is the individual's prerogative.
However, 'Jeffersonian-style' toleration must be extended culturally to a multiplicity of narratives to guarantee the generation of original and inventive story-
lines (Rorty 2007: 40). Within the boundaries of 'self-assertion', however, one
ought to liberate oneself from the vocabularies of Religion and theistically influenced Philosophy and Scientism. And once unfettered by artificial internal and
domineering external constraints posing as necessary conditions, one can give
oneself free reign to be an agent of creativity.

But does such a pragmatic hermeneutical stance (Rorty 1979: 321, 346–47)
allow for serious inquiry into matters of deep human importance? In moving
away from transcultural and interpersonal rationality, do we also depart from
a serious study, philosophical, scientific or otherwise, through which we have
made real, measurable progress?

Rorty does not believe that 'when we say something we must necessarily be
expressing a view about a subject. We might just be *saying something* – partici-
pating in a conversation rather than contributing to an inquiry' (Rorty
1979: 371). This 'saying something' is what I have taken to be what Krausz
has called *ampliative reason*. But if we are expressing ampliative reasons, are we
thereby at risk of falling back into the quicksand of unfounded prejudices masquerading as oases of poetic creativity? Do we embrace a Cold War-style
'peaceful coexistence' in order to make room for ironic liberty? Consider the
following quote that Rorty makes concerning contrasting incommensurate
moral views:

> Our moral view is, I firmly believe, much better than any competing view,
> even though there are a lot of people whom you will never be able to convert
> to it. It is one thing to say, falsely, that there is nothing to choose between us
> and the Nazis. It is another thing to say, correctly, that there is no neutral,
> common ground to argue our differences. That Nazi and I will always strike
> one another as begging all crucial questions, arguing in circles (Rorty
> 1999a: 15).

Here Rorty restates his anti-essentialist/pro-ethnocentric views as he re-
emphasizes the pragmatic hermeneutical nature of interpretation, yet in doing
so Rorty implicitly rejects the possibility of a grounding *sensus communis* in favour
of excluding solidarities and contingent agreements. Rorty nevertheless moves
to restrain the potentially cruel contrivances of the ironic poet through a non-
bridgeable division between the public and the private spheres of an individual's life. In order to maintain his 'Jeffersonian' guarantee of the radical freedom for the self-asserting poet, it appears that Rorty must separate types of
vocabularies, radically distinguishing self-referring language-games from the
causally interactive ones. The overarching question of this book then arises:
Is this pragmatic 'world' of solidarities and centreless individuals *better* than
the traditional, representationalist one Rorty has urged us to neutralize

through his Jeffersonian Strategy, in the sense that it avoids the emphasis on power and exploitation that Heidegger asserts comes hand-in-hand with the onto-theological Singularist mindset?

Jeffersonian Strategy: Balancing Personal Freedom and Public Tolerance

Because of the blessing and the curse of linguistic ability, we humans must have two focuses. One focus must be the social use of language which serves us best, if it does, when it is 'normal' and stable in its usage. Examples can be drawn from the day-to-day practices from within the medical profession and from the educational environs where conflicting vocabularies could easily be confusing and, hence, harmful in terms of pain and humiliation. Hence, the adoption of a common vocabulary devoid of humiliating or hurtful terms would serve as a promoter of social order and potentially ease conversation away from detrimental comments.

These communal enterprises will not dovetail with the irony rising from self-assertive individuality, however. For instance, a constant questioning of their own socialization by the young would be corrosive to building solidarity, liberal or otherwise. Nonetheless, Rorty believes that the tool of irony is essential to the re-creative critique of the culture and its various normalized practices, and therefore must be allowed wide latitude. The only available niche free from the societal 'final vocabularies' is in the privacy of one's thoughts. This is the second focus of linguistic use, the one that functions as a refuge from the potentially controlling and possibly humiliating impingement of public forms upon the individual's idiosyncratic contents. Yet the well-worn adage that 'no man is an island' aptly applies here, with a twist. As Rorty writes, 'On my definition, an ironist cannot get along without the contrast between the final vocabulary she inherited and the one she is trying to create for herself . . . Ironists have to have something to have doubts about, something from which to be alienated' (Rorty 1989: 87–88). The radical, poetic reconstitution of the vocabulary one inherits must have some regulation beyond relational opposition, if only to keep the 'abnormal' narrative recognizable, well-defined, and thus potentially transmittable to a larger audience. Thus there must be a liberal solidarity incontestably built around tolerance and non-humiliation that advances the free exchange of narratives in a marketplace of opinions.

Rorty's Freudian Solution: A First Look

To ensure a solidarity embodying tolerance and non-humiliation, it appears that Rorty counts on something like Freud's 'reality principle' to check the wilder musings which emanate from the 'pleasure principle' drives of any individual. That is, the 'reality principle' (better known as the *superego*) is the inculcation of societal values and taboos into the individual's psyche for the purpose of sublimating the *id*'s libidinous drives to society's will *via* the twin stratagems of shame and guilt. But in the frustrations which arise due to the thwarting of the efforts to gratify the instinctual drives for survival, security and satisfaction, Rorty cannot hope with Freud – for now obvious reasons – that a definitive science for the grasping of the way things are will materialize. The reality principle in the hands of Rorty is the pleasure principle with the clout of numbers (i.e., the force of solidarity akin to the power of endeavour – psychological impulse or drive – essential in the construction of the Hobbesian Social Contract – see Chapter 7). Yet, as Plato noted in the *Crito*, the *Apology*, and in several other dialogues, the Many is incapable of the greatest harm and of the greatest good because they act without a definitive standard in view. To some, this lack of unchanging pattern might seem to be a freedom, but to those who have suffered cruelty and humiliation, there is an insecurity in this which smacks of arbitrariness.

People's politics, like fads in fashion, are notoriously capricious. The source of this fickleness and arbitrariness might reside in the very partition of the private inventiveness and the public hope that Rorty lauds. I believe that the political issues connected with 'soft money' contributions to the political parties in the United States only emphasize the difficulties inherent in this private–public split. Consider when we as a society have asked an individual such as Bill Clinton[1] or George W. Bush to distinguish his private interests (massive fund-raising in order to ensure their ambition of re-election) from his public presidential concerns (getting re-elected in order to ensure the continuance or the dismantling of welfare state social policy) – were we not creating unhealthy social, if not moral, ambiguities that breeched the Jeffersonian divide between the public and the private spheres?

So how can Rorty stand with Plato in opposition to the unfettered fickleness of the Many while sidestepping Plato's essentializing liberal tolerance? He does this, in the spirit of neo-Darwinism, by harnessing the forces of change instead of fighting them. In allowing unrestrained invention within the containment field of a tolerant solidarity, Rorty believes a self-sustaining equilibrium is possible, more than in any other paradigm so far constructed.

Rorty, having realized the whimsical nature of both moral dicta and social policy, may now wish to turn to a quasi-Freudian account of cruelty as mental *dis-ease* with the surrounding societal norms.[2] He might move to redescribe the relation between the human organism and the discursive poet by having the individual, as social organism, publicly bow to the 'just' causal pressures brought upon her by her society to act in the role of a tolerant liberal and, as Romantic poet, allow for the privately and contrarily reweaving of her self-description to her personal liking, even to the point of her becoming an illiberal elitist. However, as Nancy Fraser observes:

> Rorty's ... position, which I call the 'partition' position, represents a compromise. If Romanticism and pragmatism are not exactly 'natural partners', but if, at the same time, one is not willing to abandon either one of them, then

perhaps they can learn how to live with one another. Thus Rorty has recently outlined the terms of a truce between them, a truce which allots each its own separate sphere of influence. The Romantic impulse will have free reign in what will henceforth be 'the private sector'. But it will not be permitted any political pretensions. Pragmatism, on the other hand, will have exclusive rights to 'the public sector'. But it will be barred from entertaining any notions of radical change which could challenge the 'private' cultural hegemony of Romanticism.

An ingenious compromise, to be sure. Yet compromises based on partition are notoriously unstable. They tend not truly to resolve but only temporarily to palliate the basic source of conflict. Sooner or later, in one form or another, the latter will out (Fraser, in Malachowski 1990: 305).

Such a contingent compromise will simply reveal an internal, and potentially pathological, struggle within the personal arena, and an adverse conflict between the social and the personal. It will be my contention in Chapter 7 that his politico-poetic alternative, the radical partitioning of the private from the public, has the Hobbesian dilemma of the two sovereigns as its unfortunate and close parallel, reaching down even into an individual's idiosyncratic webs of belief (the subject of sections of Chapter 7 and Chapter 8). For the present, however, it will be helpful if we turn our attention to the poetic aspect of his Jeffersonian Strategy, that is, to Rorty's critique of the so-called 'Myth of the Self', to flesh out his position on the radical contingency of the poeticized self, and to set the stage for his attempt to neutralize Fraser's criticism. Towards this end Rorty utilizes Freud's theory in order to dissolve a presupposition behind Fraser's challenge: 'Freud thus helps us take seriously the possibility that there is no central faculty, no central self, called reason . . .' (Rorty 1989: 33).

The Contingent 'I' and a Plurality of 'Persons'

Rorty believes that Freud radically changed our self-image. It is commonly assumed that a single human body 'houses' a single human self, a person. Once again Rorty borrows from Davidson in noting that a credible definition of 'personhood' is to have a coherent and credible set of beliefs and desires. This definition allows a reading of Freud in which the conscious and the unconscious are alternative, mostly incongruent and competing sets of beliefs and desires within a psyche. In short, it is possible that there may be two or more 'persons' within a single human body, united in a single causal network (interlacing with each other and with the body). As the vibration of the eardrum may cause a belief to arise in an individual, so too can, say, the unconscious cause alterations in the beliefs and desires of the conscious mind. Nevertheless, these 'persons' may not have a conversation with each other – each one is not a reason for alteration and change in each other. That is, each internally congruent but incompatible set of beliefs and desires may lead to 'mechanical' effects upon each other while not being reducible to the vocabulary of the other. Their metaphors do not match. Freud claims as much in the article 'The Unconscious' found in *General Psychological Theory: Papers on Metapsychology*.[3] By analogy, it would be like being blind-sided by a bumper car driven by a person who is speaking a foreign language (i.e., the unconscious; the *Id*). You (i.e., the consciousness; the *Ego*) know something has occurred. You have felt the impact and heard accompanying sounds but you are not sure from where the blow came; who or what delivered it, or why it was issued.

Self-Creating Organism/Privilege-free Democratic Associations

Rorty, by allying with elements in Freud, (seemingly) commits himself to the rejection of the strict anti-mentalist view that the unconscious as latent recollections 'can no longer be described as mental processes, but that they correspond to residue of somatic processes from which something mental can once more proceed' (Freud 1963: 117). Consistently, neither does Rorty endorse any form of dualism (apparently), thus avoiding a descent into a 'war of words' which characterizes the physicalist/mentalist debate. Rather, he chooses to occupy the position of a non-reductive physicalist. He holds that perception and the active processing thereof, and the beliefs formulated as a result, are but two descriptions of the same process. Rorty, quoted in Hall (1994: 94), states that 'the difference between mind and body – between reason and cause – is, thus, no more mysterious than, e.g., the relation between a macro-structure and a micro-structure description of a table'. We are dealing with vocabulary differences, and not comparing or contrasting rival views about alleged substantial entities. As such, we need not be concerned with the old Cartesian troubles involving the linking of two things which have incompatible essences. All that need affect us is the linguistic inconvenience of incommensurable descriptions (descriptions that do not reduce to a common, neutral vocabulary for the purpose of a comparative analysis) among nominal essences which deal with the relation between public 'physical causes' and private 'mental reasons', or between 'persons' as incommensurable sets of beliefs and desires within an individual.

Thus, it may be plausible to assert that there is a direct line in the psychology of Rorty's thought between his anti-Cartesian–Kantian stance of denying any 'sky-hooks', from which to gain an objective point of view of reality untainted by a language-game bias (or graced by a meta-language of clear and distinct ideas), and his disavowal (established along pragmatized-Freudian lines) of any claim for a centred self. Since, for Rorty, 'human nature' reduces to an ungrounded vocabulary now in play (Guignon *et al.*, in Malachowski 1990: 342), it appears that if the vocabulary of a Rortian democracy would deny privilege, it must also deny the centres of power which may lay claim to such privilege, such as a god, an objective truth, transcendental ego, or a substantial self (in a similar manner to the political parallel in American history of abolishing titles of nobility in a republican attempt to level out of existence claims of and for privilege). It also may be cross-referenced to the Freudian attempts to humanize the 'lower' drives of passion, as well as the 'higher' powers of reason, transforming the perception of hierarchical structure into distinctly human 'voices' with roughly equal and even dissonant abilities to narrate and interpret past experiences. These considerations focus and drive Rorty's weaving of his new vocabulary towards an aesthetical culture populated by radically self-creating organisms that are free (once protected from the scourge of humiliation) to couple and recouple into ever-expanding and diverse social arrangements. Perhaps, one could liken this belief to the Hobbesian individual in the state of nature, only now with a postmodern sense of liberal optimism (more on this connection in Chapter 7). Hence, the importance Rorty places on the abandoning of any vocabulary involving the narrowing of possibilities to a single, rigidly defined human nature for another vocabulary, consequently allowing for that quality of radical and creative uniqueness in individuals. It is in this way that Rorty can argue for the broad freedoms necessary to rationalize persuasively the construction, with others of similar enough idiosyncratic bent, of associations of a particular ethno-linguistic style, and still maintain the possibility of both social cohesion and the independence of the private self-creator: his Jeffersonian Strategy. The contingent recognition of similar needs and vulnerabilities by private 'ironists' is apparently enough in Rorty's view to bind society together in a reciprocal arrangement of tolerance (Rorty 1989: 84). Thus, an analogous use of Adam Smith's 'invisible hand' seems to be at work here (Fraser, in Malachowski 1990: 305). And hence the conclusion, there need not be an appeal to a foundational metaphysical nature for there to be a possibility of a cohesive society, only an acceptance of the ethnocentric roots, which, without coincidence, are the very ones found in twentieth-century American democratic culture into which Rorty was born and raised. If it is given that all choices of past generations are based on foundationless (hence, radically contingent) decisions, and if one's 'nature' is also radically contingent and must think and act out of some culture's language-game based on those choices, then why not start with one's own? But does one then have a choice in the materials one inherits and the materials one uses to create future vocabularies?

Bhaskar's Challenge to the Jeffersonian Strategy

In order to link the discussion concerning judgement from Chapter 4 to the present topic, the discernments made by the individual ironist must be coherent, albeit idiosyncratic and manifold, by being in radical engagement with the contingencies of the time, place, culture, and so on. Thus, there seems to be a tight linkage, one denied in Rorty's narrative, between public solidarity and the private irony due, at some level, to the interactions of environment and organism. Anyone who was out of synch with the democratic ideals of personal freedom and tolerance was to be considered 'mad' by those who are embedded in that history and culture.[4] Where, then, is the personal breathing space which would allow for the 'insanity' associated with the creativity that is the rudiment for progressive change in any society? Can Rortian hermeneutics, as the interpretative study of different ways to regard and articulate experience, provide that room while preserving the linguistic cohesion necessary for intra-personal and inter-personal dialogue, as Rorty promises?

This brings out a tension in *Philosophy and the Mirror of Nature* between what he terms the 'Two Rorty's', noted by Roy Bhaskar in 'Rorty, Realism and the Idea of Freedom' (Bhaskar, in Malachowski 1990: 212–17). This is Rorty as a tough-minded 'scientific naturalist of a physicalistic cast' (leaning towards a strict interchange of environment and organism) and as an advocate of a hermeneutic/pragmatic-based existential autonomy (open to and thriving upon a humanist freedom of choice). This divide seems to be played out in the alleged Rortian non-bridgeable split between the public and the private, as the following suggests: 'My "poeticized" culture is one which has given up the attempt to unite one's private ways of dealing with one's finitude and one's sense of obligation to other human beings' (Rorty 1989: 68).

Interactions between an environment and an organism can be described in a physicalist, determinist vocabulary. Thus as social organisms, humans are subject to causal laws. But Bhaskar says (in Malachowski 1990: 213) that to hold this as described breaks apart any closed system at the level of physical microstructure (i.e., the individual as a distinct organism). So there is no closed system involving an individual as a corporeal entity in a social interaction. Yet this unrestricted enveloping of the causal system seems to limit severely the idiosyncratic nature of any social organism. The interfacing of common environments and organisms will tend to homogenize behaviours within a restricted range, or ways of life that include the use of language. This, in turn, could significantly constrict the breadth of belief systems that are developed in response to environmental pressures, and hence the linguistic freedoms necessary to perform acts of self-reinvention while embedded in a cultural environment.

To break loose of this homogenizing effect of a causally determined physical system, Rorty must establish a method of free expression that releases the organism from (or alternately, *constrains*) its *en-soi* (in-itself) bind while not abandoning his pragmatic *pour-soi* (for-oneself) position (to borrow these Sartrean terms, in harmony with Rorty's usage). (See Malachowski 1990: 218.)

An unacceptable attempt was simply to ignore the constructions of causal determinism (Rorty 1979: 354), because the question then arises: Is this act of ignoring also causally determined, or is it a free choice? We could retreat down a *reductio ad absurdum* argument, and never reach the *pour-soi*. Fortunately, Rorty does not embrace this option.

A better Rortian approach, as noted above, was to claim that despite our immersion in a vocabulary of determined physicalism – of causation – we, nevertheless, have accessible to us an independent vocabulary of non-physicalism – of discursive cognition. And it is our ability to describe and redescribe '... the already-determined world in accordance with [our] vision ...' (Bhaskar, in Malachowski 1990: 226–27) that allows for the unlimited freedom of re-creation (and, by extension, self-creation). However, Bhaskar doubts whether Rorty can avoid the same tripwire triggered by what Rorty calls Kant's 'existentialist distinction between people as empirical selves' [i.e., bodies subject to causal laws or as social *parametrics*] and as 'moral agents' [i.e., persons or interlocutor] (Rorty 1979: 382).

The question is that if a language of a deterministic 'lower order' is in place, how can a redescription of it in a 'higher order' vocabulary ever have an effect on it (as Rorty, in 'Non-reductive Physicalism', claims it must in his persistent echoing of Davidson's doctrines[5])? The vocabularies would be incommensurate (for an internal polemic of Freudian persons – see Chapter 8), and the answer would be that the 'higher order' vocabulary cannot have an effect on (communicate with) the 'lower' physical determinants captured by the physicalist vocabulary, while the 'lower' determinants will govern the selections made by the 'higher' vocabulary, implying that the independence of the 'higher' webs of belief is mere illusion. This criticism would force Rorty to choose between his allegedly simultaneous vocabularies, pressing him into either an uninteresting version of physicalism reminiscent of the early Rorty's *eliminativism materialism*, or a typical rendition of idealism. In Kant this type of pressure appears to Bhaskar to be devastating, since Kant's philosophy focused upon a 'two world model'. But does the analogy to Rorty's narrative carry?

Rorty deals in vocabularies, and as we have seen, not ontological realities termed 'realms' or 'worlds', determinant or otherwise. So it seems that the point of Bhaskar's criticism misses its mark because Rorty is merely claiming to be bilingual (as opposed to Kant's suspect ontological bifurcation). Thereby, apparently, Rorty does escape Bhaskar's critical analysis. Under the description of unfamiliar noises, utterances are unfamiliar sounds out of sync in that they do not conform to the algorithm determined by the current causal configuration. Under an alternate description they are novel metaphors not conforming to the expected and accepted use of a language by a given society. In the first instance, noises impact deterministically upon the sense apparatus of the organism, and are in themselves a meaningless cacophony. They involve oral 'mentioning' only, to which the human organism can only react. Nevertheless, the algorithmic rules are changed in minor or more substantial ways, occasioning the hearer the opportunity to adapt to, perhaps, merely a new wrinkle of what is understood under the description of metaphor as meaning, or maybe to a wholly novel game-plan. It is in this poetic free adaptation, the conscious recontextualization of the rule-changing utterance into the web of beliefs and desires, that the 'mentioning' is understood as 'use' and functions as a ground for the current justification of a new belief for the hearer. *Pace* Bhaskar, there is no literal exchange of meaning between organisms in an environment. Therefore, there is no danger of a reduction of the two vocabularies into a determining rattle of sound which is caused by physical stimuli. Nor is there any peril as a result of their being incommensurate, because it is through the lack of conclusive endorsement by physical stimuli (see underdetermination as discussed in

Chapter 4) which allows a healthy plurality of narratives within and among ironists to flourish unhindered by extra-linguistic forces.

The 'Clashing Rocks' of Physicalism and Idealism

In this fashion, Rorty believes that he avoids the 'clashing rocks' of physicalism and idealism, taking a new pragmatic route which views these linguistic strategies as precisely what they are – alternative strategies employed for the purpose of coping with one's environment. We do not lose our 'self' when we let dissolve the timeworn notions of substantial or transcendental centredness any more than we lose the experience of the world when we abandon the vocabulary of Scientism. If we may recall that in paralleling the argument there is no 'world' or reality to lose when we abandon beliefs in one overriding commensurable truth about the world in itself, Rorty wishes we would let go of the centred self in a similar manner. The stress is that there is no 'self' to lose when we come to accept his pragmatized-Freudian notion of ourselves as radically choosing, contingent webs of beliefs and desires. Active and passive choice (i.e., the use and the mention of language) seems to be transformed by Rorty into, respectively, the private (discursively inventive) and the public (causally-linked) narratives of an individual, and this in turn is interpreted as possibly competing conscious (accessible and current) and unconscious (presently unquestioned and hence inaccessible) vocabularies within the decentred self. [6]

This last point seems to present Rorty with a surprising problem. If one is free to choose one's vocabulary, then this would by necessity include Rorty's depiction of a causally determined world, as well as his characterization of the self as de-centred. While in his private, creative mode, Rorty would agree, and perhaps point to Goodman as a reminder that epistemological bedrock is merely a result from a choice and projection of predicates, and the relative degree of embeddedness these predicates attain (see Chapter 3). However, with a switch of vocabulary, we find an apparently more assured Rorty assuming the (public) fact of 'causal forces' when a need arises for philosophical support for a given argument. Does Rorty reduce the causally determined to the level of linguistic invention, while ironically advocating its power to affect an organism? It appears so. Then he treads perilously close to a causal idealism – 'everything there is, apart from minds themselves, arises causally from the operations of minds' (Kim and Sosa 1995: 227) – despite his protestations to the contrary. Paradoxically, if one remembers that one can never step outside one's historico-cultural milieu, then invention itself must be treated not as a radically free act but as if a secretion of a honey bee, which the human organism 'oozes' as it interacts within the socio-physical environment, unless with a switch of vocabulary, *pace* Rorty, one can gain distance to observe this 'reality' as a representationalist.

For example, in siding with Davidson against Sellars over the issue of truth and assertability in Rorty's 'Representation, Social Practice, and Truth', Rorty states the following:

For the Neanderthal lived *in the same world* that the omniscient user of CSP [Conceptual System of Peirce] lives in, and *the same causal forces* which led most of her and her mate's linguistic behaviors to consist of true assertions will lead an omniscient user to say mostly what she said. *The complicated causal story about how this happened goes much the same*, whether told in Neanderthal, Newtonian or Peircish; the details just get a bit more complicated at each successive stage (Rorty 1991a: 160; italics added).

For the sake of simplicity and clarity, we ought to overlook the worries dealt with by the content of the Sellars–Davidson argument as told by Rorty, and focus on the assumptions at play in the italicized phrases and sentence fragment. There do not appear to be any questions raised nor any cautions issued by Rorty concerning the contingency of his own assumptions about the constitution of the world. Of course, he can argue that this is not his rhetorical responsibility, and that, as we observed in Chapter 3, and again in this chapter, it is legitimate and inevitable to argue from one's cultural and idiosyncratic biases.

Nevertheless, one is led to wonder if Rorty's bilingualism should be taken as a sincere attempt on his part to arrive at a successful pragmatic solution to our current thorny problem about self, organism and centredness, or, with Habermas, as Rorty's use of manipulative persuasion in order 'win the day' for his way of thinking.[7] Rorty uses the term 'ironic' as a rationalization for what might otherwise appear to be a linguistic parlour game involving verbal sleights of hand.[8] In this context, it is prudent for Rorty to caution his audience that irony ought not to be used indiscriminately as a cover for any conflicts or communions existing between the very culture which spawned an individual and the individual's idiosyncratic constitution. This is especially true if that individual is oneself and not some abstract, fictional character found in one's own or another's anecdote. Otherwise, a collapse of the wall between the public and the private is immediately upon us (as it was in the political analogy of soft money to which I alluded above). On the one hand, (the organic) private narrations are necessarily being fabricated solely from the societal raw materials for public consumption. Humans are then mere factories (parametrics functioning as part of a socio-physical causal chain) for the processing of linguistic by-products. Except, that is, on the other hand, when the narrator wishes to be taken seriously as an idiosyncratic poet, if just for a moment, then the bias seems to spin the other way. We are asked to suspend our organic instincts for consumption and regurgitation, if only for a time, as persons (interlocutors) to recognize and applaud the creative powers of human fabrication.

Under the potent tension, as noted in our equivocating use of an instructive term such as 'fabrication', something has got to give in Rorty's Jeffersonian bilingualism. The competing vocabularies, the rival ways of being, clash not in an abstract manner, but existentially for the individual. And with threat of the structural failure (the breaching by the public definition into the private idiom, and vice versa [see note 1]) of the Jeffersonian wall, the possibility for *Rorty himself* to maintain that the panoply of beliefs (including causal determinism) are, in principle, freely chosen either becomes highly suspect, and the claim is crushed under the weight of 'blind press' of causal determinism (see note 4), or the claim rises to its full, unchallenged height as thought unfettered by organic determinism, paradoxically as Rorty freely employs the vocabulary of causal interaction. A reduction must occur either to a thorough-going vocabulary of evolutionary physicalism or to a supra-evolutionary narrative of radical idealism for Rorty's interpretation to remain cogent, or his justification for the Jeffersonian Strategy suffers from a lack of coherence.

Applied to practice, depending upon the interpretation Rorty wishes to endorse, the Pandora's Box of unfettered personal invention may be seen to be most able to inflict a grave cruelty upon society (consider Hitler and Stalin), leading away from solidarity and towards civil war with an ungrounded society suffering a breakdown of communications, unleashing a clash of rival forces. Or alternatively, with society imperialistically imposing its cruel inevitability upon persons through sheer inertia (i.e., the suppression of individualism by Nazism or Communism as the reactive outgrowth to historico-cultural causes) there is a pushing of the material dialectic into dynamic action (i.e., war, revolution), or the reactive repression of individual rights in the name of democracy (as found in McCarthyism). Either way, harm and humiliation can come to the individual (that is, to oneself). With unresolved conflicts at the societal level, the centreless self assumes the tension of Rortian bilingualism (the Jefferson wall of separation must go 'all the way down' through the 'self') in the form of personal psychosis akin to multiple personality disorder. If I am correct in this claim, then Rorty's radical assumptions inherent in the Multiplism of his New Pragmatism, far from opening the future to the freedoms of a democratic utopia, offer humankind the potential, dare I say likelihood, of pain and humiliation regardless of which linguistic tool is used and which outcome presents itself. As promised earlier, my final chapters will address these issues in more detail on both the social level through Thomas Hobbes, and the psychological level through Sigmund Freud, finally ending with a challenge to both Rorty's pragmatic liberalism and his understanding of the de-centred self.

Part III

Chapter 7

Hobbes, Rorty and their Common Political Paradox

The Centreless Self and its Problems

The irreducibility of the *pour-soi* to the *en-soi* (Rorty 1979: 373) is a central insight towards which this work has been moving. We have encountered at least two language-games in the consideration of Rorty's narrative, of which one vocabulary touches on the body as a described physical object in relation to other objects, and the other centres upon a vocabulary of the discursive agent or the describing self. As a *pour-soi*, the describing subject may redescribe all objects, including oneself, in ever new and 'abnormal' terms. The self as describer has the ability to redescribe oneself completely. Or does one have this capacity?

Sartre has stated that the human self is condemned to freedom of choice. It seems that Rorty has absorbed this insight into a Kuhnian framework of abnormal discourses, and has said 'anything goes' *if* what goes can be accepted by some audience. This freedom to describe thoroughly includes future interpretations we will apply to ourselves. The reason for Rorty's claim in the radical malleability of narratives can be found in his anti-essentialism applied to the self. As he says:

> There is no more of a center to the self than there is to the brain. Just as the neural synapses are in continual interaction with one another, constantly weaving a different configuration of electrical charge, so our beliefs and desires are in continual interaction, redistributing truth-values among statements. Just as the brain is not something that 'has' such synapses, but is simply the agglomeration of them, so the self is not something which 'has' the beliefs and desires, but is simply the network of such beliefs and desires (Rorty 1991a: 123).

So, with no apparent limit to the Rortian self at its borders or in its centre, due to the open-endedness of cultural narratives and the absence of a metaphysical foundation upon which to rest a firm definition of the self, for Rorty there can be no constraint as to how one redescribes or reinvents the 'self'.

Yet have we escaped the familiar Cartesian error, which is at the nub of the philosophico-scientific stance that Rorty has campaigned so hard against?

I believe not. Rorty is still enmeshed in the web of Descartes's ideas when he (Rorty) is at his strongest. The distinction between 'being' and 'having' is a critical one. Rorty states that 'The important thing is to think of the collection of those things [beliefs, desires, moods, etc.] as *being* the self rather than as something the self *has*' (Rorty 1991a: 123). He sees an important aspect of human experience, and yet, I maintain, he does not avoid drawing a conclusion in contradiction to the story he has been telling. He does this by explicitly rejecting the 'having' (possessing) of beliefs and desires while, nevertheless, he is claiming that the self 'has' (is an arrangement of) them through the systemization of the individual as a coherent web of beliefs and desires (see below and Chapter 9 *passim*).

To be self-conscious is not to *have* consciousness as if a possession or object (see Marcel 1951: vol. II). It is not some thing to 'throw out' in front of one's eyes, as it were, for inspection, for a third-person descriptive investigation. However, the analogy Rorty suggested above, drawn between the structure of the brain (as an association of synapses) and the structure of the mind (as a solidarity of beliefs and desires), suggests that (1) the physicalist metaphor is equally well suited for the mind, and (2) that there is a position on which one can stand to make such an objective analysis of either metaphor. If I am correct, then Rorty slips into physicalist imagery, reducing the language used to talk about an experiencing agent into quasi-physicalist rhetoric, thereby betraying his materialist proclivities. The harm is that in making this move he thereby undermines his much discussed central claim that one may never stand in a privileged position, that is, as a distant observer who takes a 'spectator's view' resulting in a Singularist description of objects or events (see *Response to Brandom*, in Brandom 2000: 183–90). And while Rorty often reminds his critics that they miss the point of his embrace of poetic narrative as he sets aside the language-games of metaphysics and epistemology, to have a good story one must unfold the plot in a singular meta-narrative voice or risk the end of conversation with an audience in a series of nihilistic Dadaist challenges to traditional cultural and aesthetic forms.

It is in a first-person encounter, something I might be forced by the necessity to communicate to refer to as 'the immediate self' (if I wished to make the same misjudgement as Descartes does when he takes the 'Cogito ergo sum' too literally as evidence of a thinking thing), that gets lost in the Rortian shuffle. There is no *thing* as a self that can be immediate or otherwise. So far, Rorty would be comfortable with this paradoxical characterization. To utilize any such term (i.e., 'self') must be a necessary linguistic device. It is a necessary expression that *is* meant to be suggestive, and not truly descriptive. It is an ironic use of language. As such, it is not a mere fabrication but a useful metaphor. My first-person encounter is a *fact*, however, whether seen 'clearly' or 'fuzzed'. But can first-person encounters be prior to any narration or description by or about 'it'? Rorty seems to think not. Language permeates all thought; language is coextensive with thought, even thoughts about one's 'self'. Recall once again, we may never stand outside our vocabulary. Thus Rorty uses the term, 'being', to underscore this point since to 'have' is to claim to find oneself in the metaphysically privileged position as an accurate judge of what one is and is not. It is this privileging claim that must be sacrificed, according to Rorty, for reasons already stated. There may be rival vocabularies. One may be bilingual, so to speak. That is, there can be a language couched in terms of neural states of the brain which also can be redescribed (non-reductively) into the language of networks of beliefs, desires, etc. Nevertheless, *to be* is to be a lexicon of terms bonded together by desires and those beliefs derived from them. But has Rorty truly discarded the dead-ended reductionist tendencies to explain all in terms of either the language of idealism or materialism? Has he abandoned the modernist method of objectification, manifested in the spectator's view of knowledge (with its onto-theistic assumptions) applied to a descriptive analysis of the self, only to reinvent such a Singularist view in the late twentieth to early twenty-first century through a personal idiosyncratic narrative of a community of roles? And is ever such a reinvention feasible?

To take the last question first, and on his own terms, Rorty's position seems to imply that the self is this personal 'community' which checks and balances itself.[1] One part may hold itself aloof, so to speak, so as to give its input. But it is not permanently privileged to do so. No one voice of the network is the lead, or true (rational) voice. By analogy, then, one voice might function for a time as the 'strong poet' does in the larger interpersonal society, as the challenger of what is the personal equivalent of normal discourse. But following through on Fraser's observation of Rorty (cited in Chapter 6), if this type of bifurcation (poet/society) is ill-advised on a societal level, why would it not also be ill-advised on the level of the individual? For if the 'loose cannon' of idiosyncratic, elitist and potentially cruel individuality ought to be held at bay (in Rorty's estimation) so as to allow for public practice to be democratic and egalitarian, what makes it healthy for it to dominate in the microcosm of solidarity that is the de-centred self? For the remaining part of this chapter, let us examine the comparatively facile interrelational concern between the individual and society inspired by Fraser's challenge before tackling the more difficult analysis of the intra-relational dimensions of the self in the chapter immediately following. The strategic example used by Plato in the *Republic* will be a helpful guide and exemplar for the analysis below. We must understand the individual by first looking at the individual writ large in society.

Solidarity writ Large

If the success of the communitarian spirit of Rorty's Jeffersonian Strategy requires a restrictive (isolating) privatization of the radical poetic theorist, then the already noted boundary between public (pragmatic) and private (Romantic) vocabularies must develop. But, we recall, Fraser points out that, at best, it would be impossible to keep the dam between the public (interpersonal policy) and the private (personal beliefs) from leaking powerful cultural developments into the official politico-public sphere.[2] And at worst, she notes that a definite split of the kind suggested by Rorty, if successful, would tend to privatize alternative theories (e.g., Feminism), and, in effect, cut short true democratic dialogue by depoliticizing them – relegating them to the level of the idiosyncratic. What could be left is a dogmatized democracy, trapped within stale metaphors of liberal solidarity. Such a democracy would be in name only, for it would truncate the intercourse of ideas to a set of political (i.e., publicly acceptable) topics, sharply limited at the instant of the application of Jeffersonian philosophical privatization of beliefs. Fraser subsequently notes: 'The upshot of this way of mapping cultural space was to effect some significant exclusions' (Fraser, in R. Goodman 1995: 155). There was in Rorty's narrative no place in political motivations for the invention of new idioms, especially those that could overcome 'the enforced silencing or muting of a disadvantaged social group' (Fraser, in R. Goodman 1995: 155). Nor was there a place for either solidarities that engaged in abnormal discourse, or social movements that challenged dominant narratives. Fraser concludes that 'there was no place for non-standard interpretations of social needs and collective concerns. Whoever was using a non-hegemonic vocabulary had to be talking about something private' (Fraser, in R. Goodman 1995: 155).

Of course, the poetic voices could always invent new metaphors, expressing them in verbal utterances and/or physical markings on paper, with the hope of challenging and affecting other organisms within the shared political environment. This view seems to be what Rorty carried from the 1980s through the 1990s. In fact this is one of the main themes in Rorty's 1999 book, *Philosophy and Social Hope*. As Rorty says elsewhere: 'Prophecy . . . is all that a non-violent political movement can fall back on when argument fails' (Rorty, in R. Goodman 1995: 129). Yet, the visionary poets might be deemed 'mad' by their own culture, the old order which is being threatened by these prophetically novel parables. They would be maligned and perhaps ostracized for the sake of bourgeois decency and liberal kindness because ironic poetic narration can be perceived by its targets as a misguided, heartless and needlessly disturbing affair.

Rorty attempts to circumvent the issue of potential societal repression through an appeal for a solidarity of tolerance concerning what has been coined by John Stuart Mill as 'self-regarding actions'. The incommensurability of vocabularies deals with value distinctions discussed in conversation, and not as 'factual' disputes settled by scientists or philosophers. There are only those things which, due to their entrenched nature, are more familiar, more readily susceptible to agreement at a given time. Thus, in these areas the conversation tends to run smoothly, without many hitches. But which areas are more entrenched has to do with habitual practices encrusted around publicly agreed upon understandings, rules and policies. Therefore, Rorty can say:

> At certain periods, it has been as easy to determine which critics have a 'just perception' of the value of a poem as it is to determine which experimenters are capable of making accurate observations and precise measurements. At other periods . . . it may be as difficult to know which scientists are actually

offering reasonable explanations as it is to know which painters are destined for immortality (Rorty 1979: 322).

Hence, the currently accepted belief may be the highly questioned opinion in the future. Therefore, the advice is to practise tolerance towards all socially constructive ideologies, whether philosophical, scientific, aesthetic or otherwise. This is simply a reminder at the level of ideas of the moral to treat others as you would have them treat you, because the rules of the game can always change, and any subsequent alteration may endanger you and your preferred principles. This still leaves open for interpretation the question of what is to be assigned the label of 'socially useful'. And there may be times when it is socially useful to rise up in revolt in defence of one's abnormal vocabulary.

When the time is ripe it is the task of the strong poet to instigate a change in the accepted rules as encrusted in dead metaphor. This claim, however, contains unintended consequences for our strong poet. Rorty has insisted that one cannot stand outside one's vocabulary, understood to be the current expression of one's cultural matrix. Yet he seems also to claim that we must be bilingual; that our vocabulary must be bifurcated along the private/public rift. But if one cannot stand outside of the language-game in which one is involved and yet we must be bilingual, then we seem to be required to switch completely between the two sets of incommensurable vocabularies as the situation and/or the mood dictates. According to Rorty's thinking, there can be no dovetailing of linguistic roles. In describing the Romantic individual in a democratic society, Rorty stresses the division:

> For she does not think her conduct towards other human beings is the most important thing about her. What is *more* important is her *rapport à soi*, her private search for autonomy, her refusal to be exhaustively describable in words which apply to anyone other than herself. This is the search summed up in Blake's exclamation: 'I must create my own system, or be enslaved by another man's' (Rorty 1991b: 193).

The private and the public must be disassociated far enough to protect the freedoms important to the creative individual, while simultaneously shielding the public from the potentially cruel outpouring of the aesthetic spirit. This theme is his now familiar Jeffersonian Strategy.[3]

Of course, the tactic of separation of personal philosophy and state may be applied more or less cleanly when no direct conflict exists between the two spheres. However, this is not the interesting case. The test condition arises when a direct conflict occurs between the entrenched cultural beliefs and the rebellious, ironic side of oneself, or between rival identity modes (persons) within a given individual (e.g. 'Who am I at this moment, a "soft-machine" or a "creative poet"?'). In this context the ability to swing between linguistic strategies produces not equilibrium and balance; rather it generates a jostling of vocabularies causing a sort of psycho-social linguistic vertigo. In 'Feminism and Pragmatism' Rorty refers to this vertigo as a 'split'; being torn between a definition imposed upon oneself by the cultural faction with 'semantic authority' and one that is self-generated. One is caught in the whirlwinds of contradictory characterizations and cannot remain neutral to any of them. The particular example alluded to by Rorty was Adrienne Rich's characterization, in her *On Lies, Secrets and Silence*, of her experiencing such a rift in her youth. 'She was, she said, "split between the girl who wrote poems, who defined herself as writing poems, and the girl who was to define herself by her relationships with men"' (Rorty, in R. Goodman 1995: 135). The circumvention of the problem of contradictory characterizations by invoking the 'Neurath's Boat' argument will not work when competing language-games are consciously in play at the 'deep' level of personal meaning and identity. These characterizations are not mere planks of beliefs of differing sorts, but entire doctrinal sections of the vessel which must be dealt with. Because one cannot stand outside any vocabulary (one cannot bring the boat to dry dock, so to speak) — and for each conflict there are at least the two incommensurate sets of beliefs to deal with — the options are limited relative to the voice with which one need speak. Either one must be converted from one coherent web of words to another, each in their turn (i.e., Kuhn's gestalt-like shifts or 'revolutions'[4]), or one must invent a synthesis of the two webs, thus creating a novel univocal text, or again one must submit one's idiom to the dominant vocabulary used by the society-at-large. In each case, one seems driven to a reduction or submission to one voice, one vocabulary. However, none of these options has utility for Rorty since he wishes to maintain the strong distinction between the private and the public vocabularies. Therefore he must advocate that one sustains oneself in this vertigo of contingency, allowing for the possibility of a continuous and open-ended revolution of voices — now one voice is in ascendancy, then another rises to the top, and still a third, and so forth, *ad infinitum*. And he clearly does so advocate: 'But prophecy and unstable categories go together, ... [and the quote] from [Marilyn] Frye ... "we [feminists] should learn how to regard the instabilities themselves as valuable resources" is one that Dewey would have cheered' (Rorty, in R. Goodman 1995: 147, n. 32). In a Darwinian struggle for semantic ascendancy there should be no bias as to which worldview should emerge victorious: the novel view or the established outlook. But when there is a conflict, one voice must rise in preeminence out of the tumult, even in a liberal society, or an outbreak of chaos will occur, resulting in the likelihood of much cruelty, humiliation and incoherence. Nevertheless, Rorty repeatedly expresses the tendency to favour the excitement of the new and the plural as it challenges the entrenched onto-theological world picture as monomaniacal.

So far I have been trying to show how Darwin, utilitarianism and pragmatism conspired to exalt plurality over unity — how the dissolution of the traditional theologico-metaphysical world picture helped the European intellectuals drop the idea of the One True Account of How Things Really Are (Rorty 1999a: 270). But diversity itself cannot do without the unity of vision that *comprehends* its importance at the meta-narrative level in the context of social hope. I will maintain Rorty's narrative of plurality cannot be sustained on the meta-meta-narrative plane if his neo-pragmatic project is to be a coherent effort to advance as desirable the utopia of social hope.

Hobbes, Rorty and Paradox of Freedom

What I mean by this last claim can be understood through the prism of Hobbesian philosophy. If you will recall, the formation of an 'Artificial Sovereign' is designed to still the brutish use of force while providing a modicum of peace and security in service to the natural human drive for self-preservation. Thomas Hobbes states in his 'Second Law of Nature' that with individual sovereignty in peril in the State of Nature, each man's passion (i.e., the fear of death and the apprehension over the potential loss of an unfettered and commodious life) functions as a catalyst that causes each and every individual to commit themselves to the dictates of Reason. This is done out of self-interest to form a collective of similar bias in favour of a humane and honourable life. Interestingly, this is a close analogue to Rorty's definition for 'solidarity' of the liberal democratic kind. The term 'reason' is not an obstacle to the development of my Hobbes–Rorty analogy. On a close reading of Hobbes, for him reason turns out to be nothing more than a rationalization associated with the overwhelming endeavour (or drive) for survival – and not an independent process of thought capable of detached and objective observation. His Social Contract is a provincial construct, erected on the basis of a pragmatic solidarity of purpose: the construction of a well-ordered society.

For that purpose to become the object of universal acceptance, it might be necessary for the realization of the collective interest that there must be restrictions imposed to keep unruly spirits within the bounds of the contract. However, these very public safeguards could be so structured that the immediate interest of each individual is greatly advanced when he or she violates the social strictures while the others are adhering to them. In this situation, it would be allowable (even under J. S. Mill's strong defence of individual liberty) for these other individuals of the Social Contract, acting, say, in a liberal democracy directly or through their representatives, such as the 'Artificial Sovereign', to resort to compulsion. This force will be used in an effort to guarantee the wayward individual's conformity to the general will, a will that was originally expressed and uniformly recognized as a universal benefit, even by the perpetrator of the violation. The 'rational' principle of communal self-defence applied equally to all in order to protect and defend each member's voiced interest seems to justify the voiding of a given individual's will in her very act of defiant self-assertion. Paternalism seems to have its place through the preservation of the social condition when that condition serves the general welfare, as defined by and through the universal concord of the Social Contract.[5]

However, the individual's drive for self-preservation is not to be denied. Hobbes asserts that natural autonomy demands respect. Despite the 'rational' authority of the Sovereign to do whatever he/they deem necessary to an individual to avoid the circumstance of 'warre', and, as long as he/they observe the Law of Nature, never have it called unjust (Hobbes 1968: 264–65), there are some 'rights' (i.e., powers) that the individual cannot transfer or redefine:

> A Covenant not to defend my selfe from force, by force, is alwayes voyd. For ... no man can transferre, or lay down his right to save himselfe from Death, Wounds, and Imprisonment ... (Hobbes 1968: 199).

A comparison of Hobbes's theory to Rorty's pragmatism now can be made. To redefine oneself as a submissive element within the larger narrative of a society (in Mill's terms, to intentionally reduce one's status to that of a slave) is to abrogate one's future power to define oneself, and thereby to surrender one's identity into the hands of an alien final vocabulary. Or to put it another way, it would be to reduce one's discursive expressions to the level of causal chatter, rendering oneself to be nothing more than a conforming element in the grand and unconstrained movement of social evolution. But if a covenant of liberal solidarity is to preserve the individual, ironic narrator from humiliation of coerced self-denial, it would be wise to note that it is *contradictory* for any one to consent to a provision of any compact of solidarity which would have the individual agree to forfeit her literal or creative life and freedom of self-description (or alternatively, freedom from linguistic enslavement) for enthralment to the collective good. Yet, in order to maintain the conditions necessary for the preservation of a liberal democracy (the sentiment which Rorty expresses as the preference that 'our community cannot wholly die'), which it can be argued is currently the best guarantee for self-expression, the containment by the commonwealth of the allegedly 'mad' and potentially corrosive narratives within the confines of the 'deviant' verbal self-portrait must be achieved. This interpretation casts the Jeffersonian Strategy into a Fraserian light, however. The dominant cultural narrative rules as out-of-bounds any language-game which threatens to unweave the supporting strands of its belief system. This is particularly problematic for the kind of liberal democracy Rorty has envisioned. To illustrate the problem, consider the example of Oliver Wendell Holmes's 'Clear and Present Danger' decision.[6]

In *Schenck v. United States* 1919, the Supreme Court ruled that the lower court judgment against the defendant Charles Schenck, the general secretary of the American Socialist Party, for obstructing the war effort (World War I), should stand.[7] In his opinion for the majority of the court Holmes established the 'clear and present danger' rule:

> Words can be weapons ... The question in every case is whether the words used are used in such circumstances and are of such nature as to create a clear and present danger that they will bring about the substantial evils that Congress has a right to prevent (http://www.law.umkc.edu/faculty/projects/ftrials/conlaw/schenk.html).

Schenck's anti-draft stand directed against the United States's involvement in World War I and his adamant expression of this through the Federal Post was deemed an improper and incendiary public expression of beliefs, thus one that was not covered by the First Amendment's Free Speech clause. That Schenck's assessment of the connection between the war effort and business interests (significantly, the financial sector and the munitions industry) has been substantially supported by the Nye Commission hearings (1934–36), as well as an assortment of historians, is telling. Interestingly, Schenck's call for civil disobedience and the method used followed a venerable pattern as old as the pre-Revolutionary War Committees of Correspondence.[8] That there was an official silencing by imprisonment of a dissident voice (Schenck's) by a pragmatic Justice (Holmes) acting, in accordance with local sentiments of his time, to protect the constitutional republic from a perceived internal threat is not only ironic in the Rortian sense, but is incoherent. That is, it was an assertion that is on its own terms a self-contradiction.[9] Being so, the net effect of this constitutional affair was arguably a grievous disservice to both the nation (consider the domestic and the international outcomes of the post-Treaty of Versailles era) and the right/power to express unpopular views in times of societal duress.[10]

   The incoherence in this sort of irony is not merely that a conflict between factual situations exists or appears to exist (e.g., is a virus a chemical compound or a biological organism?). Nor, obviously, is this conflict masking an underlying harmony, a simple misplaced difference of opinion (e.g., a dispute as to which is the brighter celestial object: the Morning Star or the Evening Star?). It should not be due to a manifold of interpretations (i.e., whether the best music is European Classical, or American Jazz, or Japanese Kabuki, etc.). And while irony such as that suggested in the claim 'The first shall be last, and the last shall be first' can cause one to freeze, wondering if one should go to the middle in order to avoid consternation, there is no incoherence. It is clear, if one buys into the belief, that in some fashion the rear is the place to be. Rather, it is a pervasive, persistent and inextricable internal turmoil deep within a particular web(s) of belief that gives us an inconsistency that borders on, if not actually trips over to be, a performance contradiction, *assuming* there is a persistent unity to the 'self'. I suggest this condition inherently exists for all liberal democracies that have abandoned appeals to the (unprovable) Lockean *law of nature*. And it exists particularly for Rorty's anti-foundational brand. As long as majoritarian mores must be limited at the edges of libertarian integrity, and liberality must be checked by the preponderance of opinion, and where there is no impartial standpoint, an irresolvable tension presents itself to the concerned.[11]

   If we return to our Hobbes parallel, a further consequence will make the depth of the paradox clearly relevant for our topic. The Sovereign (in our case the popular will as represented in the fiduciary role of our constitutional government) is appointed as the power to oversee and enforce the Social Contract. If the Sovereign creates and is identified with Law, and if the Sovereign (not as an abstract concept but as flesh-and-blood individual[s]) is nothing more than a person or group of persons subject to the same crosscurrents of drives and

passions that affect any pre-contractual individual, may it not happen that the
Sovereign will at some time have as his/their top priority the use of 'reason' (i.e.,
the cosmetic extension of the passions) as expressed in written law and in legal
action, which is designed to ensure his/their self-preservation (as would any
Contract-breaking prisoner of the state, if he could, in the defence of his natural
life and liberty) over and above the good of the Commonwealth? And if so, will
not this preference of the Sovereign subvert the original purpose of the Commonwealth, conflating the public good with their collective and personal survival, thereby placing the population's well-being and security in jeopardy
when private interests diverge from social interests? This would cause the population to set themselves, in whole or in part, against their own stated will in the
form of their 'corrupt' Representatives – an action which is, paradoxically, an
extension of each individual's right to preserve themselves. Then it would follow
that the compact which requires a clear differentiation between the public
Sovereign and the individual contractors to avoid the violence and humiliation
of anarchy would be the cause of the very thing such a distinction was designed
to prevent – a loss of life and liberty due to unrestricted assertion of autonomy – this time as seen in the struggle between the two sovereignties, the natural (individuals) and the artificial (the appointed Overseers). Here is the
internal contradiction in its full flower. This is the heart of what can be called
the Hobbesian Conflict. Hobbes's theory, which is completely dependent on
linguistic solidarity *via* the Social Contract, constructs the same conditions
which it was meant to prevent – *Civil Warre*. Hobbes's theory turns back upon
itself and logically self-destructs – of course, since the statement form $p \cdot \sim p$ is
self-contradictory, so the substitution case $C \cdot \sim C$ ($C = Civil\ Warre$) forms a
contradiction as well, given the Principle of Contradiction.

Turning to Rorty's 'principle of sincerity' (a principle derivable from Rorty's
ethnocentrism), each person or entity has a right (due to the sovereignty of self-
asserting poetic creativity) to hold and to insist that their vocabulary-choice,
beliefs and desires *ought* to come first in the order of importance in common discourse. For example, in twenty-first-century American culture, the solidarity
formed by each individual member of the culture's citizenry around the democratic themes of individual freedom is (usually) the starting point for all dialogue. This is not an arbitrary proclamation (allegedly) but, Rorty maintains, a
sincere elevation of democratic voices above elitist Philosophers, which allows
for a cultural conservatism while leaving open the possibility for radical questioning of the culture. This advocacy for the twenty-first-century American
democratic culture can be characterized in unflattering terms, however, by
saying that Rorty's liberal is merely a person who conserves liberal values.
Therefore, this liberality *per se* is assailable, especially when it is clothed in its
cultural garb, when 'socialization goes all the way down'. Then liberalism's
promotion arises from mere rote learning – a reaction of a human organism to
its environmental stimuli – or traditional sentimentality and not creative
engagement. Rorty himself chides:

For any *literal* description of one's individuality, which is to say any use of an inherited language-game for this purpose, will necessarily fail. One will not have traced that idiosyncrasy home but will merely have managed to see it as not idiosyncratic after all, as a specimen reiterating a type, a copy or replica of something which has already been identified. To fail as a poet − and thus, for Nietzsche, to fail as a human being − is to accept somebody else's description of oneself, to execute a previously prepared program, to write, at most, elegant variations on previously written poems. So the only way to trace home the causes of one's being as one is would be to tell a story about one's causes in a new language (Rorty 1989: 27−28).

Like the Tolstoy character, Ivan Ilych, to whom, on his deathbed, comes the realization that those values which he once eagerly sought, cultivated and coveted in the days past were worthless efforts to conform mindlessly with social expectations, a critical thinker must question the impositions of post-suppositions as well as the presuppositions of the cultural norms. What I mean by this rather unorthodox term 'post-suppositions' is that a future open to the possibility of new solidarities expressing an alleged limitless tolerance for a widening of the reference 'one of us' is surprisingly equivocal. This is because there is always a projection of one's values and expectations upon the range of distant potentiality, thereby cutting short truly novel projections. As Norman Geras has noted: 'Thus, not only the privilege of solidarity but, in the view he [Rorty] endorses in *Philosophy and the Mirror of Nature*, even "personhood is a matter of 'being one of us' " . . . rather than a feature of certain organisms to be isolated by empirical means' (Geras 1995: 74). This cramps and confines the future admission of likely candidates into the definition of the 'we'. Thus we need to concentrate our attention not only on the effects of the historical upon our present way of thinking and believing, but also our (or more concerning, some other's) current mindset's impact upon how we structure our future expectations. Otherwise we might fall into hypocrisy or, worse for Rorty, mere repetition.

Take, for example, Rorty's statement of hope about the building of a multicultural global utopia. He muses that over the next few centuries, people

> will unravel each culture [as shared habits of action] into a multiplicity of fine component threads together with equally fine threads drawn from other [such] cultures, thus promoting the kind of variety-in-unity characteristic of rationality [as tolerance] (Rorty, in Hall 1994: 180−81).

But who will choose the threads, and who will reweave them? Whose narration will dominate as the pattern? In the special context of feminism, Fraser, in response to Rorty's article 'Feminism and Pragmatism', asks the telling question of who will have 'semantic authority' in the liberal society that Rorty conceives:

Out of all the available candidates, *which* new description will count as 'taking the viewpoint of woman as women'? *Which* women will be empowered to impose their 'semantic authority' on the rest of us? (Fraser, in R. Goodman 1995: 157).

This question can easily be broadened from its original context to a more general political query, as Rorty does in the following comparison of pragmatism and deconstructionism:

Pragmatists and deconstructionists agree that everything is a social construct and that there is no point in trying to distinguish between the 'natural' and the 'merely' cultural. They agree that the question is which social constructs to discard and which to keep, and that there is no point in appealing to 'the way things really are', in the course of struggles over who gets to construct what (Rorty in *Hypatia* [1993b: v. 8, n. 2]).

Of course, our ethnocentric socialization will cause any of us to frame all future 'final' vocabularies in concordance with our current narrative. This is simply the social version of Rorty's 'principle of sincerity'. Will we individually or collectively, in an Ethical Egoist vein, be knitting the fabric of the global society for our own benefit while speaking, disingenuously, in the rhetoric of inclusiveness about the general welfare, as President George H. W. Bush did in coining the phrase 'New World Order'? But, of course, in the case of Rorty, there is no difference to tell concerning one intention or the other. Speaking for the New Pragmatists, Rorty surprisingly asserts: 'We are not attempting the impossible task of developing a non-hegemonic discourse, one in which truth is no longer connected with power. We are not trying to do away with social constructs in order to find something that is not a social construct' (Rorty, in R. Goodman 1995: 130). Power relations in the form of freely evolving linguistic solidarities are the focus here. The extent to which Rorty accepts power relations is made evident in the following quote:

From a pragmatist angle, neither Christianity nor the Enlightenment nor contemporary feminism are cases of cognitive clarity overcoming cognitive distortions. They are, instead, examples of evolutionary struggle ... guided by no immanent teleology. The history of human social practices is continuous with the history of biological evolution, the only difference being that what Richard Dawkins and Daniel Dennett call 'memes' gradually take over the role of Mendel's genes. Memes are things like turns of speech, terms of aesthetic or moral praise, political slogans, proverbs, musical phrases, stereotypical icons, and the like. Memes compete with one another for the available cultural space as genes compete for the available *Lebensraum*. Different batches of both genes and memes are carried by different human social groups, and so the triumph of one such group amounts to the triumph of those genes or memes. But no gene or meme is closer to the purpose of evolution or the nature of humanity than any other – for evolution has no purpose and humanity no nature (Rorty, in R. Goodman 1995: 128).

Linguistic hegemony threatens even within the good intentions of our thought-ful professor as the spectre of Hobbes's paternalism casts its shadow in neo-pragmatism.

Reminiscent of the paternalism found in the Dawes Severalty Act, passed by the US Congress in 1887,[12] are Rorty's several attempts to finesse the limitations of ethnocentric socialization. By allowing the uninitiated to be 'shepherded into the light by the connoisseurs of diversity', the stranger and the disenfranchised are raised to the point where they can be 'treated just like the rest of us'. Here, there is the appearance of inclusiveness under the guise of dispassionate, liberal comprehensiveness. The inner circle labelled by Rorty as 'we liberals' expands its ranks in an ever-widening circumference of inclusion once the proper educa-tion in tolerance and diversity is impressed upon those currently on the fringe. Nevertheless, the expectation is that 'the other' will already be close to, or be readily redefined into, our image and likeness. If they are too removed from our criteria for solidarity, too independent of the principles democracies advo-cate, those in question will appear as 'mad' as Loyola or Marx and the anti-democratic cultures their rephrasing spawned. As Geras correctly observes:

> If, as Rorty insists, the force of any 'we', any sense of moral community, must depend on the contrast with a human 'they', on enclosing something smaller and more local than the human race; if someone's just being part of human-kind gives at best a weak reason for treating them generously, at worst no possible basis at all for imaginative identification and moral concern; then you can make 'we' larger, but you cannot make it large enough to get rid of the aforesaid ethnocentric curse (Geras 1995: 76–77).

'They' will be spurned as pariah by a society which feels justified in its repudia-tion through arguments based on self-defence. This seems truly arbitrary when it is realized that Rorty endorses an insight shared by William James and Sig-mund Freud to the effect that there is 'a certain blindness in human beings' which prevents many from seeing, as Rorty puts it, that 'the private poems of the pervert, the sadist, or the lunatic [are] each as richly textured and ... as continuous with our own activities' (1989: 38–39). So it would appear that the supposed preservers of what is of most value in a diverse, liberal culture undermine the principles upon which they claim to stand the moment they function in the twin roles of guiding shepherds and defenders. It is at the moment that the anti-foundationalists proclaim as universally valuable (at a meta-meta narrative level) that which they know is merely contingent (i.e., all meta-vocabularies) that they engage in an act of obfuscation. And it is in the strenuous defence of that democratic culture which is as equally contingent as any perceived threat to a liberal society that their actions turn capriciously cruel and self-destructive due to reflexive intolerance.[13] Again, turning to

Geras, he worries that a loss of foundational constraints under Rorty's liberal view augurs potentially cruel and often 'bizarre results'. Geras writes:

> But I am more interested here in how Rorty would have us turn back from what his softened consequence otherwise seems to permit and threaten. We may not treat the child like an animal because ... well, because it is not 'our' tradition to do so. This is to command the form, having evacuated it of its content. It is to give the tradition itself as a reason after rejecting the reasons of the tradition. It is first to put forth, as your own view, matter challenging, casting aside, the component principles and arguments of another given view; which latter you then uphold nevertheless as being, quite generally, 'our' view (Geras 1995: 82).

The parallel between Rorty and Hobbes may now be drawn tight. Without a foundational basis (earthbound or celestial, logical or transcendental) for actions of a sovereign, whether it is embodied by an enlightened dictatorship or a democratic solidarity, Rorty's principle of sincerity must be invoked. But as we have just seen with Hobbes, an inner contradiction is exposed when the descriptive distinction between self-interest and the general welfare is blurred by the practical need for a community in solidarity to sustain itself especially in times of conflict. The idiosyncratic ideas of an individual may be suppressed when it is in the interest of a liberal democracy to preserve that which it cherishes: tolerance, liberty, decency and kindness. Yet the proclaimed (and often the self-proclaimed) arbiters of this interest are, under Rorty's interpretation, also idiosyncratic individuals subject to the same physical and psychological forces as anyone else. Therefore, from within Rorty's narrative, a clash of final vocabularies must ensue between those individuals who nominally represent the rough solidarity currently in the majority in a given society representing the voice of 'semantic authority', and those unorthodox individuals – as revolutionaries or in the guise of the leaders who claim to front the minority solidarities – who are at variance with the generally accepted societal myths. Rorty himself states 'I cannot see anything wrong with power grabs ...' (in *Hypatia* [1993b: v. 8, n. 2, fn. 9]). Hence, paternalism is unavoidable, if, along with his proclaimed hope for a liberal democratic future, one accepts as the definition 'power' as 'one force acting upon another force'. And apparently for Rorty a definition something like this seems desirable, as each narrator struggles with all others to either impose their 'final vocabulary' upon the rest of humanity, or perish by means of absorption into an alien and alienating definition[14] – ironically, Rorty's own definition for 'humiliation', and the manifestation of the later Heidegger's warning about pragmatism being the culmination of the onto-theological power paradigm.

In an interesting fashion, Rorty further contributes to the last point in 'The contingency of selfhood', when he claims:

> The difference between genius and fantasy is not the difference between impresses which lock on to something universal, some antecedent reality out

there in the world or deep within the self, and those which do not. Rather, it is the difference between idiosyncrasies which just happen to catch on with other people – happen because of the contingencies of some historical situation, some particular need which a given community happens to have at a given time (Rorty 1989: 37).

What initially seemed to be a public/private issue devolves into an interpersonal struggle for an audience, divided along the fault lines of rival idiosyncratic interpretations with alleged utility. Then, what comes to be termed 'the public' out of this struggle is nothing more than Nietzsche's *Das Mann*, a colony of dominated individuals redefined (through coercion or persuasion – the socio-physical causation referred to in Chapter 6) as 'subjects' or 'citizens' by an imperious voice (the voice with semantic authority), which is heard to utter: 'This is for your own benefit' or alternatively 'this is for society's good', as it remakes, through its paternalistic zeal, the other lost poets into its own image by way of the citizens' involuntary redefinition (*via* a strong misreading) by the dominant poetic voice(s). This view is implied by Fraser as she critiques Rorty's pragmatized view of feminism. She claims that 'the club' as Rorty constructs it is a self-appointed, elite cadre that undemocratically determines what is to be labelled 'correct' for the community (and, if successful, for the entire culture) it claims to lead (Fraser, in R. Goodman 1995: 158).

The judicious Jeffersonian-styled bifurcation of the radical agents for change (the ironic poets for liberalism), from the advocates for relative order and stability (the liberal establishment), fails once the barrier Rorty has carefully arranged between the public and the private has been found to be a mere tissue of narrative. As in the *Wizard of Oz* when Dorothy draws back the curtain, the illusion of public authority of a given solidarity vanishes when the person(s) behind the curtain is (are) revealed to be all too human (viz. idiosyncratic pragmatist). With no foundational support for any given narrative and only the random association of individuals into socio-historical assemblages ('exclusive clubs'), the pretence of a unified entity that might be termed 'solidarity' has to be abandoned. Rorty has counselled us to renounce all other claims for ontological commitment: they are but mere fiction. I believe that a dedicated pragmatist would not object to his advice. As with all other assertions about so-called metaphysical substances, a pragmatist must maintain that a solidarity is merely a useful, and perhaps self-serving, myth, a construct that, it may be argued in our present case, is explicitly designed to persuade otherwise unaffiliated persons into one of innumerable circles of cultural resemblance. This unique manner of lashing together into a narrative whole what may be equally characterized as points of view descriptively distinct from each other is being catechized to us by one distinctive narrator, that is, Rorty himself. His take on the matter, therefore, can be viewed as ironic, indeed. For Rorty's counsel against ontological commitments to an item such as 'solidarity' stands simultaneously with his proclamation to act *as if* we sincerely believed in its reality (presumably metaphysical); *as if* solidarity has a force beyond his assertions about it;

as if Rorty had semantic authority at the meta-narrative level to advocate for his interpretative understanding of the term.

However, his view is not merely ironic, but self-referentially incoherent without the assumption of Singularism. Rorty's promotion for a thorough-going pluralism is Singularist in its advocacy. In effect, we have been asked by Rorty to yield any claim to grounded knowledge while we are being enticed to give over the possibility of creative freedom to his pragmatic worldview. If this sounds a little too harsh and without warrant, then perhaps it would seem more acceptable to maintain that there is a vicious circle involved in Rorty's New Pragmatism. Rorty is claiming that to be free socially we must submit to the revamping of our webs of belief to accord with his pragmatic take on Western culture's definition of bourgeois liberty, and by doing so be rid once and for all of the old, unworkable onto-theological metaphors, that is, metaphors that cannot be justified to 'us democrats' – said to not to work for us, the pertinent audience – because the paradigm has shifted towards Rorty's pragmatic view.[15] In short, in order to be free poetically, one must sacrifice intellectual independence as far as the very idea of what currently works as metaphor has all but been decided aesthetically by Rorty in the meta-meta-interpretation.

This claim is captured and reinforced by Sissela Bok in her book *Lying: Moral Choice in Public and Private Life*, when she writes:

> Just as skepticism denies the possibility of *knowledge*, so determinism denies the possibility of *freedom*. Yet both knowledge and freedom to act on it are required for reasonable choice. Such choice would be denied to someone genuinely convinced – to the very core of his being – of both skepticism and determinism. He would be cast about like a dry leaf in the wind. Few go so far. But more may adopt such views selectively, as when they need convenient excuses for lying (Bok 1979: 23).

It would be textually incorrect and morally irresponsible for me to suggest that Rorty is in any way intentionally engaged in the sort of manipulative deception to which Bok refers. However, as we have seen, he is sceptical in the extreme about any knowledge claims that propose to be a set of necessary truths, including his own. And he seems wedded to a vocabulary of causal determinism for at least the public sphere, and to extend this view to a degree into the private, as far as sounds and marks cause the individual to react (albeit creatively) (Rorty 1989: 41).

If, as I have just pointed out, the splitting off of the public language from the private vocabulary fails due to the artificiality (constructed nature) of 'solidarities' as well as of 'selves', and consequently since there is only an array of final vocabularies competing for semantic control over the use and aim of the linguistic tools at hand (memes), then the radical ability to freely create and recreate local truths (a task of the poetic ironist) and causally deterministic impact of the forces of history and culture that 'go all the way down' run headlong into each other in a manner reminiscent of the classical dilemma between freedom and determinism. And Rorty's Jeffersonian Strategy provides no exception. Still the New Pragmatism claims that it has the theoretical mechanism to handle this threatened dilemma. Once one allows for the incommensurability of vocabularies in diametric opposition in society, then, without the possibility for the appeal to foundational support, opposing voices within any given spatio-temporal frame may state concurrently their rivalry without contradiction or recourse to coercion. Why? Because it *can be* argued that there is no judgement point except from within one's own cultural paradigm. And, one might add, that in a culture of tolerance judges in the liberal democracy, Rorty envisions it would be expected for them to be particularly broad-minded in their embrace of pluralism.

Notwithstanding this, with the vocabulary Rorty wishes to establish, it would take a most tolerant individual to embrace concurrently, as having warranted assertibility to the same audience, nearly the entire set of incommensurables available in a complex, modern, democratically free society. Thus the question of self-reference surfaces again when it is asked: How is it possible coherently to maintain the multiple values, replete with their clashing concepts, within *one* belief system (e.g., Rorty's New Pragmatism) without an appeal to either a definitive Singularism or paternalistic Multiplism?[16] This question will be considered in the next chapter.

Chapter 8

Freud's and Rorty's Internal Cartesian Paradox

The Solidarity of the Mind

At this juncture of the book we seem to have come full circle on the societal side of his Jeffersonian Strategy with apparently little to show for Rorty's efforts. Thus, the inherent circularity of the last question from the previous chapter – How is it possible, if Singularism is rejected, to coherently maintain the multiple values without an appeal to a paternalistic Multiplism inherent in Rorty's Jeffersonian Strategy? – leaves us but one place to go to explain how pluralism can be the basis for a pragmatic worldview: into what may be termed 'the solidarity of the mind'. By this phrase I mean the multiplicity of narratives within one individual which can be tied to Rorty's abandonment of the hope for a metaphysically unified self. He states the concept of the unity of the self is not a matter of ontology, but

> a way of putting the familiar point that the same human being can contain different coherent sets of beliefs and desires – different roles, different person-alities, etc. – correlated with the different groups to which he or she belongs or whose power he or she must acknowledge (Rorty, in R. Goodman 1995: 144, n. 22).

Thus, with different sets of webs of belief drawn from the variety of solidarities one considers influential, the de-centred Rortian self may be conceived as a Humean bundle of, at times conflicting, Freudian drives and desires. For the remainder of this chapter we will explore the implications for the second part of Rorty's Jeffersonian Strategy, the de-centred self.

The Babel of Freudian Voices

The clash between individual and society can be reduced to, at minimum, a conflict between an individual's two manners of expression, as a creative self which functions poetically, and as an individual who participates causally as a member of a liberal society. Therefore, one might seek a possible escape route from a paradox of clashing vocabularies discussed in the previous chapter by positing multiple 'persons' for any one organism. That is, one might adopt the previously mentioned Rorty–Davidson position of a mind as a solidarity comprised of a manifold of narratives – multiple descriptive story-lines of the various 'persons' or characters which comprise the novel entity (see Chapter 7). In this way, Rorty can avoid the theistic-inspired traditional view of divine/ animal (rational/ passionate) bifurcation of human life, and the assumption of an absolute, Singularist criterion by limiting 'the opposition between rational and irrational forms of persuasion to the interior of a language game, rather than to try to apply it to interesting and important shifts in linguistic behavior ... [W]hat matters in the end are changes in the vocabulary rather than changes in belief' (Rorty 1989: 47). Thus the metaphor of a self as an epic poem containing a number of characters might allow for the possibility of incommensurable vocabularies to exist side-by-side within an organism capable of continual redefinition without Rorty's Pragmatism suffering the risk of incoherence.[1] The exemplar of a technical composition that would assist Rorty would be a version of Freud's psychoanalytical model. Rorty advances this notion as follows:

> On my account of Freud, his work enables us to construct richer and more plausible narratives of [an] ad hoc sort – more plausible because they will cover *all* the actions one performs in the course of one's life, even the silly, cruel, and self-destructive actions ... He thought that the traditional oppositions between reason, will, and emotion ... should be discarded in favor of distinctions between various regions of a homogeneous mechanism, regions that embody a plurality of persons (that is, of incompatible systems of belief and desire) (Rorty 1991b: 161–62).

Hence, it would profit us to look to Freud for the simple reason that Rorty himself has often appealed to this Viennese therapist, and because Freud offers us a fairly lucid and thorough account of the dynamics of a multifarious mind. As Rorty further suggests, '[Freud] thereby makes it possible for us to see science and poetry, genius and psychosis – and, most importantly, morality and prudence – not as products of distinct faculties but as alternative modes of adaptation' (Rorty 1989: 33). Therefore, I believe a brief digression into the psychoanalytical world of Freud will provide instructive insights into what seems to be the bedrock paradox in the thought of Rorty. I ask the reader's patience while I develop this supplementary material.

In his studies of *parapraxes* (slips of the tongue) and dreams, Freud discussed the human mind as a dynamic of conflicting tendencies, which should not be misunderstood as a progressive revelation of what the univocal subject wants, but rather as a playing-out of an antagonism between at least two expressions within a human organism.[2] In discussing *parapraxes*, and after having dismissed the possibility of their being accidental (i.e., non-intentional) and having made the distinction between intentions which are 'disturbed' and those that are 'disturbing', Freud goes on to intimate that slips of the tongue can be purposeful, albeit unconscious, attempts at self-contradiction. He notes:

One of the two, the purpose that is disturbed, is of course unmistakable: the person who makes the slip of the tongue knows it and admits it. It is only the other, the disturbing purpose, that gives rise to doubt and hesitation ... In a number of cases this other purpose is equally evident (to the observer of these cases). It is indicated by the *outcome* of the slip, if only we have the courage to grant that outcome a validity of its own (Freud 1966/1989: 57).

There is a sense in the quotation that there are rival forces at work within an organism with no independent arbiter to adjudicate the contentious issue. In an earlier period of his writing, Freud offered an important vehicle for the understanding of this last point: the tension between the *pleasure principle* (later, the *id*) and the *reality principle* (later, the *superego*). In order to keep the nervous system at equilibrium, a discharge of nervous energy must be negotiated (Freud's *constancy principle*, subsequently, the *ego*). However, the pleasure principle marks an instinctual drive for satisfaction (i.e., the immediate discharge of nervous tension), while the reality principle keeps the disburdened energy at desirable levels through the postponement of motor discharge. The temptation at this point is to search out an intentional subject as a regulatory agent of both principles. But for Freud, as is true for Rorty, there is no overarching, rational element in which the objective decisions are made.[3] This is made clear in Freud's later writings, with the introduction of the *id*, the *ego* and the *superego*.[4]

The closest element in the mind to self-consciousness as arbiter is the *ego*. It falls to the *ego* (now associated with the conscious will) to try to moderate or refuse the unconscious gratification-seeking instincts of the *id* (the subsequent archetype for the unbridled drive towards pleasure). The ultimate achievement for the *ego*, and the stated purpose of Freudian psychoanalysis, is the gradual conquest of the *id* through the raising of the unconscious impulses to the level of consciousness.[5] Nevertheless, Freud contended that the *ego* is not a master in its own house; it is a result of 'the necessity to mediate between the regressive strivings of the pleasure principle operating within the *id* on one hand, and the demands of reality and the reality principle on the other' (Singer 1965: 46). The *ego* is responsible for the repression of the wishes and desires which conflict with its stated ideals, values, etc., and their transformation into socially acceptable forms (*via* sublimation). This repression by the *ego* is said to be the unconscious function of the *ego-ideal* or the *superego*.[6] Therefore, there are regulating elements of the unconscious within the *ego*. This seems to make the *ego* part of the *id*, and not a distinct arbiter, as far as the *id* and the *superego* interact at the unconscious level as impulses – the impulse to pleasure and the impulse to please are *id*-related (recall from the Hobbes section that societal restraints have their source from the idiosyncratic, often *id*-driven, machinations of the individual(s) functioning as Sovereign). Thus, the *ego* seems to be both the leading edge and the dependent of the *id*. If this is so, the reality principle as employed by the *ego* is used both in the regulation of and in service to the pleasure principle. It would follow that the independence of the reality principle in the *ego* is possible but only at the indulgence of the pleasure principle or the *id* (see Freud 1961/1989). This seems like an untenable situation. The *ego* is driven either to fit into the societal mould or is impelled to satisfy the desires emanating from the *id* in order to manage anxiety and to maintain constancy.

There appears to be, if I may borrow a political phrase, a conflict of interest, one which demands clarification. The *ego* appears to be called upon to serve one of two masters (the *id* or the *superego*), or, against Freudian theory, to transcend both into a position of objective judgement (even in relation to the 'external world'). Consequently, we have to consider the question of whether a constructive tension exists between three distinct elements in dynamic relation, *or* is there an ultimate reduction of the *ego* to the *id* (given that from the current perspective of this work and in the last analysis, the *superego* may be blended into the *id* since both demand from the *ego* a submission of itself to the pleasure principle – through the seeking of pleasure and the disburden of the discomfort of guilt or shame – of which the *id* is the model)?

Let us assume for the moment that the Freudian distinction between the pleasure principle and the reality principle fails to holds true. Then the *ego* as the expression of the reality principle is an outgrowth of the *id*, the manifestation of the pleasure principle, as a result of the latter's reaction to the frustrations generated by its being thwarted by the 'outside', causal world, which gets internalized as the demands and regulations of the *superego*. And if the *id* is a blind (instinctual) drive, then the Freudian *ego* is merely a front for the *id*, and a reduction of the *ego*'s functions to a supporting role for instinctual impulses must follow. Survival and, as Rorty often puts it, 'getting what one wants' are the prime goals for all humans, whether in a direct grasp by acting out of impulse, or a more roundabout and subtle rationalization when dealing with that which seems to be the intrusions from powers beyond one's immediate control.

The reason why one can say the *ego* is a front for the *id* can be stated as follows. On the one hand, it is widely recognized that the highest accomplishment of the conscious mind (i.e., *ego*) is the construction of science. However, if the *ego* is not autonomous, but rather the former is a projection from the *id*, all of science ultimately would be predicated upon the pleasure principle. It is the nature of the *id*, in obedience to this principle, to seek the satisfaction for its desires through the discharge of tension without regard for the consequences, either present or future. The unbiased objectivity and future-directedness necessary for the scientific endeavour would be absent. In its place would be self-serving rationalizations posing as objective pronouncements. It might be manifested in either a personal drive for a new pet theory ('abnormal', or what Rorty calls revolutionary science), or as a desire to conform to existing patterns of theory ('normal' or entrenched science). Hence, science as an independently functioning protrusion of the *id* would be a ruse played to further the satisfaction for the *id*'s desires. Therefore, the more we are induced to believe in the objectivity of science, the more effective the ruse. This may be easily construed as an alternative way to state Rorty's opposition to scientism (see Chapter 4 *passim*). Thus, a close parallel between Freud and Rorty on this point might be forged.

On the other hand, if the *ego* can be maintained in adequate separation from the *id*, then science is possible. The *ego* must be a detached master in its own house, far enough away from the deterministic impulses of the *id* in order to be sufficiently free to make impartial judgements in association with the reality principle. The scientist is then the model of an *ego* which is controlled by the weight of evidence rather than its own impulse-driven proclivities. Therefore, the liberty necessary to be capable of delaying its own sense of urgent gratification in disinterested pursuit of the facts at hand must be part of the make-up of a psychoanalyst-qua-scientist. More than a mere projection of the *id*, the *ego* would be a successful emergent property which has significantly altered its function to achieve a modicum of autonomy of purpose, sufficiently independent from the determinism of the *id*-impulses to be emancipated from their influences. Ironically, this appears to be the formulaic parallel for Rorty's ironic and private poet (that is, an organism which has its roots firmly implanted in the historical-social milieu, but which manages to express itself in Promethean ways).

It appears that Freud wanted to have both understandings of the relation of the *ego* to the *id*. Of course, he could not sustain this pairing.[7] To do so would have meant the unravelling of many of his theoretical constructs, for example, the theory of fixation and the psycho-sexual stages of development (see Singer 1965: 46). These and other Freudian structures depend upon the expectation that the *id* is conservative in that it has inherent instinctual tendencies to avoid undue stimulus and to be regressive to the point of self-destruction. However, with the autonomy of the *ego* the possibility for human expansion is possible without being spurred on by pressures from the *id*. Self-fulfilment, or *Eros*, could then rise above *Thanatos*, the much older drive in humans towards self-elimination. As explained by Singer, an independent *ego* would replace the gloomier Freudian view (Singer 1965: 23). However, Freud would have seen any refusal to recognize this 'truth' about life and the limitations of the *ego* as a sign of a pathological avoidance, and not the inventive insight which some psychologists (e.g., Singer mentions three: Hartman 1939; Erikson 1950 and Rapaport 1951) believe theories about an independent *ego* to be (Singer 1965: 24). Freud again dovetails with Rorty's stated position. Language is the epitome of symbolic gratification. The bilingualism which Rorty attempts through his Jeffersonian Strategy seems to allow pragmatists to have their public 'cake' (a democratic social order) and privately 'eat it too' (creative self-assertability). Hence, while the causally-bound, social realm has set the cultural parameters of personal expression, forcing the need-driven individual to adjust creatively through adaptive behaviour, the poetic side of that individual is entirely free to respond through novel, self-gratifying metaphors.

But what about *Thanatos*, the drive towards self-annihilation; how does this fit into Rorty's gloss? Perhaps conformity to theological, philosophical and scientific edicts might qualify as a suitable match. The surrender of one's own final vocabulary to an alien worldview is to give up one's own personal narrative and to allow oneself to be absorbed into another's take on matters.

It would be to submit to the paternalism of one of these three engines of asserted semantic authority.

Now is when the digression into Freudian theory bears fruit. As noted above, only if the *ego* is an independent entity, capable of standing back, so to speak, and dispassionately assessing the pushes of the *id* and the pulls of the *superego*, then objectivity in science is possible, and the only means to achieve the requisite objectivity (i.e., the basis for scientism).[8] But the foundational claims of scientism are the main targets for attack by Rorty. If we accept Rorty's stated position, and if we blend in Freud's views about the *id* and the *ego* just discussed, then it follows that the *ego* must be reducible to the *id*'s instincts and the correlative *ego*-ideals of the *superego* to avoid an establishment of a rational, *ego*-driven 'skyhook'. There seems to be an obvious difficulty looming for Rorty's position, however. If the *ego* merely is an extension of the web of desires that is the *id* as it struggles to engage sundry outside (causal) influences, then the combination of the mechanistic impulses and the deterministic traditional strictures of society would overwhelm the creative impetus, or reduce such a structure to a hoax. Reflex would completely submerge re-creation. This result cannot be taken too far for Rorty, however, if he wishes at some level to maintain his Jeffersonian Strategy of the separation of creativity from political solidarity, as well as his advocacy for a truly free, poetic voice for the ironist, which is at the core of his anti-foundational polemic. To do so would endanger the constructive anarchy whose reign is the engine of novel metaphor, and whose loss would effectively reduce personal activity to a determined repetition of frozen patterns of behaviour.

If I have been correct in my argument, then there is only one option left for Rorty to escape this untenable situation. That is, he must opt for a multiplicity of voices within the ironic poet which, not conjoined to a centrally dominated federation, are associated in a loose and centreless confederation. Otherwise, an advocacy for a strong, central and independent voice must follow in order to sustain Rorty's desired separation of the creative element from the invasive and paternalistic dominance of church, science and academic philosophy. As we have recently seen in the Freudian context, and as we have previously encountered in Chapter 2, Rorty must reject and repudiate any suggestion of a Kantian-styled transcendental *eg*/self. Then the only path left him in his effort to avoid a wholesale absorption of the discursive language of aesthetics into the causal vocabulary of science is to embrace a multi-'person' association within the individual; to consolidate the disjunction of disparate components into a cohesive constituency of webs of belief. And he must do this unequivocally! In another reference to Rich, Rorty wonders what caused the experience of a 'split' Rich suffered while being a young woman in the 1950s. He rapidly ends speculation as follows:

The various true descriptions which she applied did not fit together *into a whole*. But, she is implicitly suggesting, a young male poet's descriptions would have fitted together easily. Rich was, in her youth, unable to attain the kind of *coherence*, the kind of *integrity*, which we think of as characteristic of full persons [:] . . . seeing themselves steadily and whole. Rather than feel that splits are tearing them apart, they can see tensions between their alternative self-descriptions as, at worst, necessary elements in a harmonious variety-in-unity (Rorty, in R. Goodman 1995: 136; emphasis added).

Thus, to recognize one's own 'harmonious variety-in-unity' there must be a mirror image on the psychological level of the solidarity of purpose (e.g., tolerance, non-cruelty, etc.) which Rorty has claimed is essential for a liberal society. I make this claim despite Rorty saying, in an apparent contradiction, that the 'demand that our autonomy be embodied in our institutions' is a *misguided* desire, one that is impossible to fulfil (Rorty 1989: 65). By this assertion, Rorty does not thereby eliminate the possibility of reducing 'the desire to avoid cruelty and pain' to within the solidarity of the mind (and to a form of idealism). For the 'mirror' reflects the society and not the other way around. This is an unavoidable implication of Rortian ethnocentrism. Therefore, anything short of this contraction would be to abandon some crucial aspect of his philosophical enterprise, for example, his opposition to all ontological claims for the existence of a material essence and of a substantial self. Furthermore, Rorty cannot hesitate in embracing a variety-in-unity to avoid the detrimental rending of the individual which would place her in a state of psychosis (multiple personality disorder). It seems then that not only is it plausible to suggest that there must be a plurality of 'persons' in the organism as Rorty thought, but that this plurality must be a community in solidarity if the individual is to be said to be in healthy equilibrium. Therefore, does it follow that, for Rorty, the language-games in conflict must be brought into harmony by something other than an overarching principle (or 'person'?) under pain of mental illness if he fails to find a plausible alternative to essentialism, foundationalism or Habermasian internal convergence?

The Rortian 'Self': A Distorted Mirror

What would such a suggestion look like at the personal level? How could there be a privatization among our Freudian 'voices' required in such a psychological solidarity? What would the principles of tolerance and non-cruelty look like at the intra-personal level? Consider the following analogy:

Imagine a circle of chairs, all of them occupied by distinct personages which make up your psyche. As in a discussion group at a seminar, various voices expressing differing points of view can be heard. Some are a local representative of poets; others philosophers, clergy members, lawyers, parents and so forth. Still others are a particular version of free-loaders, disabled beggars, highwaymen, prodigal sons (daughters), and 'unsavoury' types. Many are basically in accord with one another, while others are at odds with a member or perhaps the entire group. There may be a member, at the periphery, mumbling to him- or herself. Perhaps there is, at this unusual seminar, another 'participant' lying on the floor under a blanket, unseen by the group, yet influential in that she causes some to trip over her, and still others to move awkwardly around the obstruction (perceived as a natural part of the room's environment). Of course the list of characters and their conditions could be lengthy. The point is that in the Freud–Rorty–Davidsonian sense of 'persons', each one of these 'persons' would be you, and that no one of them is wholly you. In fact there is no 'you' outside this motley collection of 'persons'. The unique assemblage is that to which the label 'I' is attached (by you?). This is my metaphorical understanding of what an advocate for a psychological solidarity must envision as the mindscape of a human organism.

What is interesting, however, is not the composition of the participants, but their interrelation and interaction. If, as Rorty claims, convergent rationality is not a possibility in the justification of political action,[9] perhaps we should rule it out in the microcosmic 'society' of the individual. This poses a daunting problem. Which voice(s) is (are) to rise up to a leadership role? Unified order, in the form of a hierarchy of values, must be sought to ensure mental health.[10] Hierarchical order allows for the avoidance of the mental anarchy of neurosis and psychosis. Even if there are two or three incommensurate systems in play at one time (as is pictured in a 'good angel – bad angel' polemic), an elimination or, more likely, a repression of an assortment of other systems of beliefs has been already accomplished (pushed under the rug, so to speak), leaving competition among the remaining, dominant vocabularies to be oligarchic in form. Conceivably, the language of the narrative poet in us could become the spokesperson for the cerebral assembly. This may even be accomplished by some internal form of the Hobbesian Social Contract. The question is why should the ascension of this voice be the preferred choice from among the other voices? This question is not meant to rekindle the nature/nurture debate. Rather, it is asked to stress the point that there is no grounded reason for this, or any other, preference in a Rortian narrative. The choice endorsed by Rorty (i.e., the poet) is a troubling one in that it allows the strong, oft-times cruel and intolerant, attitude to dominate the choruses of beliefs and desires. Elitism, which is not to be tolerated in the political sphere, is apparently allowable and seemingly encouraged by Rorty in the mindscape of an organism. This may be safely implied when Rorty says that the ultimate triumph of the metaphor of self-creation over the metaphor of discovery '. . . would consist in our becoming reconciled to the thought that this is the only sort of power over the world which we can hope to have. For that would be the final abjuration of the notion that truth, and not just power and pain, is to be found "out there"' (Rorty 1989: 40). How else could the creative element be given full throttle if not by means of repression and sublimation of the rival language systems, among which are the superstitions of religious dogma, the glorification of rational thought in foundational philosophy and the reification of the world in scientism? For the usual option to coercion and intolerant action, education, in the hands of a New Pragmatist, would be in the form of persuasion either to a cultural norm (and conformity to the *ego*-ideal of the *superego*) or to an intuitive insight (and surrender to the instinctual demands of the *id*), albeit with the intention of altering and controlling behaviour for the benefit of the group and the individuals therein. Neither alternative allows for the sense of personal liberty implied in Rorty's Jeffersonian Strategy. Nowhere in the selection of language-games open to individuals can an actual choice be called *free*. This absence of freedom, and in fact suggestions of its opposite, may be seen in the following Rortian point:

> If one takes Freud's advice, one finds psychological narratives without heroes or heroines. For neither Sartrean freedom, nor the will, nor the instincts, nor the internalization of a culture, nor anything else will play the role of 'the true self'. Instead, one tells the story of the whole machine as machine, without choosing a particular set of springs and wheels as protagonist. Such a story can help us, if anything can, stop the pendulum from swinging between Aristotelian attempts to discover our essence and Sartrean attempts at self-creation *de novo* (Rorty 1991b: 161).

In a decentred pragmatic solidarity such as Rorty's, whether of the political or psychological variety, there will be a paternalistic coercion of such a magnitude that any meaningful sense of freedom of choice is negated. And with its elimination we return to a materialist narrative ('the story of the whole machine as machine'), the reification of the self reminiscent at the political level of Hobbes and hinted at the psychological level of Freud. It is with this critical insight that the shortcomings of Hobbes and the revelations of the internal contradictions of Freud conspire to severely compromise Rorty's Jeffersonian Strategy even when understood as the use of distinct vocabularies.

There seems to be an imperfect mirror working here, reflecting a distorted image of the possibility of solidarity in society upon the concept of the self as a centreless 'community' in microcosm. Unwillingly and perhaps unconsciously, Rorty's ethnocentrically-inspired ambition to extend the language of liberal democracy as far as possible leads him to mimic the structure of Plato's *Republic* in that the state and the individual are seen to be of the same character, only differing in scope. Rorty seems compelled to take on all the drawbacks inherent in this Platonic strategy, not the least of which is the reduction of the organism to a neat package which may accord with the promoted social theory but may sacrifice as unruly important elements which do not quite fit the package, that is, the very ones Rorty wishes to defend – self-assertion and autonomous creativity.

What seems to be distorting the image might be hidden epistemological and metaphysical assumptions. On a preliminary level, the question can be asked: How does Rorty know there can be, in fact, no yet-to-be-discovered neutral observer role from among the collection of Freudian voices, except by fiat or by some strong ('outside') justification? Rejecting essentialism and foundationalism and arguing that his positions are not arbitrary but culturally based, Rorty must state that he is merely voicing as a preference a suspicion sceptics have been uttering for centuries. Nevertheless, a claim that a neutral observer role for the psyche has not been found across millennia by him or anyone else is not a strong enough argument to prove the point against foundationalism's transcendent self. For while it is possible that there is nothing to be unearthed, so to speak, it can be equally possible that the 'Rosetta Stone' of these incommensurable voices lies just below the surface of our awareness, repressed in the unconscious (a distinct twist on Freudian thinking). With its exhumation, the reconciliation of the various language-games would be at hand. In short, there might be a emerging element, hitherto unrecognized within the mind-scape by human thought itself. Even a future that has been unhinged from all (allegedly unsurpassable) final vocabularies by the New Pragmatism cannot preclude the possibility of this unifying metaphor from our language. Rorty should recognize this when he admits that we may know only the possibilities which have been actualized to date (Rorty, in R. Goodman 1995: 127). Thus Rorty runs headlong here into N. Goodman's problems of induction if he tries to deny the possibility of a 'Rosetta Stone' explicitly or implicitly in order to maintain his Multiplism.

Furthermore, the claim against the possibility of either a Platonic or Kantian neutral observer, whether made explicitly or tacitly, itself must lead Rorty to a paradoxical objectivism of the kind he speaks against. Is the claim of thorough-going plurality not an attempt to hold at a distance, that is, to have a self, or some component 'person' thereof, constantly available as a neutral inspector to view as valid all Multiplist claims? And is this being done paradoxically at the very moment Rorty asserts that there is not, nor can there ever be, any privileged neutral observer role? Any attempt to sidestep this issue by claiming that all there can be is a dialogue of roughly coequal aspects of a web of belief (or 'persons') is either to fall once again into the general point previously argued by Fraser that Rorty would depoliticize alternative theories to neo-pragmatism and thus curtail authentic democratic dialogue, causing a vicious circle to form, or to covertly and illicitly introduce a metaphysical 'God's-eye' perspective or an epistemological neutral observer solution in the language-game of decentralized holism.

To avoid the horns of this dilemma, Rorty must opt for a form of Dewey's notion of 'funded belief', that all 'persons' within the matrix of an organism are successively capable of occupying a privileged standpoint from which to make judgement about another aspect (person) of the organism's psyche. The 'Neurath's Boat' argument seems to apply adequately to the Deweyan strategy until one remembers that the planks of the ship do not remove and replace themselves, and that the 'carpenter' in charge of the replacement is not part of the vessel itself, but is a crew member of one. And as the crew member, to continue the metaphor, the 'carpenter' in his function must stand apart when deliberating the systematic removal and the methodical replacement of each and every plank. However, this kind of detached agency *is* being implied by Neurath's metaphor. Nevertheless, in the early part of the twenty-first century it may be easy to imagine a fully automated ship equipped with a computerized plank-replacing mechanism akin to a Dennett system of algorithmic evolution outlined in *Darwin's Dangerous Idea*. This would seem to bypass the suggestion of a substantial self or Kantian Ego contained in the suggestive metaphor of a human carpenter. However, the danger of buying into the 'self-less' metaphor of full automation delivers one to the harbour of reductive materialism, for the discursive space may be rendered in the long run as merely the epiphenomenal hum of the mechanism leaving no room for any conscious creativity, poetic or otherwise. This is a port which Rorty does not wish to visit (see 'Response to Dennett', in Brandom 2000: 101–108). He also implies this when he argues for both the 'double describability' of a noise, as a cause and as a reason, and for the differentiation of the pragmatist from the idealist by the former's accepting the brute resistance of the physical but not as fact captured by language and used in sentences (Rorty 1991a: 81 and 171).

Nevertheless, Rorty's stance for an autonomous and free de-centred self opens him to a criticism which James Conant terms 'epistemologism' – the obsessive fixation on doctrines of epistemology, despite insistent claims to have moved beyond them as unproductive and unprofitable controversies (Conant, in Brandom 2000: 270). One such fixation is Descartes' *Cogito*.

Rorty as a Closet Cartesian

This brings me to the deeper issue with Rorty's narrative. I hold that he harbours a tendency to be a 'closet Cartesian' when it comes to his non-reductive physicalism.[11] I believe this is due to the fixation which Conant has identified as *epistemologism*. In challenging Descartes too ardently on the one hand, and following him too closely on the other, Rorty has denied that there is, in any significant vocabulary, a self-described entity as a thinking substance while maintaining that there is a causal world beyond linguistic description. That this thinking, substantial self can be denied and replaced by terms that redescribe the traditional self as an idiosyncratic arrangement of various 'voices-in-solidarity', to coin a term, seems to be enough of a rationale to gain acceptance for the other Cartesian substance, a 'physical organism', the material self as part of the causal world of brute physical resistance. In other words, it was and is my contention that Rorty continues to follow Descartes's narrative in moving from the original 'Cogito, ergo sum' first-person insight to a discussion about the establishment of the 'Cogito' (the third-person descriptive analysis of Cartesian self), and in doing so depersonalizing that which is under observation (e.g., Rorty himself) by redefining it with objective vocabulary (e.g., as a physical organism). Or to put it into Rorty's terms, to take intentionality and to look upon this vocabulary as one more attempt to predict behaviour; to be another attempt at forming a useful *descriptive* vocabulary (Rorty, in Brandom 2000: 372–73). Rorty seems Cartesian in his surprising uncritical acceptance of this method of analytic approach. It also appears that Rorty's subsequent denial of the 'Cogito' (i.e., having a third-person representational description of a free-standing self) is simply to follow Descartes too closely by (covertly) accepting the distinction made by Descartes (i.e., between intentional and extended objects), and to choose sides about it, in favour of his brand of materialism. To be consistent, it appears that it would be necessary for Rorty to deny the distinction inherent in Cartesian dualism altogether, and to follow his (Rorty's) pattern, noted earlier, of dismantling the various dichotomies (e.g., the objective and the subjective; the outer and the inner, etc.). And it *appears* this is what he has recently done.

I agree with Isaiah Berlin when he recognizes that if, in principle, objectivity was unimaginable, the term subjective and objective, no longer contrasted, would mean nothing; for as correlatives they stand and fall as one. Rorty often speaks as if he has realized this need to dissolve such dichotomies, and that his philosophical stance is specifically designed to realize this sort of deconstruction.[12] For example, in his article, 'Philosophy in America Today', Rorty consistently advises anyone with the pretension to be a philosopher dedicated to the search for wisdom to 'give up the rhetoric of the sage' and to adopt the attitude of an engineer or a lawyer (See Rorty, in Saatkamp [1995: 199] and Rorty [1982: 222 and 227]). He is claiming to be applying his tool, metaphor, to the very philosophical tool used to make the metaphor: the *vocabulary-vocabulary*.

Nevertheless, Rorty has reacted to this sort of critique offered in Bjorn Ramberg's essay (cited in Chapter 1) by acknowledging that there is a normative element of speaking to (and not just about) each other. Ramberg (in Brandom 2000: 372) has underscored, echoing Davidson, the privilege of intentional vocabulary. The privilege is due to its inescapability, i.e., that as interlocutors we cannot stop proscribing and merely describe each other. As humans we have a *voice*. We obey norms even as we challenge their existence. This insight applies to Rorty's practices, as he acknowledges; but old habits die hard. Upon a closer reading, it can be argued that Rorty betrays his earlier tendency to take sides in favour of materialism, such as in 'Representation, Social Practice, Truth'. Therein, Rorty makes use of the phrases 'the *same* causal forces' '*in the same world*' (see 1991a: 160). It seems that the ability to radically redescribe experience, personal or societal, does not apply to the background causal forces. My question is: Why is there this (arbitrary) limit to poetic licence? To which clientele is he an apologist? Members of our Western culture are split on this matter. So why does he readily project this materialist viewpoint? Perhaps it is the habitual reflex to the call of dualism so present in the philosophies of Descartes and Locke. That is, for him to claim that we live in the 'same world', Rorty may mean this literally, and hence embrace either physicalism or some form of transcendental idealism. *If* he does not speak in a literal fashion, however, he must employ the phrase 'same world' in some metaphoric manner, and hence equivocate on the meaning of the concept 'sameness'. And this seems to be the case when he writes nine years later:

Would there still be snow if nobody talked about it? Sure. Why? Because according to the norm *we* invoke when we use 'snow', we are supposed to answer this question affirmatively. (If you think that glib and ethnocentric answer is not good enough, that is because you are still in the grip of the scheme-content distinction.) (Rorty, in Brandom 2000: 374).

Therefore, the phrase in question becomes a rhetorical device without a common referent to speak about. So, in order for Rorty to avoid speaking in a meaningless, solipsistic way, he must enter into the cultural debate concerning dualism, asserting a position for *neither* materialism nor idealism, to be consistent with his claim that he has given up 'the rhetoric of the sage' and foresworn the scheme–content distinction.

It has been argued above that Rorty tried to dissolve the dualist dichotomy by the appeal to the use of coherent vocabularies in place of correspondence theories, hence, his favouring of a multi-personed organism. And on one level the appeal works. Correspondence as a means of justification for true sentences drops out and is replaced by cooperative sets of belief. Yet by denying all 'Cogito' claims to an ontologically unified self on one side and by asserting the efficacy of causal forces on the other, Rorty need not deny the immediate and inescapable self-encounter of the 'Cogito, ergo sum' insight. Nor need he eschew the first-person presence to the world that is this insight – the 'taken-for-granted background of purpose' from which descriptions emerge as descriptions of some 'x' – even if 'it' is depicted as a bundle of beliefs and desires expressed as vocal sounds or as scratches of ink upon paper in response to episodic causal interactions with 'the world'. To talk about 'it' in the vocabulary of contingent personhood or as an organism, or again as a bundle or web of beliefs, is to hold 'it' out for inspection as a description; is to have it in some quasi-Cartesian, third-person, objectivist fashion.[13] This form of having a language-game forces the maintenance of a subjective/objective split.[14] This sense of *having* would be the inspector function of the stealth carpenter on 'Neurath's Boat' alluded to earlier. Thus, we still appear to be well within the Cartesian–Kantian Enlightenment language-game despite Rorty's protestations to the contrary.[15]

This normal (Singularist) discourse within his avowedly abnormal (Multiplist) approach to Philosophy can now be judged to be more entangling than Rorty seems to be aware, even after his response to Ramberg (in Brandom 2000: 370–77). It is as if Rorty thinks that by relocating the spirit of Humean empiricism into a language motif, he would then escape its sceptical grasp, while at the same time cracking the Cartesian 'mirror' along the same lines as did Hume. This attempt notwithstanding, I contend that Rorty simply carries a privileged point of view deep within the language-game he plays (e.g., in the guise of the unnoticed Neurathian carpenter), unintentionally paralleling Kant's transcendental strategy on one side, while holding on to the realist materialism on the other. For by becoming aware that all there is are language-games, the awareness one must have to make this claim requires a 'step-back' to a non-embedded point of view, as Harris implies (see Chapter 3). For what else is it to move from an *en-soi* to a *pour-soi* but to become conscious of the limitations of the present moment and to move consciously beyond them into a new configuration, ideally through dialogue with other interlocutors or agents who do not simply 'make noise' but intentionally offer interpretative descriptions of a common world, as Habermas suggests? Therefore, the move of becoming aware cannot be a mere blind, predetermined reaction of an organism (as argued by Bhaskar earlier in Chapter 6). A freedom vocabulary must be grafted to complete the picture drawn by Rorty. Rorty did attempt the hybridization through his Jeffersonian Strategy. Nevertheless, as Rorty clearly understands, to have a vocabulary (or many) is to create a tool, in a Wittgensteinian sense that to have a concept is to use a word, and to master concepts is to be able to use a language (Rorty 1982: 222).

As previously noted and reinforced by the following quote, Rorty holds that we are basically tool creators and users: 'For even if we agree that languages are not media of representing or expression, they will remain media of communication, tools for social interaction, ways of tying oneself up with other human beings' (Rorty 1989: 41). The question arises: How far are we defined by our tools (understood as inner 'persons')? Completely, and thus we are entirely reduced to our language-game, with no remainder – even after the recognition is made that we humans are norm-followers? Or, alternatively, are we somehow independent of the language-game we play so that we must always be holding on to one vine (paradigm) until we can grasp a new one, 'Tarzan-style'? In other words, are we fully delineated by our tools, or are we transcending agents confined to expression through one or another language tool at any given moment? To put it yet another way: are we reducible to a sequence of third-person observations (in either a causal or a discursive language mode), or is there room for an irreducible first-person self-encounter (prior to language) within all the observables? For if we can stand outside ourselves enough to describe the causal aspects of self and world, even for a moment, then we would be where Rorty says we cannot be – in the first-person, objective relationship to my '*self*' and '*the world*'. That is, we would be in the privileged position he claims does not and cannot exist for a language-user except in a limited sense within any given cultural paradigm. Otherwise, we are forced back to the solidarity of 'persons' with its attendant shortcomings.

This restrictive intra-normative judgement sheds light on Rorty's often made claim that no area of culture and no period of history gets Reality more right than any other. Rorty's assertion about the epistemic constraints upon culture and history may be stated with confidence only from within the limits of his particular paradigm. If Rorty means his statement to be a trans-paradigmatic one – and he appears to be making the more general claim in his quote – then he is illicitly importing an imperative Singularism into neo-pragmatic thinking. If he is speaking to convert the non-believer, then he is advocating Singularism akin to a religious faith. How can Rorty avoid Singularist ontological commitments or onto-theological metaphor and yet speak to present and future audiences? Can he go to the well once too often; can his Jeffersonian Strategy bail him out here?

If, as I suspect, Rorty wants to say descriptions about first-person narratives and third-person explanations are both possible, albeit incommensurable language-games, he is still in the *spirit* of Cartesian dualism; there are two incommensurable vocabularies (two Freudian 'persons') linked through the 'pineal gland' of the neo-pragmatic interpretation.[16] If Rorty wishes to avoid this conclusion he would have to say that we are the vocabulary and it is us. But then we will be lost in the *en-soi* (i.e., a causal version of language[17]) and are only ignorant of our condition. The loss of freedom in the public political sphere and, by extension, in the private psychological realm, would be the price we must pay for a dogmatic solidarity (as Fraser argues) and physicalism (as Bhaskar suggests). Or if Rorty wants strong poets and novelists, creators of self-assertive narratives, to be the order of the day (Rorty 1989: 27), then he must find an escape out of the cycle of *en-soi* determinism by means of discursive language open to self-creation and freedom. However, this option seems to be a new mask for an old solution. To attempt to describe an individual in the language of community is to speak just as metaphorically as when one speaks of 'soul' or of a 'mind'. Rorty, I concede, realizes this when he remarks that

> [E]very human life is the working out of a sophisticated idiosyncratic fantasy, and as a reminder that no such working out gets completed before death interrupts. It cannot get completed because there is nothing to complete, there is only a web of relations to be rewoven, a web which time lengthens every day (Rorty 1989: 42).

Nevertheless, to try to cover the issue by saying that we are limited to a language-game of one sort or another is to bow to a subtle form of objectivism, albeit allegedly provisional. To hold that all our experience is thoroughly framed by our language and the norms found there within is to be locked, now and forever, within schemes of representing (holding at a distance for inspection, i.e., *having*) something, even if it is other aspects of our language-game. It is never to be, in the sense of a truly fresh first-person encounter – an encounter, I trust, you are enjoying as you self-consciously read these words. The liberty one has then in 'inventing' new ways of conversation must be to merely arrange and rearrange a very elaborate causal cage. Rorty has fought hard to eliminate this limiting type of 'givenness'. He wants there to be always 'something new under the sun'. Nevertheless, the creative possibilities, though expansive, are still finite once bound by and to the use of a tool. One can easily turn the caustic comment of Nietzsche's, 'I fear that we shall be unable to get rid of God, since we still believe in grammar', back upon Rorty, who cited the quote for his own purpose (Rorty 1982: 229).

To emphasize my creative use of Nietzsche's point, it can be noted that automatic syntactical rearrangements can be done today by a relatively crude computer, a tool itself, separate from the persons who might attach meaning to them. In all its sophistication and subtlety language, especially in its Apollonian form, is precisely a distance-making, portable tool, whether it is used by a computer, or by theologians, scientists, philosophers, or even poets who seek justification through (conversion with) their current audience. Carried with us and

replaceable (when made obsolete by some better adapted tool), language functions as a factory which churns out sentences as 'my mind is a gathering of
voices', holding the entire proposition as if at arm's length, or as seen from a
God's-eye point of view. It is precisely this distance which can allow Rorty to
agree with Stout's distinctions between the eternal truth of a sentence and its
being made true. We are forced to be quasi-Cartesian dualist, or else reductive
materialists, in the moment we try to say along with Rorty that the self is simply
the network of such beliefs and desires. We are prised away from our 'self', the
first-person encounter of freedom however 'it' is characterized, in the very
attempt to describe it literally *or* metaphorically as a *system of beliefs and desires*.

Caught in this fashion, we seem to be constrained, despite Rorty's protests,
to choose the systematic language-game of an autonomous self (a non-
Freudian *ego*) independent from the physical world (i.e., for idealism or dualism) or to opt for a language of reductive materialism – which is inherently
systematic. And we must linguistically describe the 'self', however it may be
characterized, according to Rorty's way of thinking or fall into onto-theological
mysticism. In this condition of linguistic dependence with no possibility to
appeal to a higher authority, it must be inevitable to believe and speak as if
our final vocabulary is objective and should be considered as an irreplaceable
plank in 'Neurath's Boat'. In this condition, it is inevitable to speak and act in
the paternal fashion of a high priest proselytizing one's faith, even if only for this
moment, and in this place, holding out, for instance, the 'civilizing' hope of New
Pragmatism for the foundationally-inclined 'savages'. Geras strikes home the
point when he says:

> But if we are not then also given something in favour of the content of this
> tradition or vocabulary, we are given no more than a name. It is as if we
> were to be told that we may not, or must not, act in a certain way because of
> *The Word*. Or it is to be offered *Our View* as a reason without any reason for
> *Our View*; or without any reason from within *Our View* such as to make it actu-
> ally a view and not an incantation. Perhaps there are traditions which this
> style of exhortation models, but it scarcely seems apt to the traditions
> Richard Rorty wants to call his own (Geras 1995: 86).

Thus, Rorty must contradict himself whenever he asserts to others both the
social virtues of pragmatic liberalism and the indispensable reformist value of
the free and creative poet for human life. Impossible as it is for him to call upon
foundational grounding to justify the veracity of his incommensurable claims, he
must advocate his positions as a sophist might by the invocation of cultural
assumptions as axiomatic. He wants to have his cake and eat it when he speaks
in the colloquialisms of a philosopher about the advantages of poetic language.[18]

Rorty believes his promotion of poetry *via* philosophical channels to be ironic,
in the spirit of Socrates. However, I believe that I have shown him to be caught
in a contradiction, a 'split', that is, in Rorty's words: 'The various true descriptions which ... did not fit together into a whole' (i.e., a failed argument for

'justification for a belief', as described in his own terms [Rorty 1991a: 171]).
This split is one that is internal to his final vocabulary – a language-game
which unequivocally extols on the object level, the meta-level *and* the meta-
meta-level (as a Singularist) the private virtues of the poetic 'word' while,
with equal strength, it advocates the value of the collective good (of democratic liberalism); a split of a nature which Socrates revelled in exposing in
the *Apology* when he cross-examined Meletus, the spokesman for the poets
(Grippe, forthcoming).

Chapter 9

Neither Liberal nor Free:
The Singularism of New Pragmatism

The Rortian Faith

My work thus far has been to favour the Rortian language-game whenever it was plausible to do so within the context of this work's ongoing dialogue among the various and diverse philosophical voices. Hence I have pulled some punches and have generally erred on the side of caution when calling Rorty's narrative into question. However, this coincidence of opinion has been maintained only as long as:

1. I was in solidarity with Rorty, i.e., I was within Rorty's language-game as he has defined it, and
2. The idiosyncratic differences between Rorty and myself were not pushed to their logical ends.

If, for the sake of argument, we agree with Rorty that self-assertion is a pluralistic enterprise (assuming that there is more than myself in existence and that my interpretative assertion plays against a backdrop of multiple, distinct assertions), there can be only a family resemblance between the distinct webs of belief which characterize individuals. Like human fingerprints or the DNA of any organism, the neural 'mindprints' of an individual's brain and the singular patterns of linguistic expression that the configuration of the neural pathways engenders are unmatched and unique. Thus, a consonance of opinion among individuals is the fortunate result of contingent circumstances and not attributable to a Kripkean externally fixed essence or a Habermasian internal convergence of opinion around a core of reason. Therefore, the parameters of a given solidarity must be in the eye of the pragmatic beholder. Otherwise, there would be what Richard Bernstein calls the 'nostalgic' sentiment for the story of pragmatism, which takes the past achievements of Peirce, James, Royce, Santayana and especially Dewey as the unquestioned standards by which to judge all would-be current and future pragmatists (Bernstein, in Saatkamp 1995: 66). Bernstein goes on immediately to make a crucial distinction concerning the idea of pluralism, one that I believe reveals the impossible position in which the New Pragmatism is lodged:

We must also take seriously our commitment to pluralism – even a pluralism in what is appropriate from the pragmatic legacy. Such a pluralism is not to be confused with what I once called 'flabby' pluralism – where one falsely assumes that one story or narrative is just as good as another ... The pluralism that I take to be characteristic of a vital pragmatism is an engaged vitality and a frustration for those trying to define it (Bernstein, in Saatkamp 1995: 66).

It seems to follow that the only method available for a New Pragmatist to discern if a person is to be included as being among 'we pragmatists' is for that thinker to use his judgement concerning present and future practices, derived from what he unsentimentally holds to be the relevant focus on the classical texts of this worldview. Consider what Rorty writes in his 'Response to Bernstein' found in the same text:

When we use the phrase to which Bernstein refers, and to which my critics object – 'we pragmatists' – I am implicitly saying: try, for the nonce, ignoring the differences between Putnam and Peirce, Nietzsche and James, Davidson and Dewey, Sellars and Wittgenstein. Focus on the ... similarities, and then other similarities may leap out at you. To grasp my nonce, idiosyncratic sense of 'pragmatism', ... [b]racket ... [the] doctrines that strike me as wrong, or parochial, or tangential, and repackage what is left. The sort of repackaging job which such nonce usages permit seems to be an important element in the construction of narratives (Rorty, in Saatkamp 1995: 69).

Again, it seems to me that Rorty is asking for the reader to have faith in his, Rorty's, idiosyncratic repackaging of 'pragmatist', and if one does then one will understand, among other things, 'an important element in the construction of narratives'. Yet this is the pattern of request all religious faiths make, as I have noted earlier: 'believe and you will understand'. Only, now we are being asked to come within Rorty's personal gloss, his 'pragmatic creed', where the good is uniquely (dogmatically?) defined by and through his narration. Rorty wants us to adopt his values on the matter. If there were a way to measure these values to some objective standard (be it, for instance, God's, Nature's, or the Kantian rational self's), then Rorty's suggestion would be linked to the basic Enlightenment assumption in Millean democracy: that reason well applied – that is, when it is allowed to be self-assertive in an open forum of an unfettered exchange of ideas – will discern the objective truth of any matter of human importance. However, the only constraint that Rorty has left us with is the dyad of values he impresses upon us, the current audience within a liberal democratic society, that is, that these assertions not be cruel or humiliating to others, and that private inventions be unfettered by undue social restraints.

The experience of the twentieth century's atrocities and violations of human integrity predisposes even the less informed persons to agree readily with these constraints. This offering of values, like the suggestion to the reader in the quote immediately above in which Rorty moves from his 'nonce, idiosyncratic sense' to the allegedly general insight about the fabrication of narratives, is done with a most subtle paternalism. Rorty wishes to share his insights into matters of human importance, and claims to place it before the reader in the spirit of democratic dialogue. Yet, just as the corner preacher who quotes the Christian Bible as advocating, say, righteous retribution, by citing 'an eye for an eye, a tooth for a tooth', plays on the common Judeo-Christian-Islamic beliefs of passers-by while recontextualizing the quote's meaning for purposes of conversion to his or his group's interpretation of scripture,[1] likewise, Rorty equivocates on generally accepted terms such as 'integrity' or 'human rights' to achieve persuasiveness in the pursuit of semantic authority for his particular pragmatic ends.[2] The Enlightenment sense of reason, rights and the like has no part to play in either the street-corner preacher's or Rorty's goal of conversion.

Like a religious belief (Hall refers to it as 'the invisible Church of the New Pragmatism' [1994: 8]), it is the spirit of the New Pragmatism, rather than any final vocabulary (meta-narrative) peculiar to himself, which Rorty wishes to insinuate into intellectual discussions, and through these debates into the conversations (narratives) of the general public. Thus, his stated goal is not the winning of a philosophical debate, but shifting paradigms, reconfiguring webs of belief. As Rorty has said, this activity of paradigm-shifting calls not so much for discussion based on traditional reason as it does for an all-or-nothing change of perspective, a change in the way one views all: 'understand my story and you will see':[3]

> But the pragmatist does not try to justify his metaphors by philosophical argument ... Instead, like Dewey, he tells stories about how the course of Western thought has been stultified by the metaphors he dislikes (Rorty 1991a: 81–82).

Having dismissed most major foundational metaphors, our pragmatist, Rorty, is free to create a new paradigm. But please remember that, under his own terms, the paradigm of New Pragmatism is merely an element in Rorty's unique narration *unless* he can stand astride multiple paradigms to speak about the creation of a new, bridging paradigm. If this ability to transcend paradigms is impossible, as Rorty seems to suggest, his is not a movement based on any ground beyond the Rortian meta-narrative, for as Rorty has often asserted there is nothing more than dead, dying or nascent similes. And each of these similes, on the judgement of Rorty alone, is assigned to its 'proper' category.[4] If I am correct, then the New Pragmatism's greater goal of liberating humankind from the allegedly deleterious effect of Western philosophical tradition is, at last call, a mission based squarely on the preferences of its author, and all those who are willing to be persuaded by his paradigmatic vision. Therefore, the strong ethnocentric misreading that is intentionally executed for desired effect of 'grabbing hold of causal forces and making them do what we [read: Rorty] want' (Rorty 1991a: 81) can be fairly characterized as both idiosyncratic and paternalistic in nature.

The Pain and Humiliation from Strong Misreadings

Paradoxically, despite what has just been said, I would suggest that from Rorty's idiosyncratic perspective there can be no paternalism. Rather, in the spirit of the Darwinian–Mendelian struggle for semantic space (see Chapter 7), it is simply a competition among equals over the meaning to apply to the blind impresses of causal activity. However, I argue that Rorty's efforts are as hegemonic as the efforts of, for instance, the Crusaders to convert the Muslim 'infidels' in order to have the God utopia on earth, because his paradigm is involved in the unregulated struggle for semantic space as is the onto-theological paradigm. If this characterization is apt, then Rorty's Jeffersonian-style separation of the self-asserting, often intolerant, poet from the public arena, where cruelty and humiliation are never an option to be tolerated, is an impossibility because there can be no middle ground, no neutral standpoint from which to achieve public tolerance that respects another's autonomy and intellectual integrity, except nominally. To assent to the view of tolerance Rorty espouses one must become intolerant of rival paradigms (see note 4) for the reason that Rorty argues that the rivals are the wrong tools for today's job. But, as Hall has noted, the strong misreadings of others' narrations that Rorty practises can be potentially humiliating.[5]

Take, for instance, Fraser speaking of Rorty's characterization of herself and other feminists as 'prophets' of linguistic and cultural change. At first glance it seems that he is offering the pragmatic equivalent of a reversal of the traditional heterosexual relationship; as Fraser puts it, Rorty is offering to do the housework in order to free-up the women for reformist activity in the public sphere. Fraser continues with extreme caution:

> [M]any of us have learned the hard way that when men offer to help with the housework there are frequently hidden costs. In the case of Rorty's proposal, the hidden cost is the implication that feminists ... are not philosophers. Granted, we're something bigger, grander, more important – prophets .... So I can't but think that the division of labor between pragmatism and feminism that Rorty is proposing is yet another way of putting women on a pedestal (Fraser, in R. Goodman 1995: 154).

But, of course, Rorty does read feminism through the prism of his own frame of reference, transforming feminism (or any other 'ism') into a metaphoric utterance within his own vocabulary. And through his transformation of all narratives into the aesthetics of literature, including narratives about feminism's identity, everything gets pulled into Rorty's meta-narrative, where the outside world is turned into a Rortian symbol, and the inside realm of the self transmutes into general commentaries about that symbol. Even criticism of Rorty's view, feminist or otherwise, is sublimated by being pulled into his paradigm. For instance, Rorty, speaking about his ideal pragmatist, says of him:

His own technique in philosophy is that same Homeric, narrative style which he recommends to the literary critic. His recommendation to the critic is thus not grounded in a theory about literature or about criticism, but in a narrative whose details he hopes the literary critic will help him fill in (Rorty 1991a: 82).

My point here is that Rorty recognizes that he may be appraised on the literary structure of his text and the cogency of his narrative, and he may even accept this criticism as important to his future work. However, the advice is given at the level of aesthetic judgement. Hence, Fraser's critique of Rorty's take on feminists as prophets must fall on philosophically deaf ears. It will never be construed by Rorty as having philosophic importance, if by philosophy one means at least a Gadamerian analysis inclusive of an alien culture's point of view. Therefore, Fraser's views on Rorty only can be *tangential* to Rorty's narrative, and thus these views can be recast by him. It is here, with this sort of misreading that seems classically Rorty, that he is most condescending, proving Fraser's point concerning his faint praise about feminist 'prophets', as well as mine about the destructive re-characterization found in Rortian misreadings.

To become dismissive of those views deemed tangential is but a small step away from being intolerant of that which is deemed 'mad' in relation to one's own cherished beliefs. Both attitudes place the *core* of one's system of beliefs and desires beyond question. For the New Pragmatist cannot say that one's beliefs are objectively wrong; they only can say that they are not theirs, wrong only in Putnam's 'innocent' internalist sense. Therefore, I can say that in structure, but *not* in commitment to a supernatural entity, there is a similarity between this aggressive faith in one's beliefs and the kind of faith that is found in fundamentalist religions. A crucial difference between religious creeds and the aggressive faith Rorty displays for his New Pragmatism is that Rorty rejects the possibility that his ideology will be proved true by an appeal to a force beyond his web of beliefs or the community's aesthetic judgement to which he appeals. By now it ought to be thoroughly obvious that his faith is based upon nothing foundational, nothing metaphysical to which it corresponds; nothing which it epistemologically represents. It involves the systematic coherence of beliefs and desires that is Rorty's own; that *is* Rorty. And this web of beliefs' power rests completely on the tensile strength of his narrative's weave. If the plait unwinds, so does the entire Rortian Multiplist approach.

I contend that the deep problem within Rorty's New Pragmatism is precisely this weave, this systemized plait of idiosyncratic beliefs and desires. Unlike the 'nature–nurture' controversy, for example, where questions about the source of human personality are compressed into the single issue of whether genetic structures or the alignment of environmental factors play the crucial role in determining what one becomes, Rorty refuses to reduce what it is to be a human in society to a single rubric drawn, allegedly, from external causes or internal structures. Rather, in his now familiar pattern, he maintains that we seem to be both the product of the cultural solidarities (old metaphors) to which we belong and the separate interplay of the idiosyncratic assertions (new metaphors) that are the creative and challenging responses to causal impacts of society and that society's 'world'. Nevertheless, Rorty's narrative falls under the spell of systemization like that found within the physicalist's 'nature–nurture' debate, only on multiple and incommensurate levels, leaving him vulnerable to my analysis of Freudian voices from the previous chapter.

The Rortian Anti-System System

What I mean by Rorty being vulnerable is that on the one hand, by Rorty reading the Freudian model of the idiosyncratic self into his narrative, he embraces a view of the individual as a system of dynamic psychic tensions ('persons') striving for equilibrium. On the other hand, in the interrelations among language users, Rorty borrows from Rawls when he claims that solidarities are also in 'reflective equilibrium' (Rorty 1991a: 183, n. 20), rendering society as a whole as a self-referential dynamic system of competing vocabularies. Furthermore, in a third way, at the natural level of organism and environment, there is a causal web, a deterministic complex involving the seamless flow of stimulation and response (or more basically, action and reaction). In each case, for the self, for society and for the world, Rorty characterizes that which is currently in his focus as an element of a centreless system, grounded upon nothing more than the poetic prose of a good conversationalist and an audience's approbation in response. Yet even the inventor of metaphor is a semantic system, coherent – when he is – in his network of beliefs and their interpretation. To communicate, he (or his interlocutor) may need to convert, radically and completely, in order to change the paradigm to which he (or they) cleave(s), otherwise:

> ... the view that human beings are centerless networks of beliefs and desires and that their vocabularies and opinions are determined by historical circumstances allows for the possibility that there may not be enough overlap between two such networks to make possible agreement about political topics, or even profitable discussion on such topics (Rorty 1991a: 191).

As recently suggested, the power of Rorty's meta-narrative is its reflexive nature's tensile strength. His story-line folds back on to itself, conch-like, in concentric hermeneutic circles. That is, his narrative purports to be coherent with itself based on its own criteria. For example, the creative poet as a semantic generator (*via* the minting of new metaphor) in the face of the 'hold-fast' quality of 'normalized' (e.g., theistic, philosophical or scientific) meanings encrusted in the 'dead metaphors' of a culture's vocabulary, can also be spoken of as the Freudian *ego* as it strives in its own unique fashion to maintain its balance among contending psychological forces. The psychological forces are the combination of the weight of internalized societal expectations and demands (the *superego*) and the drives and impulses which arise from the organism itself (the *id*). The relationship of the individual and the forces beyond his/her control may also get interpreted as the causal interplay between an organism and its environment, where deterministic laws affect both equally. The choice of narrative venue is an aesthetico-pragmatic decision made by the idiosyncratic poet in relation to his/her milieu in order to get what he/she wants. And in Rorty's case, what he wants is to institute the spirit of the paradigm he is currently using to ensure its adoption on the meta-meta-narrative level (the paradigm presupposed by Multiplism at the meta-narrative level).

Yet this freedom to slide among levels of interpretation has a serious and perhaps fatal flaw. It becomes most noticeable when we realize that Rorty must not only converse about the human organism, the Freudian *ego*, or even the ironic poet, but he must *live* the metaphors as well. In some way, and in some suitable proportion or sequence, he must be each of them (recall the notion of the self as a solidarity of persons). Otherwise, Rorty would be as detached from his discourse as any priest, any scientific or philosophical 'spectator', who claims to gain a third-person, privileged position over the matter at hand. He would simply be weaving, so to speak, fables about distant lands and peoples he has never seen, or stories concerning emotions he has never felt. This, of course, would be a novice's error, one that, under different circumstances, Rorty would quickly repudiate, as he seems to be in the following, a continuation of the excerpts cited in Chapter 7:

> But once we drop the notion of 'consciousness' there is no harm in continuing to speak of a distinct entity called 'the self' which consists of the mental states of a human being: her beliefs, desires, moods, etc. The important thing is to think of the collection of those things as being the self rather than as something which the self *has*. The latter notion is a leftover of the traditional Western temptation to model thinking on vision, and to postulate an 'inner eye' which inspects inner states. For this traditional metaphor, a non-reductive physicalist model substitutes the picture of a network of beliefs and desires which is continually in process of being rewoven (with some old items dropped as new ones are added). This network is not one which is rewoven by an agent distinct from the network – a master weaver, so to speak. Rather, it reweaves itself, in response to stimuli such as the new beliefs acquired when, e.g., doors are opened (Rorty 1991a: 123).

Notwithstanding this, as I argued in Chapter 8, Rorty is unaware of the distance he takes when he speaks of 'the self' as being coextensive with the network of one's beliefs and desires or as being embedded in a culture. This is because throughout Rorty's writings his challenges to the traditional assumption of 'an inner eye of the mind' and its alternative form, the 'God's-eye point of view', lead him to think that by identifying and critiquing these 'looking-glass metaphors' he thereby has moved beyond them. This is not so. When Rorty offers his culturally engendered beliefs and desires for the reader's consideration (i.e., inspection), he objectifies them, and puts them at a distance from himself as surely as Descartes disengaged from the 'Cogito' when Descartes began to describe himself as 'a self' or a 'thinking thing' – an object open for critical inspection. Rorty, by fuzzing the lines between creative fiction and claims about reality, has made himself into a narrative character ('that which reweaves itself'), not only for his readers but apparently for himself. Thus as a highly fluid and centreless complex, Rorty inadvertently take himself to be an impersonal – i.e., 'third-person' – system, which responds with new adjustments (reflexive or projective in nature) from within that system to stimulations presented by other systems (be they identified as 'physical', 'political' or 'cultural'). This distancing takes on a spectator-like quality and is evident despite his frequent employment of the language of personal 'I' – 'the first-person' perspective – of idiosyncratic individualism. A denial of this by Rorty would be disingenuous as long as he maintains that humans must be culturally embedded webs of beliefs devoid of anything like Kantian 'personhood'. I trust he will continue his views on the matter, hence, I am also confident (given supporting arguments from Chapter 8) that Rorty is alienated from himself in a most incoherent way, especially when he insists (and I believe that the language of his quote above substantiates this) that such objectivist alienation – as he claims to find not only in the philosophies of Plato, Aristotle, Descartes and Kant but also within the thoughts of Locke, Berkeley and Hume – is an impossibility within a pragmatic vocabulary.

What is even more astounding about this alienation is that with Rorty's elimination of the representationalist metaphor of the rational mind as the pure mirror of reality due to its outlived utility, he has also precluded the possibility for him to appeal to his creative self, that is, the agent of unification for the web of beliefs. That is to say, I can see no way that Rorty's thought, as a system of 'persons', can reflect upon the aggregate (i.e., himself) as a whole to establish individual identity. In his judgements, he must always occupy a position at some point of the web, and never move beyond its bounds to achieve a 'God's-eye' view of himself. Thus Rorty's 'universe' is restricted to the dynamic assemblage of the various elements which comprise the idiosyncratically arranged bundle to which the label 'Richard Rorty' applies (see Chapter 8 and below). He ought never to reach a point where he can achieve enough distance to establish the *ego*-identity he has unjustifiably presupposed for himself. To do so would require that he disembedded himself from his environment. That is, Rorty must be able to differentiate himself from that which is, for him, the non-self: society, the culture, the environment, and so forth. But Rorty's trade in the alleged impossibility to step back and gain the requisite point of view, godly or otherwise, prevents him from establishing any definitive boundary between his private self and that which is supposedly outside him in the social and the natural world.

Where can Rorty position himself so that he may be sure that there is a boundary between the two, himself and the non-self? It seems that the suspect standpoint of the rational objectivity is necessary not only to distinguish self from other-than-self, but to conceive of a self at all. Perhaps the creative poet is but one point, one node in that vigorous, extensive but solipsistic web. But then that web in all its aspects and with all its nodes would be, as implied in Rorty's writing, both his idiosyncratic vision of himself as the poetic crafter of narratives and the narrative of self as toolmaker, the result of evolutionary adaptation to the opposing socio-causal forces. His personal identification and the public description of self would be coextensive. In short, Rorty is the New Pragmatist just as Aristotle's ideal human was a Greek like himself, and New Pragmatism is Rorty, in the same way that the Transcendental Ego and its categories was Kant and his organizational idiosyncrasies.

The Loss of Perspective; the Loss of Voice

From this angle, the ability to gain perspective about one's culture, to analyse its shortcomings and to project a new linguistic construct to overcome its obstacles to pragmatic satisfaction – that is, to be an autonomous individual capable of offering utopian reform – seems to require more than a mere assertion that a sheltered private realm exists, for the claim itself might be a causal happening (and not an agent's act) due to the determination of evolutionary forces. That is, the autonomy necessary for critical evaluation cannot be understood as a simple matter of there being a cul-de-sac of idiosyncratically arranged beliefs and desires, a contingent system within the larger contingent system of society, all driven by an evolutionary impetus. While in self-assertion there might be relative liberty – immunity from 'outside' impediments and constraints – for individual systems to spin their webs, there cannot be freedom – the ability to discern with spontaneity – solely 'within' each individual system (see Chapter 8). Being an enclosed system (for example, a web of beliefs and desires labelled 'Rorty') should not include the reflexive fact that such a peculiar system happens *to be* independent of its environmental entrenchment, not from inside a Rortian perspective at least. The act of self-assertion should never include the discovery of the conditions of this fact of entrenchment; a Rortian self could never establish its *factual* embeddedness, for it is so firmly rooted in the Heraclitean flux as to not gain perspective on itself or its surroundings.

So an essential element in self-identity, that factually 'I am', cannot be accounted for by the Rortian self *per se*. The self is, at most, a cultural artifact, a definition imposed upon the individual by his society, a facticity. Then, defining the individual as a centred or a centre-less self would be a Darwinian struggle between rival utterances (algorithms of memes) and not a conceptual issue open to reflective conversation about what, if anything, is the 'nature' of selfhood.[6] Therefore, the necessary distance to evaluate critically one's personal condition of embeddedness and to decide which of the rival narratives *works* best for one's self ironically is missing from Rorty's pragmatic account; lodged as the Rortian 'self' is in a non-disquotational relationship to itself. Since there is no fact-of-the-matter about himself to counteract projections about himself by other poets, Rorty the ethnocentric must *always* decide in favour of his ultimate worldview (principally about centreless selves) or surrender his descriptive autonomy to these other narrators. Thus, Rorty can never be in the kind of error Davidson and Ramberg cited (in Chapter 1) as a necessary element for being a norm-following human.

Furthermore, to assert that a particular sort of self, the poet, is currently more authentic a metaphorical tool than its Enlightenment predecessor (the philosopher) or its Modern alternative (the scientist) on the basis of its utility might be an important insight for Rorty himself as a pragmatist. But to expand this claim into a critique of a large part of the intellectual world's manner of organizing its thinking into ontology and epistemology is for Rorty to move beyond the creation of a quixotic narrative and to believe in and engage in reformative powers of determinative debate with those other forms of life that lean on the Platonic–Cartesian–Kantian discriminations (that is, if he is attempting anything meaningfully interpersonal, and not merely ampliative, through his narrative). And by its nature, such a debate must be demonstrative if it hopes to be interpersonal. Yet, Rorty denies the efficacy of this philosophical approach. Still as a reformist, it appears that Rorty must adopt more of the Gadamerian position concerning a rational, non-polemic, interpenetration of horizons in order to transcend the cul-de-sac of idiosyncratically arranged beliefs and desires in which his narrative approach seems to lodge him.

Perhaps at this point Rorty may stir and say that I, Ed Grippe, am engaging in a strong misreading of him. But if I were to take Rorty seriously, by not misreading him and accepting that truth is relevant to a culture, and that unqualified 'right' and 'wrong' have become *passé* with the adoption of the neo-pragmatic language-game, then I cannot be accused of prevarication. I ought to be construed as a poet simply offering a different gloss, one that might or might not compete well in the struggle for logical space and semantic authority. I am confident he would agree and endorse my poetic licence. Nevertheless, Rorty could dismiss the importance of my offerings for himself. But he cannot dismiss it for anyone who has not joined their voice to his in paradigmatic solidarity. In short, ultimately Rorty can only speak for himself to those whose beliefs share a family resemblance to his own, and engage in eristic exchanges with others who do not stand within the space of his meta-narrative. Once he, as a neo-pragmatist, extends his thoughts to cover humanity not already part of his solidarity, he is being either paternalistic, hegemonic or philosophic. If he is being philosophical, he should, as I suggested, embrace the Gadamerian dialectic approach to hermeneutics (see Chapter 6). That is, Rorty ought to envision his web of belief (his 'fore-meaning') as not only projectable and contiguous to similar projections, but to be open to the projection of others as well in dialectic open foreplay; and to recognize that the give-and-take play of unforced dialogue opens us all to interpretation that reaches beyond isolation into an emerging common ground. That is, he, like Gadamer, ought to allow for the interplay of systems of belief beyond the Darwinian–Mendelian struggle for survival, and thus move beyond conversion to conversation, the kind of conversation that involves unforced dialogue, that is non-polemic at its core, to allow the possibility of general understanding or agreement, a *sensus communis*, as Habermas and McDowell[7] have suggested in their distinct ways. Otherwise, conversation becomes impossible in the polemicized environment, leading to the paternalism of manipulative persuasion, with its potential for humiliation and other more extreme forms of harm.

Why paternalism? Unforced dialogue requires an individual that has voice. And voice requires *free* agency. Rorty uses the rhetoric of freedom but fails to account adequately for this sort of self-determination beyond the royal 'we' as in the phrase 'we pragmatists'. Why is this so? My claim that for Rorty the idiosyncratic and the collective are coextensive can be linked with Rorty's zeal to eradicate the metaphor of privilege from late twentieth-/early twenty-first-century discourse about science and philosophy, based on the Jeffersonian model for the removal of religious beliefs from public policy. While in theory Rorty's reformist endeavour borrows its democratic flavour from the Jeffersonian model (itself derived from the Enlightenment's advocacy for equality over supremacy, and autonomy over conformity), Rorty's attempt cannot sustain itself as such because of his anti-essentialist stance.

Conant's Critique of Rortian 'Newspeak'

Equality of worth is the cornerstone of a liberal democracy. This insight must be a discovery about those who participate in the human community. For the participants, equal voice is not something that may be conferred upon them like membership in a church, or citizenship in a society, or association in a cultural solidarity. Voice is part of the participant's human 'inheritance'. James Conant offers three internally-linked, non-transcendent concepts necessary for human voice: freedom, community and truth. He argues that in the absence of this interlocking troika, an alternative triad arises: solitude, uniformity and an Orwellian double-think prevail (Conant 2000: 311). This latter threesome force upon those inculcated into an Orwellian social order barren conformity to a paternalistic meta-ideology that denies the very ability to reformulate language in ways that might threaten the veracity of that order. This is accomplished by relativizing truth; by reducing 'truth' to the status of empty compliments and by utilizing cautionary doubt as a method by which each individual replaces inconvenient memories with group 'justified' assertions. Conant associates Orwell's warning in *1984* about the dangers of socially caustic and depersonalizing totalitarian 'Newspeak' with Rorty's New Pragmatism project as far as Rorty wishes to instil a new vocabulary that excludes the possibility of meaningful language use associated with the onto-theological vocabulary of rival paradigms.[8]

Nevertheless, Rorty would have us believe that, to the contrary, democracy is to be made solely in the formation of a solidarity based on a shared vocabulary where one's opinion, community sentiments, and hence truth, coincide. He infers from the 'old coherentist chestnut'

... that you can only get at 'the facts' by way of conciliating beliefs, memory-images, desires, and the like – to the view that there is no procedure of 'justification in the light of the facts' which can be opposed to concilience of one's own opinion with those of others (Rorty, in Brandom 2000: 343).

Yet this take on justification within a democratic setting strikes me (as it did Fraser) as being more like admission into an exclusive country club which is anchored in a system dedicated to the conferring of nepotistic privilege; where inclusion is decided on the basis of some contingently historical criteria by those already in the club. Thus, one's value as an individual is determined by this status of inclusion (or exclusion). Rorty refuses to admit a basis for an encompassing communion (*sensus communis*) or a sense of belonging for who you *are*, essentially. With the elimination of a grounding core as an area where commensuration is possible, there emerges a paradoxical threat of a loss of the autonomy that is necessary either to avoid the tyranny of privileged superiority (i.e., become one of them) or to avoid conformity to its dictates (i.e., knee-jerk rebel against authority). The third Socratic option of autonomy as the social manifestation of an eternal principle is summarily ruled out of court.

Even if care is taken, with the abandonment of a centre, inequality must become the norm, ironically as exemplified by the neo-pragmatic tendency to be ethnocentric. The 'us over and against them' strategy employed by Rorty throughout his works plays into this divisive and potentially condescending tendency. It suggests that the elitist and excluding – and hence potentially cruel – aspects of the ironist cannot be contained in the private sphere. It leaks out to taint Rorty's entire public project, turning personal interests into rival ways of life. Rhetoric of liberal democracy and the equality of narratives only serve to mask Rorty's unspoken intent: to get what he wants and what he can 'get away with' with the current audience: a world ostensively pluralistic yet ultimately governed by the Singularism of the Rortian gloss.

Rorty's Singularism: Evolution

Let me expand further. Without grounding, democratic dialogue is transmuted into the Darwinian survival struggle, where the clever and the quick minds absorb the slow and the weak by means of a Calliclean power-play.[9] Rorty's role in this narrative is likewise transformed into one like that of a demagogue and not a democrat. He 'follows' by leading at the meta-meta-narrative level. If I may characterize the attitude as follows: 'I want only what you want. And this is what you want ...' This attitude might be innocent enough and perhaps a courageous assertion for a person who is committed to the discovery of that essential way of being which will bring all of us, including the speaker, personal and societal satisfaction. However, when the hope for a *sensus communis* has been discarded, that same assertion assumes a less altruistic and more egoistic character;[10] it becomes a Sartrean projection of the idiosyncratic lifeworld – in this case, Rorty's – as an authentic mode of life to be considered as a plausible narrative for humanity. The 'I want only want you want ...' assertion self-consciously identifies a paradigm with one's personal creation rather than locating one's vocabulary within a 'naturally occurring' paradigm (a.k.a.: The One Reality). This, of course, is a valid source of invention and innovation, one that Copernicus and Galileo chose to follow when they questioned the validity (and objective truth) of the entrenched 'natural' Aristotelian theories of their times. And while such acts of creativity in others are overtly lauded by Rorty, and even encouraged by him on the narrative level, covertly he must be careful to isolate and camouflage his most basic premise from future intellectual Vandals lest they, in their own act of creation, sack and burn not only his metaphoric construct and the meta-narrative he has been using (as he readily and consistently expects them to as part of his meta-narrative) but also the Singularist paradigm set above both by which the narratives and meta-narratives of past, present and future are to be narrowly framed, that is in exclusively pluralist terms.

Let me clarify even further. *If* Rorty is to be true to his own narrative, his interpretation of God, the world and the self must be as 'mythical' − a contingent artifact of his time, place and culture − as any of the theories he dismisses. As such, his story is compelling only if we, the readers, make it so through the lending of our belief to it. We must become the *paparazzi* − the sustaining force of a transient image − for his narrative. This is so because, consistent with Rorty's own belief, his narrative cannot have any inner power, no extra-lingual force (see Chapter 1), or duration beyond its current popular (aesthetic) appeal. Paradoxically, for Rorty's narrative to work there must appear to be more to his project than the touching on the periphery of 'centerless networks of beliefs and desires' (see relevant Rorty quote above). And that 'more' must appear to involve a motivating dynamism that goes beyond his words as auditory disturbances of the eardrum or as graphite scratches on paper to reach and influence the minds of others. In short, there must be, or *appear to be*, a sharing of meaning at the narrative level among different interpretative groups. For otherwise without an impelling force (not unlike the power of self-evidence associated with a necessary truth), Rortian vocabulary would be less than the babble of babes in its power to motivate change in others (i.e., conversion to a new paradigm), in that, unlike Rorty's self-consciously contingent professions, a baby's evolutionary-tested cute prattle might ensure our concern for her survival. So, to sustain his point of view, Rorty must create the appearance of 'impelling force' similar to the physical energy found within the theories of Galileo, Newton and Einstein, and of the psychological impetus Descartes putatively discovered in the 'Cogito ergo sum' insight, in order to promote and sustain his foundation-less meta-narrative. To this end he associates his narrative and meta-narrative with evolution itself, and the notion of purposeless production of diversity as the creative force in the universe. He is attempting to ride the horse as the horse runs on its own. That is, he speaks as if Darwin's theory is yet another image created by the coping human mind and that this creativity is *in fact* part of the evolutionary adaptation mechanism. Thus the claim sitting behind his meta-narrative of New Pragmatism is that regardless of the growth or the demise of his and all other meta-narratives, he has identified and articulated the confluence of human thought and random evolution. This is his paradigm: a conversion to the Darwinian future 'to produce an ever-expanding profusion of new sorts of human lives, new kinds of human beings' (Rorty 1999a: 269).

In summary, in making the case for anti-foundationalism, Rorty must resort *at the end of the day* to the rhetoric of Singularism that is designed to contain and anchor assumptions about the world and ourselves in the very way his New Pragmatism strongly denies is possible. Rorty's approach is like a marketing strategy that creates the appearance of an endless Multiplism, while cleverly prodding us to a singular consensus about the unfeasibility of convergent consensus on the basis of evolution as an open-ended flux of diversity in and among individuals.[11] To deny his thesis without supplying criteria for the acceptance of truth in its disquotational form, an omission that Rorty thinks Conant is culpable for, appears to reinforce the Rortian Multiplist perspective. That is, to deny the truth even about the realism of evolution as Rorty does, to treat it as yet another intuitive image, is to reinforce the notions supporting evolutionary forces driving both the intuition and all counterintuitions as *fact*.

An Odd Sort of Fact

This is an odd sort of fact, however. It seems to allow Rorty to effectively be an anti-essentialist and anti-foundationalist while keeping Conant's idea of the facts of the matter alive. How is this possible? John McDowell attempts to answer this question.

McDowell suggests a refinement of Putnam's internal realism by offering a distinction that actually makes Rorty, Putnam *and* Kant allies! (McDowell, in Brandom 2000: 112). He attempts this feat by distinguishing the fear of a contingent life and the subsequent appeal to a Freudian, father ike force that provides us with iron-clad answers and norms to live up to *from* the desire to have us answerable to the way things are. McDowell suggests that Kant too wished to combat the denial of human finitude and the consequent withdrawal from contingency into the safety of an eternal realm by claiming that *appearance* was not a barrier preventing us from gazing at reality objectively but is the very reality we as rational human beings aspire to know. In this way McDowell thinks that Kant, admittedly anti-metaphysical, was as anti-priesthood as Dewey – extending the Protestant Reformation's idiosyncratic connection to a non-human reality into Philosophy – and in line with Rorty's anti-epistemology stance, in that we are always ensconced within the human frame of reference. The upshot of McDowell's distinction of objectivity from epistemic escapism is that even as we are located inextricably within a meta-narrative there can be joined a unified discourse where the combination of a disquotational, descriptive use of the word 'true' and the use of 'true' that treats this term as a norm of inquiry is possible (McDowell, in Brandom 2000: 116–17).

Persistently, Rorty resists McDowell's notion of objectivity in favour of solidarity. He stays with the belief that we can make ourselves answerable to only the verdicts of our fellows and not any facts in themselves. Rorty believes that when consensus evades interlocutors, as it must when they do not share a common vocabulary, the advocates for objectivity attempt to assure themselves with the conviction that the grounds for consensus exist even when ambiguity and shortsightedness are rife among interpreters. Rorty offers that such a position embraces the idea of climbing outside our minds and into a 'God's-eye' perspective. The question 'Did X happen?' and the question 'Can saying X happened pass muster in the current practice' are not the same question and seem to demand two norms: a sociological norm and one that appears to be independent of social practice. But, Rorty continues, that is a difference that makes no difference. There are not two norms, only one. Upon close inspection the objective norm is reducible to the sociological norm (Rorty, in Brandom 2000: 125).

But why can't we hold McDowell's and Rorty's views simultaneously? We are embedded in our time and place, governed by some sociological norm unable to deny our finitude, not capable of climbing out of our minds to a supermundane standpoint. Yet we make this observation as if we can step outside our current condition, avoid Goodman's *Grue Argument*, and state that our current condition is the human condition for the duration of the existence of the race. We seem to be embedded and able to transcend this entrenchment somehow.

The last observation leads directly to the more basic question: What prevents Singularism and Multiplism from profitably interfacing? The Multiplist would argue that a plurality of perspectives would be undermined if there were a definitive interpretation in place to be a standard against which all other interpretations would be measured and hierarchically ordered. The only way for this situation to be avoided is to accept that there is no privileged interpretation, no one perspective that has access to what is real and thus coincides with what is the one and only truth. But this view then rises to be the standard by which we judge all other interpretations, rejecting all views that claim to be singularly correct and true. To sidestep this obvious performance contradiction we may allow all forms of interpretation, letting popular opinion decide from the plethora of language-games which one best serves them at the present moment. But popular opinion sometimes can be enormously destructive to the health and mental well-being of individuals.

But why care about anyone other than oneself and significant members in one's life? Could this extended care be motivated by self-interest? This appeal to the extension of self-interest will only work if one is personally at risk, or perceives a threat to one's interests (including peace of mind). When there is no perception of risk then there will be no concern for the pain and humiliation suffered by the other due to a lack of awareness. The promotion of the utilitarian goal of human happiness, approvingly cited by Rorty as the key reason for his placing the pursuit of truth as a tributary purpose in *Philosophy and Social Hope*, will seldom be applied as a general principle, but usually as a personal aim for oneself and those of which one is aware and attached to in some way. So the happiness of persons and their community can be made a pragmatic aim and still be narrowly ethnocentric. But the need then is to expand the ethno-centric sense of the communal 'we' to include an ever-increasing number of others. Why? Again, could it be enlightened self-interest? But what if there are some who firmly believe that their true happiness is the submission of individual self-interest to some greater spiritual or ideological entity in direct opposition to your 'enlightened' sense of self-interest? Is this not part of the bliss-producing 'ever-expanding profusion of new sorts of human lives, new kinds of human beings'? If not, why not? Is it because this mode of life is Singularist in its intent and thus a dam to the flow of the 'infinity of equally valuable ways to lead a human life' (Rorty 1999a: 268)? As noted in Chapter 1, Multiplism may have appeal to singularity of interpretation. But this is peculiar because the Multi-plist opposition to any Singularist position must contain a conviction that there is not an equality of value among *all* the ways to lead a human life. The Multi-plist must limit the infinite number of worthy forms of life to some finite number. In addition, the criterion for limitation must assume a selective plurality based on the utilitarian good of human happiness as conceived by the Multiplist himself. And does not the Multiplist's perspective then carry with it an air of authoritative morality that extends beyond simple preference to call for social reform and human progress? And is this not ethical Singularism under the guise of Multiplism?

This is where even Rorty must stand both inside and outside his embedded perspective. He must advocate Multiplism and the poetic freedoms it implies as a singular goal. To be creative, one must project oneself beyond the confines of the present context. Therefore, to reject McDowell's view on objectivity, Rorty must argue not only that his, McDowell's, view does not pass muster within Rorty's interpretation, but that it can no longer be maintained as a viable position *per se* among the current audience. Yet since Rorty acknow-ledges that most people agree with McDowell that Rorty is missing the point concerning objectivity, Rorty's interpretation of justification as solidarity is the abnormal narrative, as 'mad' as Loyola's or Nietzsche's to contemporary society. Thus to challenge innovatively the present understanding with abnor-mal language, Rorty must step beyond the limits of the moment and consciously create a new way of life. This move obliges something that Rorty has at times seemed to deny and at times seemed to require: a self capable of mundane trans-cendence of the current context to a wholly new state of affairs that nevertheless is open to convergent consensus around that illusively odd fact. Perhaps due to a pre-existing physicalist prejudice – for I would scarcely think it was a lack of nerve or imagination – Rorty takes back into his pragmatism elements which he has thought he had discarded: the dogmatism associated with religion; the philosophical tendency for privilege by 'treating the self as something one "has"'; the systemization of the self and disassociation of power from a lived human life prevalent in representationalist theory. By doing so, Rorty demon-strates first-hand the necessity and the pitfalls of the use of language.

Much like New Pragmatism itself, language serves to pull individuals into close proximity as it erects simultaneously the barriers that prevent their achieving commonality. Thus, while a pragmatic analysis of the self might throw useful light on much of our human desires and preferences, the discussion itself must also distance the experience from the encountering 'I' at the moment the former is conveyed and/or the latter is described in language. Therefore, despite all his protests to the contrary, the ultimate inconsistency of Rorty's narrative is that it is an attempt by different means to stand apart and elude the embedding effects of language and culture while decrying all such attempts. This ability to achieve an observer standpoint is embraced by Rorty at the moment he pens his *determinative* reasons for the rejection for its very possibility. For as he writes he does not simply fabricate an abstraction often labelled 'the self', but he asserts his unique presence in the act of self-generation. This kind of authorship requires a platform that is more significant than can be found in the redefining of a vocabulary about the public and the poet for mere ampliative reasons. And it requires a centrality that is beyond any (meta-)theoretical posit.

Let me first explain the need for a platform by way of an allegory:

Imagine a hall of mirrors. You have never experienced anything other than the hall. On every mirror, no two of which are alike, is reflected your image in a unique fashion. For a long while you entertain doubt; you are not sure which of those images really represents you. But suddenly you realize that while some reflections are contrasting in their appearance they are all of you. Soon thereafter you begin to believe that there is nothing more to yourself than those reflections in the contingently arranged hall, for this is all you have ever encountered. Moreover, the hall turns out to be nothing more than the sequence of these mirrors. With this realization it seems that the distinctions between the sequenced reflectors and the multifarious reflections of yourself on them fade. As this happens, you believe that at your pleasure you can play with the images, thinking now that they are part of the mirrors and alternatively that they are more independent of them, and that, perhaps, collectively they are you and that the mirrors are defined by the play of your dancing images. You are liberated by the thought that there is no outer and no inner, only the creative play of images looked at this way or taken that way according to the dictates of your fancy and desires.

There is a problem within this allegory. How were you sure that the image in the mirror was you? What made the image stand out as a self-image and not merely an integral part of the looking-glass? Furthermore, if somehow an *ad hoc* distinction was made between image and object, how could you be sure that the quasi-independent image was you, and not an epiphenomenon of the system of mirrors, or some other presence altogether? Again, how could you ever be sure you were ever seeing yourself (-selves) and not someone else's projection which you mislabelled, or, for that matter, even a cardboard cut-out caricature of you placed between you and the mirror by someone out to redefine you?

If we take the system of mirrors to be alternatively the 'world' or one's home culture, and the collective images to be the Rortian self as a centreless web of beliefs, and furthermore, the substitute projection and the caricature of you as society's initial contributions to 'self-image', then as the allegory plays out, it ought to become obvious what is missing from this analogy – *you* as the focal ground or platform for the appreciation of the images and as the wellspring of the creative projection of word and world. Without you in the sense of your first-person (perhaps mysterious) origin of self-awareness, there could never be self-assertion or self-creation (see above). Our identities would be hopelessly embedded in utterances, absorbed by the mirrors of culture produced by the utterances of other equally unaware 'selves' as surely as when, in total oblivion, a lower primate encounters its image unaware that the reflection in the looking-glass is its own. Therefore, I conclude that Rorty, despite a valiant effort, has missed his mark. Upon close inspection, the basis for his anti-foundational narrative concerning the self is undercut by his inadvertent underscoring of the expectation of centredness when his insistence to the contrary is played out to its own logical conclusions.

A 'Hovering' Truth

And with the possibility of some kind of centred self, the possibility for a *sensus communis* re-emerges. But we ought not to reinvent the representationalist's epistemology. Rather, it would profit us guardedly to embrace Rortian Pragmatism, Kantian epistemology, Platonic Forms, and the rest of the creative and well-constructed *logoi* which human minds have fashioned. These constructs are but signposts on the road to further inquiry.

'What about your own attempt in this book,' the reader may now ask. 'Are you not appealing to an audience with the arguments offered in your text? Does this not play to Rorty's claim about the sociological nature of inquiry and justification?' The answer must be Yes and No! That is my point. What has been taken to be definitive as a Singularist claim is the *having* of a philosophy, having a perspective that cannot be set aside by any audience. For Kant that would be the expectation. For Rorty it would not, yet there it is, he 'has' his new paradigm of evolutionary plurality. But the *doing* of philosophy requires first-person participation and third-person perspectives that curve back upon one's personal perspective(s) (web[s] of belief). A hermeneutics of meaning is to be found holistically in the pattern of narratives in play and not in the individual narratives themselves, mine or anyone else's. This reflective review may be achieved in an atmosphere free from polemics, one that assumes Davidsonian Charity and thus is conducive to non-eristic interpersonal dialogue. And while Davidson's Charity alone cannot narrow the possible interpretations of the blind press of causality, his notion of triangulation (discussed in Chapter 1) holds the promise of a greater concilience. Ironically, Rorty inadvertently gestures towards the sense of triangulation that opens to convergent consensus when he writes:

McDowell would be right to point out that I should not speak of 'norms of our peers'. It was a mistake to locate the norms at one corner of [Davidson's] triangle – where my peers are – rather than seeing them as, so to speak, *hovering over* the whole process of triangulation ... It is not that my peers have more to do with my obligations to say snow is white than the snow does, or I do (Rorty in Brandom 2000: 376; italics added).

Isn't the sense of 'hovering', *pace* classical Rorty, a location of a second norm beyond the 'norms of my peers'? If triangulation is to work, triangulation cannot be a concept permanently lodged in a paradigm, for that would return us to the singular peer-driven norm of solidarity and its attendant issues. And yet, triangulation *is* local to a meta-narrative, i.e., Davidson's now redefined by Rorty. We are caught in a paradox only if we follow Rorty and limit language to being a tool that is instrumental. Words can also be used intentionally, not to some transcendent idealization separate from the mundane, but to an emergent character drawn from the pulse or pattern of theory formation and destruction. It is in the construction and deconstruction of theories through non-competitive dialogue among peers and by the recalcitrance of the world that truth emerges, hovers if you will, over the entire enterprise of human thought and action.

For example, McDowell, Habermas and the later Putnam insist that while situated in the world we can reach beyond solidarity and converge on objective truth through the active exchange of interpretations. Rorty and Nelson Goodman consider talk about such things as intersubjective agreement to be locally entrenched and unavoidably transitory. Both camps have the partial picture and neither has the last word on the matter. While no narrative captures Reality-in-itself, each narrative contributes to an emergence of the pattern of meaning, hence truth. This truth remains fully shrouded within any given use of language, but, with a nod to Kripke, as a particular language-game is offered, reinterpreted and ultimately deconstructed by successive linguistic communities, the extra-linguistic referent, the emergent truth, is unconcealed. What emerges is wisdom, which is neither reducible to one or the other *logoi* and 'hence so far transcends the interlocutors' subjective opinions that even the person leading the conversation knows that he does not know'.

Like defining an invisible force field such as a black hole by observing the stars that surround it, the very stars that were born from this dynamic void and into which they will fall to be destroyed in a process that sustains the black hole, it is only with the backdrop of competing paradigmatic Singularisms that arise in search of clarity of thought and are destroyed in the light of valid criticism that Truth can be identified in profile but never completely and finally. There will always be the outpourings of the human mind that will help bring truth from the shadows to hover over us again and again in original, surprising and iconoclastic insights.

Additionally, the hermeneutical circle of meta-narratives allows for there to be the Multiplism Rorty notices when the focus is on each language-game individually or as part of a solidarity, while simultaneously permitting the contextual objectivity which Habermas, Conant and McDowell appreciate when attention shifts to that which 'hovers' over the totality of language-games, allowing for what may be construed as a *sensus communis*.

The obvious Rortian reaction to what I have just written is that it is simply another attempt to have a final word on the matter; to end the conversation by proving that I have identified the solution to the problem vexing critics and supporters of Rorty's New Pragmatism. This work ought to be considered and set aside as another one of many attempts to treat truth as a non-human power; a simply intuitive image of a mind that is insecure with the finality and contingency of human life.[12] This pseudo-Freudian critique is correct in one way: what I have written is a mental construct, one among many, more than a few quite superior to what I offer. Nevertheless, if the critique is to have any bite it must assume that I am more than a causal event amenable to auto-manipulation, and that the area for discussion between us is open to an exchange of determinative reasons. Even with these two assumptions the critic may argue that I am wrong in some substantial way, that I am in error about truth as the emergent property, or what I say is useless for our times and in need of serious retooling. To be more than an ampliative statement, this criticism must involve a genuine engagement between interlocutors that assumes an overlapping of interpretations and a field around which to play off each other to reveal the errors in logic or in tool application. In short, we must struggle with each other and the topic in the hope that through the fissures in our idio-syncratic narratives (Davidson–Ramberg notion of error) a shared awakening to that which is recurrently manifesting itself in dialogue *through* the correctives offered by sincere critics will occur.

Otherwise, if the critique is based solely upon ampliative reasons, especially in one's meta-meta narrative, the voicing of this aesthetic preference must pose as a series of determinative statements to win over the undecided (in a way par-allel to Bok's comments on freedom and selective determinism cited in Chapter 7). But this 'gimmick' underscores the importance of communal truth-seeking, and helps to frame the need for concilience in lieu of attempts to dominate opin-ion through stealth semantic Singularism and the demagoguery it spawns. Without such a ruse ampliative reason takes on the character of a passing remark about one's partiality for certain weather conditions, which is a substi-tution of habitual utterings for genuine conversation. For these reasons, the Jef-fersonian priorities of social tolerance and personal liberty Rorty has set for the New Pragmatism cannot be realized through Rortian narrative.

And with this inherent incoherence in Rorty's writings, the criticism Rorty directs towards Kant noted at the outset of this work can be reapplied to Rorty's New Pragmatism. The basis for Rorty's pragmatic narrative is ulti-mately the Singularist assertion that the evolutionary thrust therein depicted and expressed must itself fall prey to its own aesthetic and historicist critique in the same way that it is applied to Kantian theory *if* Rorty's writings, as I claim, are made as determinative reasons by a self-conscious individual. If this is not the case then the meta-narrative Rorty offers becomes merely a series of ampliative statements that can be appreciated as museum-piece art and not the leading edge of a paradigm shift. Thus a reevaluation of Rorty's Jeffersonian Strategy at the core of his New Pragmatism seems necessary and appropriate concerning not only the de-centered self but also with regard to the concept of solidarity as a replacement for objectivity in setting social practices.

Notes

Chapter 1

1. 'Dewey between Hegel and Darwin' in Rorty 1998: 293–94.
2. See 'Hilary Putnam and the Relativist Menace', in Rorty 1998: 48.
3. 'Charles Taylor on Truth' in Rorty 1998: 86.
4. 'Dewey between Hegel and Darwin', in Rorty 1998: 292.
5. See 'Pragmatist's Progress: Umberto Eco on Interpretation', in Rorty 1999a: 134.
6. Rorty believed that '. . . nothing counts as justification unless by reference to what we already accept, and there is no way to get outside our beliefs and our language so as to find some test other than coherence' (Rorty 1979: 178).
7. 'Is Truth a Goal of Inquiry? Donald Davidson versus Crispin Wright', in Rorty 1998: 28.
8. Rorty asserts: 'It is futile for human communities to ask, "Is our recent political history, the one we summarized in a narrative of gradual progress, taking us in the right direction?" as it would have been for squirrels to ask whether their evolution from shrews has been going in the right direction. Squirrels do what is best by their lights, and so do we. Both of us have been moving in the direction of what seems, by our respective lights, more flexibility, more freedom, and more variety' (Rorty 1998: 304).
9. See Rorty's take on the difference between the carpenter and the scientist (Davidson 1984: 41).
10. Davidson 1990b: 136. See also Davidson's views on 'Plato's Philosopher' and 'The Socratic Concept of Truth' respectively, in Davidson 2005: 240 and 249.
11. Rorty 1999a: 131. Additionally, in *Truth, Language, and History*, Davidson discusses Plato's struggles with the Socratic elenchus. Claiming that the elenchus as a process will yield not only consistency but truth, Davidson argues that if we assume that the elenchus ensures that among beliefs that are inconsistent there resides a false belief, and that in a coherent set of beliefs there exists 'unshakable true beliefs inconsistent with the false', then we can be confident that the method elenchus leads to the truth without forcing us to adopt one, commensurate truth. See also Davidson 2005: 239. Yet Rorty will say that we still can propose which 'truths' work for us now. Therefore if there is an inconsistency in his views, Charity fails in his case.
12. Rorty cites the work of Davidson which challenges the whole notion of the dichotomy of scheme and content – and therefore of competing conceptual frameworks – to call into question the 'obsession' with the need (Rorty 1982: 13) to ground our beliefs in some sort of foundational conceptual base. This criticism revolves around Davidson's notion of 'charity' in 'radical interpretation'. To commence communication between oneself and the members of another language group, or linguistic sub-grouping within one language, there must be supposed a

substantial number of background beliefs between the subject and the interpreter. This follows from the claim that 'knowledge of beliefs comes only with the ability to interpret words', and from a reasonable conviction based upon evolutionary theory that the majority of one of its member's beliefs could not be false. Hence, it is only possible to assume a widespread accord exists among beliefs taken as a whole between would-be communicants, as Davidson observes: 'Charity is forced on us; whether we like it or not, if we want to understand others, we must count them right in most matters' (1984: 196).

Thus, neither the posit of the 'world' as an independent thing-in-itself, nor the hypothesis of a common conceptual matrix necessary for the guarantee of rational autonomy and universality, is needed. The derivability of alternative frameworks (meta-narratives) is thereby eliminated as well, in favour of the view which takes differences among language-games as relatively minor adjustments to the rather large set of common beliefs currently being held. Correspondence theories drop out in favour of interpenetrating rationales.

Yet the spectre of relativism is not realized, according to Rorty. By adopting a restated version of Davidson's position, Rorty, in saying that 'only the world determines truth', is suggesting that we take this sentence fragment in the liberal Deweyan sense of a 'funded experience' – those beliefs which are not being challenged at this moment – while steadfastly maintaining that there is no distinction between scheme and content. To do otherwise, to label 'the world' as the given 'sense-data', 'the sensual manifold' or 'stimuli', which stands over and against the manner in which these are received and spontaneously organized and represented, is to move well within some specific epistemological theory, and out of the realm of the transcendental metaphysics. We again find ourselves dislodged from the illusory role of independent arbiter of truth and thoroughly planted within a given cultural paradigm where interpenetration among paradigms is impossible. Yet, we are not drawn into scepticism, for while overarching standards supporting representationalism are abandoned, Rorty does not desert the belief that there is justified solidarity around a historically preferred vocabulary of a specific community.

13. 'Is Truth a Goal of Inquiry?' in Rorty 1998: 26.
14. With a different focus, but in the same vein, see Rorty 1999a: xxxii.
15. 'I stoutly deny thinking that Darwin describes reality, or even just us human beings, better than anybody else. But his way of describing human beings, when supplemented ... by a story about cultural evolution, does *give us a useful gimmick* to prevent people from overdramatizing dichotomies and thereby generating philosophical problems' (Rorty 1998: 152; emphasis added).
16. D. Davidson, 'Three Varieties of Knowledge' in Davidson 2001: 207.
17. 'Once God and his view goes, there is just us and our view', insulated against a God surrogate by what Sartre called 'a consistent atheism' (Rorty 1998: 54). Yet I contest that Rorty does invent a God surrogate through his appeal to an anti-metaphysical and anti-epistemological 'atheism'. This is a Rortian faith; a faith that dismisses as meaningless all but unfettered creative production that is fit for the environment, the meaning of which is also subject to the same creative thrusts.
18. For Heraclitus to assert that 'All is change' he had to leave open the possibility that this sentence will alter to become its own opposite – the Parmenidean claim that 'All is Stability'. When pushed to its logical conclusion, this Heraclitian transformation would render all language meaningless due to its radical interpretative instability.

Chapter 2

1. Starting with Thales, Western civilization has been focused upon the search for the *arcte* – the origin or source – of all things by the use of a reasoned account or *logos*. It is this search that Rorty claims is wrong-headed.

2. Rorty says: 'It is the notion that human activity (and inquiry, the search for knowledge in particular) takes place within a framework which can be isolated prior to the conclusion of inquiry – a set of presuppositions discoverable *a priori* – which links contemporary philosophy to the Descartes-Locke-Kant tradition. For the notion that there is such a framework only makes sense if we think of his framework as imposed by the nature of the knowing subject, by the nature of his faculties . . .' (Rorty 1979: 8–9).

3. An interesting take on the original Copernican revolution is offered by Michael Polanyi in Chapter 1 of his 1958 book, *Personal Knowledge*. He presents an anthropocentric account of objectivity as lying in a greater intellectual satisfaction derived from abstract theories. Applied to Kant's revolution, we see the spirit of the Copernican enterprise in Polanyi's remarks, even if the latter's definition of objectivity might have been questioned by Kant (Polanyi 1958: 3–4).

4. Rorty observes: 'Instead of seeing ourselves as quasi-Newtonian machines, hoping to be compelled by the right inner entities and thus to function according to nature's design for us, Kant let us see ourselves as deciding (numenally, and hence unconsciously) what nature was to be allowed to be like' (Rorty 1979: 161).

5. Samuel Stumph states that the Newtonian explanation of the world, which threatened to both absorb human freedom and the notion of God into a mechanical universe *and* open the way to the problems raised by Hume that placed in jeopardy the justification of scientific knowledge, were dealt with by Kant's recognition that '. . . in principle scientific knowledge is similar to metaphysical knowledge, and, therefore, the justification or explanation of scientific thought on the one hand and metaphysical thought concerning freedom and morality on the other are the same . . . *Both in science and metaphysics, the mind starts with some given datum, which gives rise to a judgement in human reason*' (emphasis added) (1988: 302). I place emphasis upon Stumph's last sentence because I believe with him that at the root of these separate faculties of the mind in the Kantian system, Kant must assume that there is the same sort of human judgement common to them both. This is crucial, for it allows a thinker like Rorty to make the critical collapse of pure understanding into practical reason, and then slide from practical reason to aesthetic judgements (i.e., from the must to the ought to the *sensus communis*). As I will argue in a later chapter of this present work, that once accomplished, it is but a small step for Rorty to move from the *sensus communis* to his view of 'solidarity', thereby, in his estimation, disposing of the need for Kantian reason while dismantling the tripartite division of science, morality and art.

6. Wolfgang Kersting, in the first page of his article 'Politics, Freedom, and Order: Kant's Political Philosophy', makes optimistic reference to the relation of the law of reason to autonomy. See Kersting, in Guyer (1992: 342).

7. Onora O'Neill's contribution to *A Companion to Ethics* entitled 'Kantian Ethics' lends support to the idea of the supremacy of practical reason in the following way:

    'We must see ourselves both as part of the natural world and as free agents. We cannot without incoherence do without either of these standpoints, although we cannot integrate them, and can do no more than understand that they are compatible. On such a reading, we can have no insight into the "mechanics" of human freedom, can understand that without freedom in the activity of cognition, which lies behind our very claim to know, a causally ordered world would be unknown to us. Hence it is impossible for us to think freedom away' (O'Neill 1991: 181).

8. Kant offers the analogy of Reason as a judge compelling nature to answer questions posed on Reason's terms in Kant (1965: 20).

9. This is Wartenberg's point when he says: 'Kant does think that these [transcendental] ideas can be salvaged, so long as we understand that what they refer to is not an actually existing object, but rather a type of systematic unity among the knowledge that we do have.' See Wartenberg, in Guyer 1992: 245–46).

10. As Rorty notes (1991a: 83), 'Kant's point [is] that you can't compare your beliefs with something that isn't a belief to see if they correspond.'

11. See Chapter 1's discussion of Ramberg's critique of Rorty on this point.

12. In an autobiographical article from 1992 entitled 'Trotsky and the Wild Orchids' (in Rorty 1999a: 3–20), Rorty recounts his failed attempt to bring to life by way of Plato and Kant a phrase from W. B. Yeats, 'hold reality and justice in a single vision', by the merging into his life's narrative the feeling of a numinous presence, 'something of ineffable importance' with a Trotskyite socialist's desire for justice, that of liberation of the oppressed from their exploiters. Ultimately Rorty despaired of finding the neutral standpoint from which competing first principles could be appraised. He later moved to what Krausz has termed the Multiplist position, unhinging the striving for a just world from the claims of that world being necessarily part and parcel of the fibres of the universe and hitching them to the persuasive power of social justification.

13. Rorty provides a helpful illustration of conflicting intuitions (Kantian and Mystical) (1979: 154, n. 36).

14. BonJour, in an effort to preserve as rational the appeal to *a priori* intuitive apprehensions, offers sophistic and political means to ameliorate clashes between conflicting intuitions. Ironically, persuasion rather than an arrival at a *sensus communis* seems operative in his suggestion. See BonJour (1985: 209); see also note 17 below, and Chapter 5.

15. Kant must concur that there are erroneous intuitions, for when in arguing for his own project he is obliged to challenge as fallible other thinkers' intuitions, those of Newton's and Hume's.

16. In response to Ramberg's clarification of Davidson's views, Rorty concedes two major Sellarian claims: '. . . that "true" and "refers" do not name word-world relations' [and that it cannot be] 'that all our relations to the world are causal relations. I shall instead have to say that there are certain word-world relations which are neither causal nor representational – for instance, the relation "true of" which holds between "Snow is white" and snow, and the relation "refers to" which holds between "snow" and snow'. Nevertheless, Rorty holds firm to his pragmatic outlook: 'I can epitomize up [sic] what I have been saying as follows: What is true in pragmatism is that what you talk about depends not on what is real but on what it pays you to talk about. What is true in realism is that most of what you talk about you get right. Would there still be snow if nobody had ever talked about it? Sure. Why? Because according to the norms we invoke when we use "snow", we are

supposed to answer affirmatively. (If you think that glib and ethnocentric answer is not good enough that is because you are still in the grip of the scheme-content distinction. You think you can escape the inescapable, cut off one corner of Davidson's triangle, and just ask about a relation called "correspondence" or "representation" between your beliefs and the world)' (Rorty, in Brandom 2000: 374).

17. For example, when one considers Kantian beauty, whether encountered in the aesthetics of a stained-glass window or in the elegance and simplicity of a theory in physics, it seems to involve 'a sense of satisfaction, but one that is distinct from the fulfillment of any desire, or even from the satisfaction accruing to moral excellence. It is a satisfaction for itself, as it were. Beauty gives its own intrinsic fulfillment. The goal is internal' (Taylor 1991: 64). Within the Kantian picture the judgement of a theory in physics must be augmented by the logic of the categories to produce universal and objective assent to its propositions, while the non-conceptual aesthetic experience must rely solely upon a subjective principle based on feelings and not concepts, which, nevertheless, is universalized through common sense (*sensus communis*). Such 'judgement of taste' may not find agreement among various individuals, but everyone ought to agree to it (see Stumph 1988: 323). The universal necessity extends only to the person who appreciates, delights in, the beauty as such, however, if the anti-foundational intuition, as herein outlined in accordance with Rorty's views, is coherent. Any attempt to project this 'cognized' sense of necessity on to another, especially for her own aesthetic enhancement, is to act paternalistically. At worst, the *sensus communis* (akin to peer pressure) would be an imperialist tool used for the suppression of all rival opinions. At best, the *sensus communis* would boil down to a contingent solidarity among those with like values and interests. All pretences to a subjective convergence about universalized feeling would be abandoned as metaphysical speculation. A more considered discussion about Kant's *sensus communis* can be found in Chapter 5 of the present work.

Chapter 3

1. I will reserve the term 'paradigm' for what I will later refer to as meta-meta-narratives, using 'meta-narratives' to refer to what Harris and Rorty are calling paradigms.
2. Rorty has no issue with the grouping of science with art or music. The language of science becomes one of many voices available when different tastes from communities of people's sex, race or culture preferences are open to active consideration. Therefore, as far as Rorty is concerned, criticism such as Harris's misses the mark. Nevertheless, someone like Krausz who finds agreement with Rorty does not endorse the Nelson Goodman stance against The Way the World Is realism, repeatedly cited by Rorty as support for his brand of anti-essentialism (Krausz, in Ritivoi 2003: 347).
3. Goodman's desire to relinquish the possibility of ever designing a procedure or set of criteria which will yield the confirmation of a theory through its correspondence to a world with an underlying 'reality' has been lauded by Rorty, who calls Goodman 'maverick', a term of commendation (see Rorty 1982: 192).
4. In the chapter entitled 'The "Justification" of Induction' from his work, *An Introduction to Logical Theory*, P. F. Strawson argues for the inability to establish a justification for induction modelled upon, and tied to, the deductive method. In this he

underscores Goodman's concept of 'entrenchment', noting as meaningless any attempt to legitimize contingent 'regularities' by grounding them in bedrock rationality (Strawson 1968: 450).

> 'But to what standards are we appealing when we ask whether the application of inductive standards is justified or well grounded? If we cannot answer, then no sense has been given to the question. Compare it with the question: Is the law legal? It makes perfectly good sense to inquire of a particular action, of an administrative regulation, or even in the case of some states, of a particular enactment of the legislature, whether or not it is legal. The question is answered by an appeal to a legal system, by the application of a set of legal (or constitutional) rules or standards. But it makes no sense to inquire in general whether the law of the land, the legal system as a whole, is or is not legal. For to what legal standards are we appealing?' (Strawson 1968: 450).

5. Rorty believes that Kuhn himself contributed to his own criticism. Claiming that Kuhn's main point – that no algorithm for theory-choice was possible except 'one which constructed an epistemology on the basis of the vocabulary or assumptions of the winning side in a scientific dispute' – was obscured by his 'idealistic-sounding agenda' (Rorty 1979: 324).
6. A trial by ordeal was a method of justice based on the assumption that God would guarantee, after subjection to arduous physical trials, the survival of the individual who was in the truth and had a just claim. Rorty, of course, rejects this approach in the intellectual sphere as well. 'The notion of "rational support" is not apropos when it comes to proposals to retain, or to abandon, intuitions or hopes as deep-lying as those to which theists, realists, and anti-representationalists appeal' (Rorty 1999b: 5).
7. *Pace* Harris's defence of method, see Rorty (1999b: 15).
8. Rorty finds support in Hume's view of sentiment over epistemological concerns. See Rorty (1979: 140, n. 14).
9. See Rorty's objection to Putnam's position (Rorty 1998: 50).

Chapter 4

1. Rorty's rejection of any language as being privileged by its ability to better fit the world leads him to maintain that 'reality is indifferent to our descriptions of it' (Rorty 1998: 7), and that truth is fabricated and not disclosed.

   Of course, Kripke would only go as far as this. The important and relevant distinction between Kripke and Rorty is whereas the latter believes that there is no further ground to language than its use, Kripke maintains that language may be used to point to and fix attention upon a given physical entity and those properties which are associated with that entity in all possible worlds. Once this is accomplished, necessity is retro-fitted on to some arbitrary language choice. Thus, Kripke would constrain linguistic redescriptions about our experience whenever they involved mention of natural kinds.
2. An example of a definite description which is not a rigid designator would be 'The first President of the United States', for that to which the phrase refers was the man George Washington, and it refers to him contingently. It could have applied to Thomas Jefferson or John Adams in some counterfactual situation. However, the

term 'gold' is said to be 'rigid' since it must always refer to the same trans-world substance designated by the atomic number 79.

3. Daniel Dennett is a strong advocate of scientific realism, and thus to a degree an ally of Kripke. See Dennett (1997; 1998), as well as 'The Case of Rorts' in Brandom (2000: 91–100).

4. An example of a misleading case, but not dangerously so, drawn from W. V. O. Quine's 'Natural Kinds' in Schwartz (1977: 167), is of the Australian marsupial mouse.

5. Applied to natural kinds, such as gold or water, the general names would be 'rigid', referring to the same stuff independently of the superficial phenomenal properties normally associated with a description of that particular stuff in, for instance, the English language of America in the late twentieth century. The same would be true for contingent historical properties as well.

6. For example, the statement 'water is that clear liquid stuff (over there)' helps fix the reference of water, but does not give the meaning in the traditional sense of supplying a synonym for the term 'water'. Kripke, therefore, claims such statements in reality are neither necessary nor analytic.

7. Since Kant, there has been the assumption that necessity and *a prioricity* were coextensive. Thus analytic notions, which are tautologically true by definition, were thought to be both *a priori* and necessary. In contrast, all empirical discoveries were thought to be not *a priori*, nor necessary, and of course not analytic. While the possibility for Kant's synthetic *a priori* necessities was in dispute, most philosophers agreed with Kant that synthetic *a posteriori* discoveries were always contingent. However, Kripke challenged this through his severing the three notions cleanly from each other, allowing for the logical possibility of a synthetic *a posteriori*.

8. For this essentialist view of Kripke's to be correct, he must be correct in his tripartite distinction mentioned in note 7 above. In 'Identity and Necessity' (in Schwartz 1977: 87–88), Kripke argues, '. . . for although the statement that this table, if it exists at all, was not made of ice, is necessary, it certainly is not something we know a priori'. Or to put it more generally:

P > [] P – from *a priori* philosophical analysis
P   – by empirical investigation
- - - -
[] P   – therefore, it is necessary, based on *a posteriori* investigation
           (since one of the premises on which it is based is *a posteriori*)

'So, the notion of essential properties can be maintained only by distinguishing between the notion of *a priori* and necessary truth . . .' (Kripke, in Schwartz 1977: 88).

9. Putnam, originally in agreement with Kripke in his attempt to establish, by his Twin Earth argument, that 'water' refers rigidly to the stuff that we do in fact call 'water', to the exclusion of XYZ, an identical water-like substance with which we have no causal connection, switched allegiances, joining Habermas in the 'Internal Realist' branch of pragmatism.

10. Rorty's thought about Davidson's slogan that causation, unlike explanation, is not under a description is that it needs retooling to capture what should have been Davidson's intent. Rorty writes that descriptions can be explained in an almost unlimited variety of ways. See Rorty (1998: 88).

11. As we shall see shortly, Rorty's position on this matter seems to take us, at least in one language-game, towards a mechanistic account in which the phrase 'not being out of phase' suggests that an organism's deliberation independent of environmental influences is out of the question. The implication is that the whole transaction must be devoid of sense, operating as it would strictly on the causal level.

12. See Kohlberg (1981). Of course, Rorty, if it suited his purpose to engage this ethicist in conversation, would most likely argue for a rearrangement of some of Kohlberg's stages (e.g., Stage 6 – of universal ethical principles – would have to be demoted, it being too closely associated with the Kantian view) and for the expansion of the possible number of stages indefinitely. However, Kohlberg and Rorty might find a narrow solidarity on the point that once outgrown, a previous stage is shed for a new take on life.

13. This is, I believe, the essence of Kuhn's insight regarding paradigm formation. Kuhn suspects that something like a paradigm is a prerequisite to perception itself. What a man sees depends both upon what he is looking at and also upon what his previous visual-conceptual experience has taught him to see. In the absence of such training there can only be, in William James's phrase, 'a bloomin' buzzin' confusion' (Kuhn 1970: 113). Therefore, it is most plausible that it is inevitable that some worldview must be consciously or unconsciously formed to have any experience. This supports Davidson's charity thesis in that all encounters with the causal world 'teach' an organism to form workable conceptual arrangements for coping. Yet it also supports the possibility 'the original sin' of taking your sensory-conceptual experience to be the only mode of experience, freezing one in time, so to speak, by inhibiting adaptation of beliefs to changing environmental circumstances.

14. As Hall notes: 'An unfamiliar noise can function as a cause for a belief. Only after the metaphor has lost its unfamiliarity and begins to be self-consciously contextualized within one's web of beliefs and desires can it be a reason' (Hall 1994: 99). Both are used in the fixation of beliefs, but in obviously different ways. Public noises and marks can be noticed and reacted to at the level of organism (mentioning), but the *use* of them as a ground for the justification of personal, idiosyncratic beliefs falls under the heading of a poetic consciousness.

15. In 'Private Irony and Liberal Hope', Rorty underlines the contingency of all language-games. See Rorty (1989: 73–74).

16. The problem Rorty faces is that in creating a new Pragmatist paradigm, he must stand astride the new world vision and the old (as did Plato, Descartes and Nietzsche before him). But to do so is to be an insider–outsider; that is, Rorty must be bilingual not only with his narratives but also with his meta-meta-narrative. He must be a pluralist in his ability to speak from two different frames of references – from within and about his narrative. But Rorty claims that only by conversion can we ever shift these frames to appreciate the new vistas. And thus, with Rorty we tread upon a path to an infinite regress (i.e., speaking about meta-meta-paradigms, or from a meta-meta-meta-paradigm and allow for multi-lingualism at this higher level), or else stop the regress by taking a Singularist stance within and about the paradigm we are embedded in, thus shifting the same 'objects' into new arrangements without being hyper-creative and without the ability to communicate with those embedded in another paradigm.

    But, for example, Galileo and Descartes were creative in their ability to take from the old Aristotelian paradigm and project a new worldview while standing one foot in each 'world'. So it must be possible to stand above, so to speak, the meta-narratives within each paradigm and speak about them, as Kuhn did, without being absorbed by his own frame of interpretation while using the language of the paradigm with which one is familiar within a specific meta-meta-narrative. This seems to be an odd sort of 'perspective' dealing with odd sorts of 'facts'. More on this topic will be discussed in the concluding chapter.

Chapter 5

1. Thomas Jefferson's 1779 contribution to an act for establishment of religious free-dom in the State of Virginia, passed by that State's Assembly in 1786. This Act served as a model for the First Amendment to the US Constitution.

2. Augustine argues that a conversion of both the human intellect and the will are necessary to attain knowledge of the divine will, and the peace inherent in the full acceptance of God's Law (see Augustine 1960: Bk 8, Ch. 10/197). The acts of self-assertion without the benefits of the force and power of divine grace are, for Augustine, a 'perverse way' of imitating the one true and good volition (Bk 2, Ch. 6/73). The Augustinian solution was to withdraw from the tyranny of the mutable and 'contradictory phantasms' of the world and its various heretical narratives, and to submit, mind and body, to the true path of sound doctrine (Bk 7, Ch. 20/178). Thus doctrinaire tradition is placed over and above self-asserting creativity.

3. See Copleston 1985: 95. Of course, Ockham held that the Good and God's power are coextensive. This may solve the issue for a person of faith; however, it does not eliminate the challenge laid out by Plato in the *Euthyphro* (10e-11a) (Plato 1981: 16).

4. This medieval belief of Ockham's seems to have anticipated Humean thoughts con-cerning the association of ideas in the habit of constantly conjoining event A to event B. Of course, while Ockham buys into the belief in God, Hume was an agnos-tic. If, however, concentration is focused not upon the possibility or impossibility of an external (theistic) accounting for perceptual judgements, but rather upon the human perspective, one may see a parallel. Both men arrive at the opinion that this world is radically contingent, but through widely divergent scenarios. This, I believe, underlines the mythic quality of explanations, giving credence to Quine's point in 'Two Dogmas of Empiricism' (Quine 1980: 20–46), and hence, lends sup-port to Rorty's view in favour of seeing philosophy as a poetic enterprise.

5. The Cartesian irony, of course, was that once it was established that God as a 'Per-fect Being' could not create a deception, especially when it came to our judgements about mathematics, and its application to the primary qualities, then this formal notion of the divine could be relegated to the philosophical sidelines in lieu of science.

6. According to Rorty, foundational philosophy became the intellectual's substitute for religion (Rorty 1979: 4).

    The positive element arising from this substitution is the realization by the 'intel-lectuals' that it was their responsibility and freedom to identify the criteria of self-worth. While the Enlightenment thinker had separated himself from the womb of religious surrender, the umbilical cord, so to speak, to the mother of the eternally and immutably true was not entirely severed. As Rorty suggests, a yearning for the metaphysical security prevented post-Cartesian intellectuals making a clean break. The result was, and is, a gerry-rigging of the creative process of scientific hypothesis-building to a method that contains absolutely binding principles for the process of science. From an anti-foundationalist point of view, this is an unfortunate recapitulation of the much earlier pattern of submission to religion or Platonism in a way that can be characterized as a Freudian-styled authoritarian projection (Rorty 1979: 223).

7. Rorty is hopeful that finally we might abandon the Kantian idea that a 'metaphysics of experience' is needed to provide the 'philosophers' basis' for the criteria of culture (Rorty 1982: 87).

8. According to Rorty: '... the Enlightenment thought, rightly, that what would succeed religion would be *better*. The pragmatist is betting that what succeeds the "scientific", positivist culture which the Enlightenment produced will be *better*' (Rorty 1982: xxxviii).

9. Kuhn 1970: 2.

10. For the purpose of motivating edifying philosophers see Rorty (1979: 368).

11. Rorty wishes to crack the 'mirror' metaphor used by philosophy for the past 2,500 years. Based on the analogy of visual representation, philosophical discourse has been married to the notion that reality *is*, and that it is 'seen' worse or better by the mind which, respectively, distorts or accurately reflects reality's properties. Those who have polished their mirror by means of objective rational thought have the insight to the eternal, so they are the philosophical seers. In opposition, Rorty wishes we abandon the metaphor altogether (Rorty 1979: 371–72). The first step in this rebuff is to realize that there is something to reject, and that we will lose nothing and gain much by the rejection. It is here that Rorty takes the 'Jeffersonian' model and brings it to its full logical extension.

12. Rorty suggests that Kant '... managed to transform the old notion of philosophy ... into the notion of a "most basic" discipline – a *foundational* discipline' (Rorty 1979: 132).

13. See John Dewey who eloquently challenges the systematic philosophers in Dewey (1920: 25–26). See also William James's contribution to the pragmatic turn in philosophy by defining the notion of pragmatic truth in James (1982: 127).

14. Here, Rorty aligns with William James, when the latter suggests that 'the true' was 'only the expedient in our way of thinking'.

15. For a challenge to 'metaphysical realists' see Rorty (1991a: 22).

16. Kant refers to this type of containment as a 'canon'. Looking to his *Grounding for the Metaphysics of Morals* (Kant 1981: 32/424), he identifies rational, internal contradictions – those which violate the categorical imperative – as well as what can be loosely characterized as contradictions of the will. The latter issue exposes a basic assumption at work here for Kant. The transgressor would acknowledge the objective necessity of a universal law while allowing personal, subjective exceptions to it. This move avoids the first sort of contradiction and creates an opposition between the reason and the inclination. Yet this is offered as support for the validity of the categorical imperative through opposition to it. This reminds me of the alleged proof for the existence of God which argues that the very denial of God by an atheist is a left-handed assertion of the Deity, in that the topic ought never to have arisen if, in fact, there was no God. Freud has offered a plausible account through his notions of transference and projection of the infantile wish for parental protection on to the cosmos which allows the atheist her say without contradiction. In a like spirit, could we not counter Kant's assumptions about 'canon' based upon the subjectivity

of lies (and hence, their containment *via* the objectivity of truth) with Rorty's 'Davidson account of truth' (1982: 165–66), an account which brings into question the whole notion of subjectivity and objectivity regarding lawgiving veracity?

17. The point I am making here has its roots in Quine's 'Two Dogmas of Empiricism'. What Quine is saying in the often quoted passage about the equal epistemologically character of the gods of Homer and physical objects, as understood by a contemporary physicist as posits in different 'webs of belief', I would like to extend to, for example, Locke and Kant's theories. That is, even though the gods of the ancient Greeks have less explanatory power than that which is found on today's periodic table, and hence are out of vogue for the modern mind, nevertheless for Quine, they are each posits which in themselves are equally mythical or equally 'real' from an epistemological perspective. So too with entire theories seen as webs of belief; a theory's 'superior' explanatory power does not guarantee the ontological objectivity of its representational constructs. So, following the lead of Rorty and Kuhn, one could treat webs of belief as poetic narratives or value systems rather than the method of *theoria*. See Rorty (1982: 164).

18. Davidson's understanding about the epistemological scope of his principle of charity may be connected to an evolutionary theory of language development. The expectation would be that for each surviving language group an adaptation has been forced upon it to accommodate for the impingements and impacts which comprise the causal transactions between an organism and its physical and cultural environments. Survival acts as a guarantor that each language group must have an adequately adapted system of beliefs, otherwise the group would have perished long ago, and with them their failed attempt at language. Although, lacking an outside standpoint from which to assess beliefs in absolute terms, Davidson nevertheless considers it safe to hold that there is enough overlap among coherent language-games to create a social environment. See Davidson (1986: 315).

Thus, the interpreter is neither working from an absolute standpoint beyond all particular language-games, nor strictly from a unique cultural platform; he is in a radical position where, while ensconced within his group's language-game, the question 'Why couldn't all my beliefs hang together and yet be comprehensively false about the actual world?' (Davidson 1986: 309) could never come up for himself, and by reasonable extension for his or any other thriving language group, without his being able to un-embed his perspective enough to appreciate the possibility of error. See the final chapter for the implication of this observation.

19. I use the phrase 'coherent rationales' rather than the more familiar 'coherent theories' to capture Rorty's studied ambivalence about the characterization of, for him, the symbiotic notions of 'truth as coherence' and 'truth as correspondence'. To throw light on this point, see Rorty (1982: 15).

20. Rorty notes, in his introductory remarks for John P. Murphy's book *Pragmatism: From Peirce to Davidson*, that anti-representationalism – the abandonment of the spectator account of knowledge – frees thinkers from the appearance/reality distinction and hence, from the charge of relativism (Rorty, in Murphy 1990: 2). Rorty continues, claiming that truth or falsity of any given inscriptions and utterances will indeed be relative to the language in which they are held to be statements. 'However', he maintains, relativity of this type '. . . is no more dangerous than the fact that any representation of a sphere on a plane must have its accuracy judged relative to the mercator or some other projection' (Rorty, in Murphy 1990: 2–3).

Chapter 6

1. When the key legal question of the 'soft money' controversy in the late 1990s was whether President Clinton used the publicly owned spaces of the White House, rather than his own living quarters in the same building to raise campaign funds for the Democratic National Committee, there seems to be a gerry-rigged distinction being made between public action and private ambitions. While it would be ideal that the private desires and the public behaviours of Clinton could have remained separate and distinct, it is not a surprise that, apparently, they did not. To separate the office from the person holding that post seems to be the worst sort of abstract thinking. Every person redefines the public role they assume. To demand such a distinction to be all the way through an individual, as Rorty does, is to coerce the individual to repress personal ambitions for the public image. This might lead to sublimation and creative thinking, but if the 'soft money' situation teaches anything, it illustrates that such ambitions undergo a metamorphosis without translation into a truly distinct language. Rather than corrupting the vocabulary of public good, it reveals the inevitable and thorough embeddedness of the individual impulse in all public affairs where the assumptions of a common human nature are removed. The alleged wall of separation between vocabularies melts along with 'metaphysical' grounds.

2. It is of supreme importance who controls the culture. The rise of Hitler and the National Socialist Party in Germany involved the use of physical force to wrest the cultural, economic and political power from those in the Weimar Republic who fumbled to control the institutions governing the three sorts of power. The German people, tiring of economic and social upheaval, turned in large numbers towards the apparent strength of the Nazis. Had the leaders of the Weimar Republic resisted with force in the mid-1920s, the brutality of World War II and the atrocities of the Holocaust might have been averted. However, this could have been achieved in the mid-1920s only through official acts of cruelty and, when effective, humiliation directed at the violent resistance of nascent Nazi leadership. We slip towards a utilitarian calculation that may confound the New Pragmatism if we ignore the development of solidarity for the programmes of the National Socialists among the vast majority of Germans, particularly for *Kristallnacht* and the 1939 invasion of Poland. Whose cruelty should we value or disvalue more: the Nazis or a hypothetically repressive Weimar government? The German people as a society and a culture chose one way in the 1930s, and many died regretting it. Yet there is no question that at the Nuremberg rallies in 1938 solidarity was achieved through the manipulation of sentiment.

   In his 1993 *Oxford Amnesty Lecture* entitled 'Human Rights, Rationality and Sentimentality', Rorty said 'the emergence of the human rights culture seems to owe nothing to the increase of moral knowledge and everything to hearing sad and sentimental stories' and, therefore, it would be best to 'concentrate our energies on manipulating sentiment, on sentimental education ...' (in 1993a: 118–19). Since there are, by Rorty's own estimation, no neutral premises to back this argument, then it is only by means of propaganda and coercion, and perhaps ultimately force, that the visionaries of human rights will achieve their purpose. There is irony here, but I fear not the kind which Rorty usually intends.

   For an interesting discussion of this and related matters, see Geras (1995).

3. Freud, in an article entitled 'The Unconscious' (1915), justifies the theory of the unconsciousness as necessary and legitimate by suggesting that the only coherent way to understand the often disjointed conscious mental acts of healthy or sick persons, and the observable behaviours associated with them, is to posit another set of mental acts which are unavailable to – hidden from – consciousness (Freud 1963: 116–17).

4. Rorty, following John Rawls's use of the term (Rorty 1991a: 179, n. 7), indicts Nietzsche and Ignatius Loyola as examples of the 'mad' in their actual and implied ideological opposition to liberal constitutionalism. They breech the norms of local and contemporary sanity and in doing so their ideas threaten the fabric of freedom. Again citing Rawls, Rorty links freedom to justice – without, of course, an appeal to the standard of an interpersonal truth invoked by the latter Putnam – and asserts that force may be used against the individual conscience whose fanaticism may lead that individual to act as a menace to democratic institutions (Rorty 1991a: 183) specifically designed to limit cruelty, and thereby ensuring an atmosphere conducive to freedom.

5. The poet or the novelist's beliefs are the means used to affect her readers, sensitizing the latter through the use of language and metaphor to the existence and the deleterious effects of the needless infliction of pain upon another human (i.e., humiliation). It is in this way that Rorty hopes that the creativity of the private individual may affect the public behaviour of a society. That is, how reasons function as causes. There is no need for there to be a reductionist explanation to account for this. Such efforts confuse linguistic 'apples' with 'oranges'.

6. Rorty does contend that the sundry beliefs which each of us holds are like planks in 'Neurath's Boat' which are being constantly prised loose and replaced as we go along through our life. Those which have yet to be dislodged are akin to the notion of 'funded experience' (Rorty 1982: 13). This manoeuvre allows Rorty to sustain the claim that we choose all of our beliefs, even those we are not presently conscious of, as beliefs *per se*.

7. Hall captures in a significant fashion the discomfort I have with Rorty's vision and use of irony. See Hall (1994: 140).

8. See Hall (1994: 144) for a viewpoint supporting my claim.

Chapter 7

1. Rorty endorses the interpretation of Rawlsian 'reflective equilibrium', that is, Rawls's original position is not like thinking as if one has a view from nowhere, 'but rather of thinking like a lot of different people in turn – thinking from the point of view of every "concrete other" whom one might turn out to be' (Rorty, in R. Goodman 1995: 141, n. 8). This point will be of central significance in the next chapter.

2. An important distinction between freedom of speech and freedom of belief is often overlooked, resulting in a conflation of the two. Freedom of speech is a public policy issue which is intrinsically interpersonal in nature. Freedom of belief, while enshrined at the public level to ensure the protection against socially coerced participation by an individual in activities which run counter to his beliefs, is a personal, non-public issue. This distinction is the essence of the Jeffersonian wall of separation. Once beliefs are given voice in a public act of speech, however, a public policy of tolerance or censorship is or is not set into play. What Fraser seems to be

suggesting is that it is unreasonable to set down a firm demarcation between the public and the private because, unless purposely withheld, repressed or suppressed, private beliefs almost always find their way into the interpersonal realm through their public expression. Hence, to privatize these beliefs is to depoliticize them, to deprive them of a public voice.

3. Rorty differs from Mill on this point concerning the public/private dichotomy. Mill's concern for a free and rational exchange of opinions (Mill 1975: 36) was directed towards the establishing of an intellectual zone of safety for any individual whose offbeat lifestyle and beliefs might otherwise prompt those who dislike them or find them distasteful to resort to cruel and humiliating actions as a means of their suppression. It therefore follows that Mill would look unfavourably if there were any controls or censorial limits placed on public discussions. He also views with a disapproving eye any appeals to authority or general inclination in lieu of a rational position, for such appeals could circumvent his zone of safety and easily lead to the acts of intolerance.

    Rorty, on the other hand, cannot be so positioned, because of his belief that great harm may be done when one is subjected to the forced redescription by another group or individual (Rorty, in R. Goodman 1995: 129), and because he eschews all appeals to rational beliefs that are made true by reality. Therefore 'we have to give up the comforting belief that competing groups will always be able to reason together on the basis of plausible and neutral premises' (Rorty, in R. Goodman 1995: 128). Rorty must place a restriction to speech beyond that which Mill, a believer in the power of the rational to foster convergence, is willing to allow. Thus Rorty's Jeffersonian Strategy is a two-way boundary designed, as Mill's, to carve out a space for the individual's creative self-assertions, and unlike Mill's, to censor those assertions by the caustic poet who could cause the public pain of humiliation through his creation and employment of malicious redefinitions. This limit to toleration seems innocent enough except, again unlike Mill, Rorty believes that there is no fixed human nature. Therefore, what is to be termed 'malicious humiliation' is a political, and not a 'rational' question, and the censoring is determined by those who have achieved 'semantic authority' within that society. However, this seems to be the antithesis of Mill's programme, as when he writes of a society's intolerance of dissenting opinions and the accompanying assumption of infallibility (Mill 1975: 18) Rorty would concur, applying Mill's concern about societal hubris to the adherers to the onto-theological mindset. Mill would extend this warning to Rorty's pragmatism as well, and there is the key difference between the two.

4. See Kuhn (1970: 111); also see Rorty (1979: 320).

5. It ought to be remembered that each signatory to the Hobbesian Social Contract has made an explicit agreement to preserve the conditions of the collective peace and security. Implicit in that pledge is the acknowledgement that the suppression and control of any violators of the established good order − as defined in the Covenant − is a desirable and valued activity in that society. This collective power to control aberrant behaviour extends to each and every individual who freely consented to enter into the binding agreement. Therefore, when elements of the society, acting within the intent of the Social Contract, move to control a wayward member, they act paternalistically, especially when, in their view, that individual hypocritically objects to that which he or she has made a vow.

6. Holmes was the chief advocate of pragmatism in the law in his time. He held that law was not based on unchanging principles, but on human experience. Holmes

argued that even prejudice had its place in the formation of law. As people's experience changed, so too should society's concepts about jurisprudence alter in a corresponding manner. His pragmatism greatly influenced the Supreme Court in its decisions in the early part of the twentieth century.

7. Schenck had sent leaflets to 15,000 draftees urging them to resist induction into the armed forces on the grounds that the European war was a conflict spawned by capitalistic nationalism and an imperialistic desire for territorial gain.

8. In 1772, John Adams created a committee of correspondence in Boston, Massachusetts. Using letters as the means, this group of dissidents formed a political nucleus in order to make public the grievances against English rule throughout the American colonies.

9. Justice Holmes believed that 'the character of every act depends upon the circumstances in which it is done'. Apparently, a few months after *Schenck*, circumstances were altered sufficiently for Holmes to take a minority position, in *Abrams v. United States* (1919), that no clear and present danger existed in that case. Jacob Abrams, a self-described 'anarchist', an immigrant from Russia, was convicted of printing and distributing leaflets that 'insulted the United States' and interfered with the nation's war effort against Germany under the Espionage Acts of 1917 and 1918. Abrams called for, through two separate leaflets, a general strike and a revolution against the US government for taking part in the Allied intervention in the USSR. The intentions of these pamphlets were clearly for the undermining of the American industrial war effort and for the overthrow of the national government. As such they seemed to pose a greater peril to the country than did Schenck's anti-draft mailings (see note 7 above). Yet, Holmes argued that a clear and present danger must be a real and immediate threat, and that in a democracy truth must be found 'by a free trade in ideas'. Hence, the best test of the truth of even 'the opinions that we loathe' is to gain the assent of a majority 'in the competition of the market'. Apparently this argument did not apply for Schenck's opinions. The line is not just drawn very fine here. I believe Justice Holmes has fuzzed the distinction and has rendered idiosyncratic and inconsistent decisions which support my contention that liberal democracy under a pragmatic view is inherently self-contradictory.

10. Domestically, see The Palmer Raids (1919–1920), and internationally, the Treaty of Versailles 1919 and its aftermath: World War II.

11. Consider that in Freudian psychoanalytic circles homosexuality was seen to be a perversion of normal sexual activity (heterosexual intercourse with the intent of procreation). Even with the unbiased reading of 'perversion' as a deviation from the norm, it still reveals the cultural bias in the designation of a standard for human activity, one which had and is still having a lasting adverse affect on the language of western cultures.

12. The Dawes Severalty Act was a federal law that created conditions where the Native American would be assimilated into white American culture. This was in response to Helen Hunt Jackson's exposé *A Century of Dishonor*, a book which highlighted the mistreatment and official betrayals of the Native American tribes by the US government. The 1887 Act's legal dissolution of the tribal system and the division of its members into nuclear family units was seen as a positive remedy. By *Americanizing* the Indian, with the proper practical and formal education, it was thought that 'they' would become part of 'we'. However, split off from the fabric of their tribal societies, Native Americans floundered at the fringes of white society for many years. Ultimately the tribal lands, totalling 75 million acres after various

farming plots were distributed to Indian farmers, were opened for white settlement by Congress. The moral is, without some grounding principle, what seems progressive for a people, or an individual, can be tragically tinted by the socio-historic prejudices of even those who take a view of democracy akin to Rorty's view that the expansion of liberal 'we' is at its core beneficial.

13. Tolerance and compromise are virtually synonymous in American culture. Compromise between majority opinion and minority assertions are political adjustments to the tension which arises due to the divergence of their opinions, if these differences arise from incommensurable worldviews. And when they do, if Rorty's take on hermeneutics is considered (see Chapter 3) in conjunction with his adoption of Kuhn's theory on paradigm shifts – yielding the position of internally coherent yet mutually exclusive language-games which touch, only at the periphery – then there is no possibility of a true meeting of minds.

Compromise would take one of two forms: first, either a clever use of terms that serve to cover over the real cleavage between the parties to the dispute, leaving the underlying tensions unresolved in a way that the passage of time will not suffice to convert a person's way-of-life to some alien and unwelcomed social paradigm. Or second, the unlikely, yet possible, form of a wholesale conversion by one party to the other's vocabulary. This second alternative, of course, is not a compromise but an abandonment of one's position. In either case, democratic devices such as legislation, court cases, verbal adaptations of the law used for social policy change, become coercive tools, which, in the hands of a paternalistic government, force outward compliance in public behaviour, thereby achieving the effects of compromise as defined above, without the consent of the party affected. Politically incorrect speech-acts are suppressed to the level of private mutterings and idiosyncratic beliefs.

I do not believe that these are the only alternatives to the racial, ethnic or gender divides, or any other contentious debate. However, I can see no other options available to Rorty. Hence, for democratic institutions based explicitly or implicitly, the New Pragmatism I cannot envision a resolution to the potentially destructive tension between libertarian individualism and an enforced public policy of tolerance. More will be said on this topic in the concluding chapter.

14. If we follow Rorty's suggestions to the letter, we must end in a Hobbesian society where, without an authority (power) either natural or supernatural to set standards and sculpt behaviour, there must be only local persuasion and/or force to organize and maintain solidarities.

15. The inconsistency is, of course, that Rorty speaks of bourgeois liberties while he constructs a worldview which undermines them in precisely the same fashion as Hobbes did, that is, through a self-defeating internal contradiction. Rorty must claim semantic authority for himself in order to be consistent with his pragmatic programme. He takes the high ground in the discussion, thereby delimiting the choice of vocabulary available for conversation. Thus, if one wishes to enter the discussion, one must either make a Kuhnian conversion to Rorty's gloss on bourgeois liberality, or the conversation never begins. There can be no intellectual interface, only conversion or political struggle over final vocabularies. This situation of disassociation, as I have mentioned previously, springs from his idiosyncratic take on hermeneutics which makes inaccessible Rorty's language-game to those individuals whose interpretations of, say, liberal democracy differ markedly from his.

16. Even Mill, a very tolerant person, could not embrace any value which allowed an individual to compromise his liberty (e.g., the uncoerced, self-regarding choice to sell oneself into slavery) despite his strong advocacy for freedom of choice (see Mill 1975: 95).

The important part for my commentary is Mill's apparent defence of the legal and social deterrents placed upon, in any other instance, what he would term a liberty of choice or 'self-regarding act' (Mill 1975: 227). Mill seems to form a distinction between that which an individual apparently, or mistakenly, desires and that which his real, rational will ought to be. To maintain the greater part of the personal freedom that he cherishes, Mill would paternalistically check the wrong-headed or 'mad' impulse towards self-enslavement of an individual who otherwise would be judged as sane.

If, with Rorty, we abandon all hope of a commensurate rationality (Rorty 2002: 35), Mill's impulse for paternalistic benevolence would carry over, but his alleged rational justification against such 'madness' would reduce to a cultural preference against any form of enslavement under any condition. His endorsement for the legal enforcement of that preference could be seen as both an act of raw coercion and, alternatively, as an act of paternalism, which still can be justified, albeit contingently and arbitrarily. Thus, drawn within Rorty's narrative, Mill's decision for paternalistic restraint would be without that which the latter took as decisive – a common and unwavering rationality. Undistinguished, his desire for the prevention of harm would run headlong into his belief for autonomous freedoms.

Unquestionably in a Rortian world, Mill would be in self-contradiction if he chose to prevent a free and consensual act of self-enslavement, having to maintain simultaneously two incommensurate and contingent preferences (for freedom and for paternalism) regarding the very same act. I maintain that self-contradiction will always be the outcome when preferences arising from individual autonomy and societal values come into conflict within a democracy deconstructed by the New Pragmatism.

Chapter 8

1. In support of his view of liberal polity, Rorty endorses Isaiah Berlin's defence of 'negative liberty' as that which accounts for individual dynamic, better than the traditional 'telic conceptions of human nature' (Rorty 1989: 45).

2. Peter Gay says in his introduction to Freud's *The Ego and the Id*:

   The historical accident that psycho-analysis had its origin in connection with the study of hysteria led at once to the hypothesis of repression (or more generally, of defense) as a mental function, and this in turn to a topographical hypothesis – to a picture of the mind as including two portions, one repressed and the other repressing (Freud 1960b/1989: xxix).

3. While Freud has the *ego* representing reason, and that reason was important in the 'analysis of the resistance', nevertheless, it was not a concept which was identical with the Enlightenment's notion – that which can be separated from the natural order, from causes. Rather, reasons are underlain and shaped by bodily processes. As such, they are a construct, a working model of the world, which is driven by the impulses of the *id*, under the influence of the pleasure principle – the endeavour to

fulfil all of one's desires, and modified by the reality principle – the force of realization that one cannot always fulfil one's wishes. Thus, the *ego* is the dynamic equilibrium that forms in response to the bodily drives and their frustrations. A dispositional state, rather than a bracket around the abstract contents of propositional attitudes, the *ego*, impacted by the natural order, organizes around conscious narratives, as well as unconscious fantasies (as represented in dreams) to fulfil wishes while screening out painful feelings and desires (e.g., through the process of projection). One might say that the *ego*, as Freud conceived it to be (and the reasons generated by its operation), is an epiphenomenal outcome of the relevant causal forces at play.

4. In particular, the *ego*, *id* and *superego* are discussed in detail in Freud 1960b *passim*.

5. The *ego*'s relation to the *id*, Freud writes in *The Ego and the Id*, is like a man on horseback; the *ego* checks, with borrowed force, the superior strength of the horse (the *id*) but moves only where the 'horse' wants to go. However, the *ego* is in 'the habit of transforming the *id*'s will into action as if it were its own' (Freud 1960b: 19).

6. After a lengthy explanation in *The Ego and the Id* of the origin of the *superego*, Freud makes this significant observation:

> The ego ideal is therefore the heir of the Oedipus complex, and thus it is also the expression of the most powerful impulses and most libidinal vicissitudes of the id. By setting up this ego ideal, the ego has mastered the Oedipus complex and at the same time placed itself in subjection to the id (Freud 1960b/1989: 32).

7. In the final pages of *The Ego and the Id*, Freud seems to be crediting the *ego* with a modicum of independence only to withdraw that liberty less than a page later (Freud 1960b/1989: 58).

Add to this the comment from the same source that the imposition of the thinking process as a power to postpone 'motor discharges and control the access of motility' is 'a question more of form than of fact: in the matter of action the ego's position is like that of a constitutional monarch, without whose sanction no law can be passed but who hesitates long before imposing his veto on any measure put forward by Parliament', and this image of a weak figurehead gets attached to the *ego*. The ego's power as a self-regulator is hampered to the point of non-existence by the powers around it.

8. As Jeremy Leeds underscores (1993: 354), a lack of some sort of common point of reference makes hermeneutic arguments relative and at times logically fallacious, and hence unscientific – devoid of objectivity.

9. As Rorty states: 'As a partisan of solidarity [the pragmatist's] account of the value of cooperative human inquiry has only an ethical base, not an epistemological or metaphysical one' (Rorty 1991a: 24).

10. The point is supported by Freud in his discussion about the *ego*'s object-identifications (and the *ego*'s relation to the *id* through the *superego*), and the dangers of a gross multiplication of them, to the point of a multiple personality disorder. Consider the implications this comment has upon the Rortian mindscape of incompatible voices:

> If they obtain the upper hand and become too numerous, unduly powerful and incompatible with one another, a pathological outcome will not be far off. It may come to a disruption of the ego in consequence of the different identifications becoming cut off from one another by resistances; perhaps the secret of the cases

of what is described as 'multiple personality' is that the different identifications seize hold of consciousness in turn. Even when things do not go so far as this, there remains the question of conflicts between the various identifications into which the ego comes apart, conflicts which cannot after all be described as entirely pathological (Freud 1960b/1989: 25).

11. I originally argued this point in my doctoral 1998 defence.
12. Rorty advises once again against foundationalism in favour of narrative freedom. And once again, he begs the question in favour of a subtle physicalism through his decided stance against the 'nonmechanical'. See Rorty (1991b: 162).
13. In answer to the question 'Why cannot the self be a subject for inquiry?', I would first say that, from Rorty's perspective, to hold the self out for inspection, the inquirer must stand apart as if a spectator, and distance himself from his self to be able to get an objective view. Of course, for Rorty, there cannot exist a pre-linguistic self which the inspector could detach from and move about, so to speak, in order to describe linguistically it as if an object of inquiry. For him, one's self is coextensive with one's vocabulary, and there is no way to stand apart from one's language-game. I would add that in his writings, Rorty himself seems never to be engaged in the areas that he is conversing. He takes his academic distance even in discussions about the human self. In this way he falls into the same objectivist trap which all Enlightenment figures, as well as Freud, are to be found. The systemiza-tion of the self, whether by Hegel, Freud or Rorty, must treat its focus as an alien force to grasp and reckon with, and thus, forever leave out the crucial unalienable, first-person encounter that is oneself (read: me, the reader).
14. Guignon identifies as a significant and troublesome split between the two tenden-cies which Rorty exhibits in his though the Hegelian 'insider' strand, and the crit-ical 'outsider' aspect. See Guignon et al. in Malachowski (1990: 359). In itself, the incommensurability of these two strands is not problematic for Rorty. However, the split becomes paradoxical when discussed in terms of a first-person/third-person distinction relative to the self (see note 16, below).
15. Hall agrees with the assessment that Rorty is caught in the Enlightenment. See Hall (1994: 28).
16. Guignon et al., I believe, strike directly to the heart of the problem for Rorty's bilin-gual strategy by noting that implied deeply in Rorty's rhetoric is an ego-split.

> Now this bifocal vision on the situation seems to produce a type of 'ego-splitting': the self regarded as an 'empirico-transcendental doublet'. We are holistic webs of beliefs and desires engaged in an interminable process of reweaving, yet it is also up to us 'to invent a use for ourselves', to undertake the task of 'what Bloom calls "giving birth to oneself" ' by inventing new metaphors and self-descriptions. This implies a distinction between an 'I' who is the web and an 'I' who reweaves and recreates the web (Guignon et al., in Malachowski 1990: 359).

This ties into my point that Rorty is a 'closet Cartesian' in that ultimately, when one has dived deeply into the presuppositions of the New Pragmatism, one finds an old-style Cartesian dualism of first- and third-person perspectives now expressed in the rhetorical garb of the anti-foundational vocabulary shifts.
17. In 'Hesse and Davidson on Metaphor', Rorty seems to strike his usual ironic pose on the subject of metaphor by paradoxically supporting the stance by an *unqualified* appeal to an underlying causal nexus. See Rorty (1991a: 171–72).

18. I believe Rorty is at odds with himself, like the man who wishes to open the session of the German legislature but rather speaks as to betray his unconscious desire to close preemptively the assembly, caught in 'the tension between an effort to achieve self-creation by the recognition of contingency and an effort to achieve universality by the transcendence of contingency'. Why else would he engage in strenuous debate within the arena of philosophy? If, as he claims, Philosophy, with a capital 'P' for Professional, is dead, why not eschew systematic debate altogether and write poetry – or even become as silent as a Zen monk? He says that the pragmatist 'thinks of the thinker as serving the community, and of his thinking as futile unless it is followed up by a reweaving of the community's web of belief' (Rorty 1991b: 17). But why does he insist upon telling a story about his favourite and least favourite texts to an audience rife with scepticism about his narrative except to prosclytize a gospel, a thcorctical onc at that? As thc cditors of *Puzzles, Paradoxes, and Problems: A Reader for Introductory Philosophy*, Peter French and Curtis Brown note: 'But it is crucial that philosophers are not merely engaged in creative theory construction. In that case their views would be of interest as artistic creations but would not make serious claims on our belief. Philosophers do not just invent views, they argue for them' (1987: 2–3). It seems that Rorty is himself 'split' between Romantic poetic creation and rational philosophical argumentation. Thus, his writing seems like a grand parapraxis.

Chapter 9

1. The biblical sentence oft quoted in favour of divine revenge or retribution for sins is not only taken out of context from the text itself (consider *Leviticus* 19.18), but misses the wider cultural context of the command's source – the *Code of Hammurabi* where an 'eye for an eye' was meant to be a limit on retribution and not the unlimited advocacy for it.

2. Geras, in his *Solidarity in the Conversation of Humankind*, is concerned with the possibility (more to the point, the impossibility) of humanism without any human nature. In it Geras refers to a lecture given by Rorty in the *Oxford Amnesty* series on 'Human Rights' (see Rorty 1993a) which connects to my present point (see Geras 1995: 71–72). The answer to the question posed by Geras as to whose morality is Rorty referring, at first glance, seems to be referring to the solidarity of Western culture's liberals. Upon reflection, however, it would be a surprise if most of these liberals agreed with Rorty's view on the denatured self and the ungroundedness of supporting principles. Therefore, with principles being ad hoc adaptations of past norms and without the firm peg of a self upon which to hang his web of beliefs, Rorty has to be advancing his own idiosyncratic values packaged persuasively by the artful use of equivocations as part of the human right's culture based on a universalist notion of transcultural human integrity. In short, Rorty appropriates the notion of rights and intentionally 'misreads' them for his own pragmatic ends.

3. Unlike Kuhn, who writes: 'My point is, then, that every individual choice between competing theories depends on a mixture of objective and subjective factors, or shared and individual criteria' (Kuhn 1989: 157, 159), Rorty reduces the universality of shared agreements to agreements more easily reached within a cultural setting. Whereas Kuhn tried to argue for the admission of 'idiosyncratic factors of

biography and personality' as philosophically important elements in theory choice, Rorty extends these factors (read: embeddedness in a cultural matrix and a unique arrangement of Freudian complexes) to every aspect of human intellectual life.

4. Hall's understanding of Rorty throws light on the isolation of the Rortian vocabulary:

    > ... Rorty's philosophy is closed to rational analysis, critique or dialectic. I agree with Rorty that we are forever outside one another's discourse, and that language, therefore, is not a medium of communication open to rational analysis but a 'tool.' From the perspective of understanding, one person's language is little more than a vague supplement to the language of another (Hall 1994: 6).

5. Hall's perceptiveness on the point that, '[t]he refusal to take other final vocabularies seriously often leads to redescription, which threatens humiliation', proves helpful in uncovering Rorty's inconsistencies. Hall notes Rorty's 'assault upon the systematic, metaphysical thinkers is an aggressive refusal to read in such a manner as to avoid dismissing these thinkers as unworthy of conversation' (Hall 1994: 140). Here is where the potential of humiliation arises.

6. Once again, the reader should take care not to be drawn into thinking that with Rorty we are truly discussing whether the self has a centre or not. He has already asserted that the whole issue involves the dead metaphor of a substantial self. From his perspective, if you disagree with him about the self, this makes you part of a solidarity that is a rival to his own. Semantic authority is what is at stake. He has ceased discussing the issue of the self in the usual philosophical terms and thereby is trying to force the debate on to his turf. Nevertheless, Rorty has again appropriated the vocabulary of traditional philosophical discussion as a strategy for the advancement of his narrative, and tries to use it against those who are not careful to notice that equivocation is taking place, especially at critical junctures such as when he himself (apparently) raises the metaphysical question as to whether selves have centres or not (see 'Non-reductive Physicalism', in Rorty 1991a: 113–25).

7. See 'Towards Rehabilitating Objectivity' in Brandom 2000: 109–123.

8. Conant builds his argument linking 'Newspeak' and New Pragmatism upon the non-controversial claim that freedom of belief is achievable only when one can decide for oneself concerning the facts in a community that nurtures this sort of freedom. And this community can only be sustained when its norms of inquiry are not biased towards lock-step solidarity with one's peers, but are geared towards the encouragement of independent attempts at relating one's claims about the way things are with the way things are, in fact (or as Conant writes: 'turning to the facts'). Real human freedom can be expressed when one is able to believe autonomously and to test one's belief for its truth and falsity in a public forum unconstrained by sociological determinants. Freedom, Conant claims, is therefore a human capacity that emerges from the human condition and need not be attributable to any Realist thesis. Conant agrees with Rorty that there is nothing deep within us; there isn't any indestructible nature or eternal substance. Nevertheless, a systematic effort to eliminate the vocabulary containing terms such as 'eternal truths', 'objective reality' and traits 'essential to humanity' would be akin to George Orwell's 'Newspeak', in that such an elimination would render impossible human freedom by making it impossible to share in language such ideas and

concepts. The very possibility of interpretative communication and dialogue among freethinkers engaged in the search for truth would be banished by the sort of control exerted over language Rorty recommends.

9. Callicles, a Greek Sophist, discredited traditional notions of morality as a ploy by the weak masses to control their natural superiors. He suggested that the strong ought to assert their power not in pursuit of abstractions such as 'justice' and 'truth', but to get what they want: survival and pleasure. Add to this claim of another proto-Machiavellian Sophist, Critias, who taught that a shrewd ruler invents and employs scenarios (in his case, non-existent gods) with the sole intent to influence and manipulate the beliefs of his subjects towards his own advantage, and a two-tiered morality of Egoism emerges, similar to that of Rorty's. The point is that in both the ancient and modern philosophies a clever individual can weave a narrative involving, say, powerful gods or powerful principles, which will ensure law and order among the general population, even to the point of reducing cruel actions among the citizenry, while privately exempting himself from the narrative's restrictions, the very scenario played out in Hobbes's theory.

10. In *Homo Viator*, Marcel's analysis of what he called the 'pose' of a demagogue seems to be an apt description of Rorty's stance *vis-à-vis* others when he discusses democracy (see G. Marcel, in VanEwijk 1965: 70–71).

   It is the comments to the effect that language is to be used to get what one wants, applied to the interpersonal context, which caused me to see Rorty in Marcel's pointed words. For without a centre, all human activity is merely one sort of posing or another in the mirror of society.

11. What is not clear is Rorty's criterion for his Multiplism. Is he pluralizing objects of interpretation and taking a Singularist view on each of them or is he a Multiplist concerning a single interpretative object? What seems to be plausible is that he is committed to multiple interpretative possibilities about multiple 'realities'. But is he? When he claims to be a realist does he claim that there is one object, 'the real', but radically open to multiple interpretations? Or with paradigm shifts, do multiple realities open to him the likelihood of multiple Singularist views of distinctive, multiple realities? Can Rorty – given that he thinks of Reality as that which no normative terms may be used to describe 'it' – even decide whether there is one or multiple intentional objects to be considered and one or plural meta-standpoints from which to interpret? Perhaps Rorty will opt for multiple interpretations of ideals of interpretation relative to reality(ies); paradoxically, this would be a Singularist meta-meta-interpretation.

12. My suggestion can be treated like the speculation of Anaximander about the 'Unlimited'. But as unsupportable as both are, the critique of each serves the Socratic urge to continue to search for the truth even when rational argument reaches its limit.

Bibliography

Augustine (1960), *The Confessions of St Augustine*. John K. Ryan (trans.). Garden City, NJ: Doubleday.

Berlin, Sir Isaiah (1958), 'Two Concepts of Liberty', in *Four Essays on Liberty*. New York: Oxford University Press.

Bernstein, Richard J. (1991), *Beyond Objectivism and Relativism*. 4th edn. Philadelphia: University of Pennsylvania Press.

Bok, Sissela (1979), *Lying: Moral Choices in Public and Private Life*. New York: Vintage Books.

BonJour, Laurence (1978), 'A Critique of Foundationalism', *American Philosophical Quarterly* 15: 1–13.

—— (1985), *The Structure of Empirical Knowledge*. Cambridge, MA: Harvard University Press.

Bourke, Rev Myles M., et al. (1970), *The New American Bible*. Wichita, KS: Fireside Bible Publishers.

Brandom, R. (ed.) (2000), *Rorty and His Critics*. Malden, MA: Basil Blackwell.

Campbell, Joseph (1968), *The Hero with a Thousand Faces*. Princeton, NJ: Princeton University Press.

Conant, J. (2000), 'Freedom, Cruelty, and Truth: Rorty versus Orwell', in R. Brandom (ed.), *Rorty and His Critics*. Malden, MA: Basil Blackwell, pp. 268–341.

Copleston, S.J., Frederick (1985), *A History of Philosophy: Book One*. Garden City, NY: Image Press.

Davidson, D. (1984), *Inquiries into Truth and Interpretation*. Oxford: Oxford University Press.

—— (1986), 'A Coherence Theory of Truth and Knowledge', in E. LePore (ed.), *Truth and Interpretation: Perspectives on the Philosophy of Donald Davidson*. Oxford: Basil Blackwell, pp. 307–319.

—— (1990a), 'The Structure and Content of Truth', *Journal of Philosophy* 87, no. 6: 279–328.

—— (1990b), 'A Coherence Theory of Truth and Knowledge', in Alan Malachowski (ed.), *Reading Rorty*. Oxford: Basil Blackwell, pp. 120–138.

—— (2000), 'Truth Rehabilitated', in R. Brandom (ed.), *Rorty and His Critics*. Malden, MA: Basil Blackwell, pp. 65–73.

—— (2001), *Subjective, Intersubjective, Objective (Philosophical Essays of Donald Davidson)*. Oxford: Oxford University Press.

—— (2005), *Truth, Language, and History*. Oxford: Clarendon Press

Dennett, Daniel (1995) *Darwin's Dangerous Idea*. New York: Simon & Schuster.

—— (1997), 'Faith in the Truth', *Amnesty Lecture*, Oxford, 17 February 1997 at http://ase.tufts.edu/cogstud/papers/faithint.htm.

—— (1998), 'Postmodernism and Truth', *The 1998 World Congress of Philosophy* at http://www.butterfliesandwheels.com/printer_friendly.php?num=13.

Dewey, John (1920), *Reconstruction in Philosophy*. New York: Henry Holt and Co.

—— (1963), *Philosophy, Psychology and Social Practice*. Joseph Ratner (ed.). New York: G. P. Putnam's Sons.

Erburu, Robert F. (ed.) (1988), *Bill of Rights in Action*, vol. IV, no. 3. Los Angeles: The Constitutional Rights Foundation.

French, Peter A., and Brown, Curtis (eds) (1987), *Puzzles, Paradoxes, and Problems: A Reader for Introductory Philosophy*. New York: St Martin's Press.

Freud, Sigmund.

—— (1960a/1989), *New Introductory Lectures on Psycho-Analysis*. James Strachey (ed.). New York: W. W. Norton & Co.

—— (1960b/1989), *The Ego and the Id*. James Strachey (ed.). New York: W. W. Norton & Co.

—— (1961/1989), *Beyond the Pleasure Principle*. James Strachey (ed.). New York: W. W. Norton & Co.

—— (1963/1989), *General Psychological Theory: Papers on Metapsychology*. New York: Macmillan.

—— (1966/1989), *Introductory Lectures on Psycho-Analysis*. James Strachey (ed.). New York: W. W. Norton & Co.

Gadamer, Hans-Georg (1977), *Philosophical Hermeneutics*. Berkeley: University of California Press.

—— (1980), *Dialogue and Dialectic: Eight Hermeneutical Studies on Plato*. New Haven: Yale University Press.

—— (1994), *Truth and Method*. 2nd edn. New York: Continuum.

Geras, Norman (1995), *Solidarity in the Conversation of Humankind*. London: Verso.

Goodman, Nelson (1965), *Fact, Fiction and Forecast*. New York: Bobbs-Merrill Co.

—— (1978), *Ways of Worldmaking*. Indianapolis, IN: Hackett Publishing Co.

Goodman, Russell B. (ed.) (1995), *Pragmatism: A Contemporary Reader*. New York: Routledge.

Grippe, Edward, 'Plato on Homeric Justice', *The Journal of Philosophy in the Contemporary World* 14 (2) 2007 (forthcoming).

Guyer, Paul (ed.) (1992), *The Cambridge Companion to Kant*. Cambridge: Cambridge University Press.

Habermas, Jürgen (1992), *The Philosophical Discourse of Modernity*. Frederick G. Lawrence (trans.). Cambridge, MA: MIT Press.

—— (2000), 'Richard Rorty's Pragmatic Turn', in R. Brandom (ed.), *Rorty and His Critics*. Malden, MA: Basil Blackwell, pp. 31–55.

Hall, David L. (1994), *Richard Rorty: Prophet and Poet of the New Pragmatism*. Albany: State University of New York Press.

Harris, James F. (1992), *Against Relativism: A Philosophical Defense of Method*. LaSalle, IL: Open Court.

Hartnack, Justus (1967), *Kant's Theory of Knowledge*. New York: Harcourt, Brace & World, Inc.

Heidegger, Martin (1962), *Being and Time*. John Macquarrie and Edward Robinson (trans.). New York: Harper & Row.

Hobbes, Thomas (1968), *Leviathan*. C. B. Macpherson (ed.). Middlesex, England: Penguin Books.

Hume, David (1969), *A Treatise of Human Nature*. Ernest C. Massner (ed.). Middlesex, England: Penguin Books.

—— (1992), *The Natural History of Religion*. James Fieser (ed.). New York: Macmillan.

Jackson, Helen Hunt (1994), *A Century of Dishonor*. New York: Indian Head Books.

James, William (1977), *The Writings of William James*. John J. McDermott (ed.). Chicago: University of Chicago Press.

—— (1982), *Pragmatism: A New Name for Some Old Ways of Thinking*. Franklin Center, PN: The Franklin Library.

Kant, Immanuel (1929), *Critique of Pure Reason*. Norman Kemp Smith (trans.). London: Macmillan.

—— (1952), *The Critique of Judgement*. James Creed Meredith (trans.). Oxford: Clarendon Press.

—— (1965), *Critique of Pure Reason*. Norman Kemp Smith (trans.). New York: St Martin's Press.

—— (1981), *Grounding for the Metaphysics of Morals*. James W. Ellington (trans.). Indianapolis, IN: Hackett Publishing Co.

—— (1990), *Critique of Pure Reason*. J. M. D. Meiklejohn (trans.). Buffalo, New York: Prometheus Books.

Kim, Jaegwon, and Sosa, Ernest (1992), *A Companion to Epistemology*. Oxford: Basil Blackwell.

—— (1995), *A Companion to Metaphysics*. Oxford: Basil Blackwell.

Kohlberg, Lawrence (1981), *Essays on Moral Development. Vol. I: The Philosophy of Moral Development: Moral Stages and the Idea of Justice*. New York: Harper & Row.

Krausz, M. (2003), 'Interpretation and its Objects: A Synoptic View', in Ritivoi 2003: 11–24.

Kripke, Saul (1977), 'Identity and Necessity', in Stephen P. Schwartz (ed.), *Naming, Necessity, and Natural Kinds*. Ithaca, NY: Cornell University Press.

Kuhn, Thomas S. (1970), *The Structure of Scientific Revolutions*. 2nd edn. Chicago: University of Chicago Press.

—— (1977), *The Essential Tension: Selected Studies in the Scientific Tradition and Change*. Chicago: University of Chicago Press.

—— (1989), 'Objectivity, Value Judgement, and Theory Choice', in Baruch A. Brody and Richard E. Grandy (eds), *Readings in the Philosophy of Science*. 2nd edn. Englewood Cliffs, NJ: Prentice Hall.

Landesman, Charles (1985), *Philosophy: An Introduction to the Central Issues*. New York: CBS College Publishing.

Leeds, Jeremy (1993), 'Problems of Relativism in Psychoanalysis', *The Philosophical Forum* XXIV, no. 4: 349–62.

LePore, Ernest (ed.) (1986), *Truth and Interpretation: Perspectives on the Philosophy of Donald Davidson*. Oxford: Basil Blackwell.

Locke, John (1975), *An Essay Concerning Human Understanding*. Peter Nidditch (ed.). Oxford: Clarendon Press.

MacIntyre, Alasdair (1984), *After Virtue*. 2nd edn. Notre Dame, IN: University of Notre Dame Press.

Malachowski, Alan (ed.) (1990), *Reading Rorty*. Oxford: Basil Blackwell.

Marcel, Gabriel (1951), *Mystery of Being: Faith and Reality*, vol. II. René Hague (trans.). South Bend, IN: Regnery/Gateway, Inc.

Margolis, Joseph (ed.) (1968), *An Introduction to Philosophical Inquiry: Contemporary and Classical Sources*. New York: Knopf.

Mill, John Stuart (1975), *On Liberty*. David Spitz (ed.). New York: W.W. Norton & Co.

Murphy, John P. (1990), *Pragmatism: From Peirce to Davidson*. Boulder, CO: Westview Press.

O'Neill, O. (1991), 'Kantian Ethics', in P. Singer (ed.), *A Companion to Ethics*. Oxford: Basil Blackwell, pp. 175–85.

—— (1992) 'Vindicating Reason', in P. Guyer (ed.), *The Companion to Kant*. Cambridge: Cambridge University Press, pp. 280–308.

Plato (1981), *Plato: Five Dialogues*. G. M. A. Grube (trans.). Indianapolis, IN: Hackett Publishing Co.

Polanyi, M. (1958), *Personal Knowledge: Towards a Post-Critical Philosophy*. Chicago: Chicago University Press.

Quine, Willard Van Orman (1980), *From a Logical Point of View*. Cambridge, MA: Harvard University Press.

Ramberg, B. (2000), 'Post-ontological Philosophy of Mind: Rorty versus Davidson', in R. Brandom (ed.), *Rorty and His Critics*. Malden, MA: Basil Blackwell, pp. 351–69.

Rawls, John (1971), *A Theory of Justice*. Cambridge, MA: Harvard University Press.

Ritivoi, Andreea Deciu (ed.) (2003), *Interpretation and Its Objects: Studies in the Philosophy of Michael Krausz*. Amsterdam: Rodopi.

Rorty, Richard (1979), *Philosophy and the Mirror of Nature*. Princeton, NJ: Princeton University Press.

—— (1982), *Consequences of Pragmatism*. Minneapolis: University of Minnesota Press.

—— (1989), *Contingency, Irony, and Solidarity*. Cambridge: Cambridge University Press.

—— (1991a), *Objectivity, Relativism, and Truth*. Cambridge: Cambridge University Press.

—— (1991b), *Essays on Heidegger and Others*, vol. II. Cambridge: Cambridge University Press.

—— (1993a), 'Human Rights, Rationality and Sentimentality', in Stephen Shute and Susan Hurley (eds), *On Human Rights: The Oxford Amnesty Lectures 1993*. New York: Oxford University Press, pp. 111–34.

—— (1993b), 'Feminism, Ideology, and Deconstruction: A Pragmatist View', *Hypatia* 8.2 (Spring): 96–103.

—— (1995), 'Feminism and Pragmatism', in Russell B. Goodman (ed.), *Pragmatism: A Contemporary Reader*. New York: Routledge, pp. 125–49.

—— (1998), *Truth and Progress*. Cambridge: Cambridge University Press.

—— (1999a), *Philosophy and Social Hope*. London: Penguin Books.

—— (1999b), 'A Pragmatic View of Contemporary Analytic Philosophy', at http://www.standford.edu/~rrorty/pragmatistview.htm.

—— (2000), 'Response to Bjørn Bramberg', in R. Brandom (ed.), *Rorty and His Critics*. Malden, MA: Basil Blackwell, pp. 370–77.

—— (2007) *Philosophy as Cultural Politics*. Cambridge: Cambridge University Press.

Saatkamp, Herman J. (ed.) (1995), *Rorty and Pragmatism: The Philosopher Responds to His Critics*. Nashville, TN: Vanderbilt University Press.

Schwartz, Stephen P. (1977), *Naming, Necessity and Natural Kinds*. Ithaca, NY: Cornell University Press.

Sellars, Wilfrid (1991), *Science, Perception and Reality*. Atascadero, CA: Ridgeview Publishing Co.

Singer, Erwin (1965), *Key Concepts in Psychotherapy*. New York: Random House.

Singer, Peter (ed.) (1991), *A Companion to Ethics*. Oxford: Basil Blackwell.

Strawson, P. F. (1968), 'The "Justification" of Induction', in J. Margolis (ed.), *An Introduction to Philosophical Inquiry: Contemporary and Classical Sources*. New York: Knopf, pp. 444–53.

Stumph, Samuel Enoch (1988), *Socrates to Sartre: A History of Philosophy*. 4th edn. New York: McGraw-Hill.

Taylor, Charles (1991), *The Ethics of Authenticity*. Cambridge, MA: Harvard University Press.

VanEwijk, Thomas J. M. (1965), *Gabriel Marcel: An Introduction*. Glen Rock, NJ: Paulist Press.

Index